THE POLITICS OF URBAN CHANGE

THE POLITICS OF
URBAN CHANGE

DAVID H. McKAY and ANDREW W. COX

CROOM HELM LONDON

© 1979 David H. McKay and Andrew W. Cox
Croom Helm Ltd, 2-10 St John's Road, London SW11

British Library Cataloguing in Publication Data

McKay, David H
    The Politics of urban change.
    1. City planning – Great Britain   2. Great Britain
    – Social policy
    I. Title   II. Cox, Andrew W
    309.2'62'0941   HT169.G7

    ISBN 0-85664-436-6
    ISBN 0-85664-847-7 Pbk

Printed in Great Britain by Biddles Ltd, Guildford, Surrey

CONTENTS

FIGURES, CHARTS, TABLES AND MAPS

PREFACE

It is probable that important aspects of British urban policy are still the subject of admiration in many countries. American observers, in particular, continue to look with something approaching awe on our Green Belts, New Towns and regional policies. In recent years, however, disillusionment in Britain with the effects of more than a generation of state intervention in housing, land-use, transport and other aspects of urban life has increased perceptibly. Interestingly, the criticism is generally not that we have had too much government intervention in urban society, so much as that government policies have been insensitive, misguided or misdirected. This book was written with the specific intention of explaining why governments have pursued what have often been poorly conceived or inefficiently executed policies. While it is not always a depressing story, the record is not encouraging. We are not so pretentious as to believe that our analysis will lead to a re-appraisal of policy or policies. But we can hope that it will clarify why governments have so often failed and expectations have so often been dashed.

We owe a debt of thanks to a variety of individuals and institutions. The study has its origins in an EEC sponsored project into the National Urban Policies of the Northern Member States of the EEC. David McKay was the author of this project's British Report, and we are grateful to the Commission for providing us with the stimulus to study this general area. We are also grateful to Carl-Johan Skovsgaard of the University of Aarhus who helped coordinate the project and provided comments on the British Report.

Douglas Ashford, Barry Cullingworth and Peter Hall read various chapters in draft and provided valuable comments. We are especially indebted to Anthony Barker and Andrew Milnor both of whom gave a great deal of time at short notice to read and comment on our final draft. None of the faults that remain are, of course, theirs.

Finally, thanks to the Western Societies Program of the Center for International Studies, Cornell University for providing excellent facilities and support during the final stages of the study.

June 1978   David McKay, Ithaca, New York
                             Andrew Cox, Hull, North Humberside

13

1 GOVERNMENT AND URBAN CHANGE

> If to do were as easy as to know what were good to do, chapels
> had been churches, and poor men's cottages princes' palaces.
> (Merchant of Venice, Act 1, Scene 2)

Urban crisis is not new to Britain. At least since the Industrial
Revolution British cities have been a subject of concern and of various
attempts at reform. But the most recent crisis, centred on the plight of
the inner cities, is different in one fundamental respect: it follows a
period of massive state intervention in urban society based on certain
principles of urban change and growth. The latest crisis must in part,
therefore, be attributed to a failure of government. On a wide front,
government activities are under fire. Among the more important
criticism are claims that state housing provision is characterised by
social and spatial inequalities; that land use planning policies have
resulted in urban blight and decay and have aggravated the disparities
between inner cities and suburban and New Town locales; that land
values policies have failed to stem land price inflation; that transport
policies have done little to halt the environmental damage wrought by
the rising tide of motor vehicles; that policies designed specifically to
improve the lot of the urban disadvantaged are hopelessly underfunded
and possibly based on false empirical assumptions; and finally that
governments of all shades and at every level are unresponsive to citizens'
demands and needs. Not all of these accusations are fully justified, and
by no means are all contemporary urban problems a consequence of
government actions. Non-Marxists and Marxists alike agree that some
degree of territorial injustice and exploitation is inevitable in industrial
societies, irrespective of particular forms of economic and social
organisation. Scholars also agree, however, that wide differences
between capitalist societies exist, including the role of the state in
urban life.[1] Where the disagreement and confusion occurs is in the
analysis of the specific role of the state in relation to social classes and
urban change. This is true of debate within Marxist urban sociology,[2]
within liberal social science,[3] and between Marxists and non-Marxists.[4]

As far as urban politics and policy is concerned, political science has
probably contributed less to this debate than has urban sociology. In
Britain, the study of urban politics has become virtually synonymous
with the largely descriptive study of local government, and although

some rather more ambitious studies of local politics have appeared in recent years,[5] few political scientists have shown much interest in broader structural questions about the general role of the state in urban areas, and especially how this role has changed over time. Perhaps the most glaring omission is research on the formulation and implementation of *national* urban policies. Wherever we look in contemporary urban Britain, policies initiated by national governments in planning, housing, transport and urban renewal appear to be a source of, or are closely related to, urban problems. While Marxist urban sociologists have linked policies to class relationships and resource distribution, they too have tended to focus on local politics, or on grass roots social movements.[6] Given the conviction among many Marxists scholars that social reform must come from the efforts of social movements and that no independent reformist role can be attributed to the actions of the state, this focus is understandable.[7]

Among those urban sociologists such as R.E. Pahl and John Rex[8] who do accept some independent state role, research has tended to concentrate on broad theoretical questions of definition, or on how (mainly at the local level) official rules and procedures can affect class relationships. Understandably with their sociological perspective, they have not traced the political forces involved in the evolution of policy over time, or attempted to explain what accounts for changes in policy. A major objective of this book is, therefore, to help fill this gap by studying the ways in which different governments have formulated urban policies since 1945. The central focus will be on national legislation and on assessing which forces have been responsible for the policies adopted at particular times. In other words, our overriding concern is to explain how and why the policy agenda changes over time. We are, therefore, centrally involved in the analysis of political power and conflict. With E.E. Schattsneider we accept that:

> Political conflict is not like an intercollegiate debate in which the opponents agree in advance on a definition of the issues. As a matter of fact, *the definition of the alternatives is the supreme instrument of power*, the antagonists can rarely agree on what the issues are because power is involved in the definition. He who determines what politics is about runs the country, because the definition of alternatives is the choice of conflicts, and the choice of conflicts allocates power.[9] (Italics in original.)

We now know enough about British government to include the role of civil servants and organised groups in any analysis of the policy agenda.[10] Surprisingly, however, few scholars have attempted to trace the role of political parties *in government* with respect to specific policy areas. Studies of particular governments are legion, and there is a growing literature on the ideological, organisational and historical development of parties.[11] The critical question of whether, at the national level, parties in government make a difference to policy, has received much less attention. Few dispute the political importance of political parties as mobilisers of opinion and as the vehicles for the translation of opinion into policy. As David Robertson notes: 'To talk today about democracy is to talk about a system of competing political parties,'[12] and most recent criticisms of liberal democracy focus on the role of parties and their alleged failure to convert contrasting programmes into policies.[13] Indeed, for democratic theory the relationship between the state and class relations in society hinges fundamentally on the role of political parties, for we have few other mechanisms of representation which in the context of modern industrial states have the same potential for mobilising and responding to class interests. Notwithstanding some recent variations, a competitive two party system has existed in Britain since the Second World War with each party ostensibly adhering to a distinctive position on how society should be organised and resources distributed. Under these conditions, responsive party government is at least theoretically possible, and the analysis of the policies pursued by different governments can provide a crucial indicator of the performance of government. Such an analysis must involve weighing the influence of the complex of forces bearing on policy — interest groups, civil servants, the broader economic and social environment, as well as parties. In so doing we will be joining a debate on the state of liberal democracy in Britain. Some scholars have already gone so far as to claim that Britain (along with most industrial societies) has already ceased to be a liberal democracy as policy is no longer determined by citizens transmitting their preferences to policy makers via parties and elections. Instead, they claim that Britain is corporatist; or is characterised by a polity where the shared interests of parties, bureaucracies and organised economic and professional groups dominate policy.[14] Unfortunately, corporatist theory is relatively undeveloped and little relevant empirical work has been undertaken. We know little, for example, about which policy areas are most susceptible to corporatist decision-making. We do not even know whether Britain is moving towards conservative corporatism (as in fascist states) or what has been called redistributive corporatism (as in

Scandinavia). While we cannot provide answers to these questions, we can throw light on the debate by showing which forces have been important in determining policy in a range of policy areas.

A further dimension of government which we will examine in this book is the way in which party principles and ideologies influence policy over time, and whether they adapt and change in response to changes in social structure and citizens' needs and demands. It may be, for example, that a coherently thought out party policy conceived in response to a particular social need is appropriate at one point in time, but remains unchanged some years hence when social and political conditions have changed. In this situation, which party is in government may be important, but the party role may be quite inappropriate to the needs and expectations of party supporters and particular social groups. What we cannot do in our discussion of parties is to analyse in detail intra-party decision making processes outside government. Our objective of studying policy formulation and implementation in broadly defined areas of urban policy is already ambitious, and while intra-party decision making structures will be referred to when relevant, this will not be a major focus.

In our analysis of national urban policies we intend, therefore, to pay particular attention to the role of party in government, and to assess the extent to which party programmes and ideologies have influenced both the formulation and implementation of government programmes. Each chapter will describe changes in a particular policy area over time and will assess the role of parties, interest groups and central and local bureaucracies in this process. We will also attempt to place policy in the broader economic and social context by demonstrating the ways in which macro-economic constraints and also certain ideas about the nature of urban society have had a direct influence on policy. Perhaps obviously, this latter exercise can rarely be precise. The sheer complexitiy of the policy process blurs many causal relationships and renders systematic analysis with the precise factoring out of particular influences impossible. However, what can be achieved through careful scholarship and the utilisation of what is now a large body of related research in each of the policy areas covered, is an identification of the *main* influences on policy, together with some explanation of why particular influences have been important at particular times.

National Urban Policy: A Definition

Our concern with national policy derives partly from a perception that

in Britain the policies pursued by central governments have been crucial
in affecting resource allocation in urban areas. If there is a distinctive
feature of the British central/local system, it is the functional rather
than territorial division of powers.[15] Considerable variation in policy
outputs between different local units does exist[16] and in some policy
areas local discretion and local power is significant.[17] However, as
judged by government statements and legislation, as well as broad aims
of urban policy such as containment or regional revival, central rather
than local interactions are perceived by most participants as the key
determinants of urban policy. Local units are very much the recipients
of central dictates in specific policy areas such as housing and education,
and the local policy agenda — the issues and policies debated and
discussed at particular points in time — is greatly influenced by
functionally distinct national policies. We do not, however, want to beg
the question of local influence. As Douglas Ashford notes, we still have
much to learn about the central/local system,[18] and one of our main
aims is to place local political and bureaucratic power in national
perspective. But this book is not primarily about central/local relations.
It is a study of the ways in which the national policy agenda has
changed over time, and of the relative influence of various actors —
including local authorities — in shaping this agenda.

With over 90 per cent of its population living in urban areas, Britain
is truly an urbanised society. Why, then, should it be necessary to
distinguish policies which are primarily urban in character? After all,
every aspect of public policy touches on the urban population from
defence to education to law enforcement. There are two ways in which
this problem can be approached. First, we could attempt to discuss
urban policy in terms of a definition based on a universally applicable
set of urban characteristics. Such an exercise would be problematical,
to say the least. Sociologists and urbanists have struggled long and hard
to define 'urban' but have yet to agree on a definition.[19] Admittedly,
we are familiar with the main forces responsible for urbanisation and
urban change. Among these, migration[20] and patterns of industrial,
commercial and infrastructure investment[21] are the most important,
but we are still unsure of the precise relationship between migration
and investment. Given the difficulties involved in agreeing on a basic
definition of urban, defining urban policy is an even more awesome
task. As noted, to a greater or lesser extent all aspects of public policy
affect the urban population. Again, existing theory provides us with
little guidance. To rely on recent Marxist urban sociology, for example,
and accept that capitalism based on 'collective consumption' determines

spatial forms,[22] would confine us to the spatial aspects of urbanism and would require us to analyse all those aspects of public policy which impinge on urban investment patterns. To be consistent we would, therefore, have to study not only planning, housing, transport and regional policy, but also other infrastructure investments (such as education) as well as general monetary and fiscal policy. The causal links between many of these policies and particular aspects of urban society and form are highly complex and often tenuous.

Because of these problems we do not rely on a theoretically independent definition of urban or urban policy. Instead — and this is the second way in which the problem can be approached — we will examine those policies which, in their functional division of responsibilities, politicians and civil servants themselves consider essentially urban in nature. While there is no rigid view on what is and what is not urban, broadly speaking the areas covered by the Department of the Environment (DOE) on its creation in 1970 — housing, transport, planning, land values, conservation and central/local relations — are accepted as part of the urban purview by politicians and bureaucrats. In addition, programmes concerned with urban decline or 'deprivation', although until recently in the domain of the Home Office, must be included within any 'official' definition or urban policy. The justification for respecting this definition is that by studying these areas the adequacy or otherwise of national urban policies can be assessed either in terms of officially stated policy objectives, or in terms of some broader criteria based on social justice or economic efficiency. Since 1945, many urban policies in Britain — and especially land use planning — have been based on certain values concerning the nature of urban growth and change. These include the 'containment' of urban sprawl, the 'decrowding' of overpopulated cities via dispersal to New Towns and growth towns, and the use of an extensive public housing sector to help achieve these broad objectives. These policies do not add up to a national urban policy in the sense that physical, economic and population planning have been co-ordinated to achieve certain goals. Among capitalist or mixed economies we have to look to France or Holland for such attempts.[23] However, British policy does represent a major intervention by the state in urban society. Note that with the exception of 'deprivation' policies, British urban policy has been conceived almost entirely in terms of the *physical* aspects of urban society. Education, law enforcement and social services are recognised as having an urban dimension but, at the level of national policy making, rarely have politicians, civil servants or academics considered them

primarily urban areas. It is perhaps obvious that if the stated objectives
of urban policies are to be achieved — and these almost always involve
resolutions to reduce inequalities in the provision of services and
resources between individuals and between and within areas — *all*
aspects of domestic policy must be involved. In no sense, therefore, do
we accept the 'official' definition of urban policy as complete. On the
contrary, in our concluding chapter we argue strongly for a broadening
of British urban policy to include most domestic policy areas. But the
book's immediate purpose is to analyse those issue areas which have
been an express part of urban policy: land-use planning, land values,
housing and slum clearance, urban transport and inner cities policy.
To this list we add regional economic and industrial location policies.
Although at first this area might appear to sit slightly uncomfortably
with our other policy areas, there are at least two very good reasons for
including it. First, correcting regional imbalance was a major part of
post-war reconstruction policy. Together with the dispersal of
population and the containment of urban sprawl it was part of a general
(if not very carefully worked out) strategy with profound implications
for migration and investment patterns and therefore for urban growth
and change. Second, the directing of industrial, commercial and
infrastructure investment is arguably among the most powerful tools
available to governments in their efforts to control, regulate or
transform urban society. Since the Second World War, British
governments have pursued regional revival with more consistency and
vigour than any other area of economic planning. Again, this has had
important consequences for the British pattern of urban change.

   Like all advanced industrial countries, Britain has acquired a vast
and complex administrative machinery to implement the various
urban-directed policies and programmes and, as will be demonstrated,
administrative changes can have a profound effect on particular policies.
Governments have sometimes recognised the interconnectedness of
different policy areas in their reorganisations, and have edged towards
the creation of a 'national urban policy'. Our definition of urban policy
must include, therefore, relevant administrative innovations and
reforms, including changes in central/local relations. In sum, national
urban policy is defined as including:

(a) *Land-Use Planning.* This includes both the framework of local plan
making and broader national planning objectives such as regional policy
and dispersal and containment. Because of the central importance of
land-use planning in affecting other urban policies, some of the more

important administrative changes within central government and
between central and local government will be covered in the land-use
planning chapter.

(b) *Land Values Policies.* Attempts by governments to collect
betterment on development land and to compensate owners whose
property has been purchased by agreement or compulsion, are included
in this category. Land values are often treated in conjunction with
land-use planning. Our attempt to distinguish between the two reflects
our conviction that land values, because of their effect on investment,
are a critical (and also an under-researched) area of urban policy.

(c) *Housing and Slum Clearance.* All aspects of central government
policy affecting the public and private housing markets will be covered.
Some reference to conservation policies will also be included.

(d) *Urban Transport Policies.* Central government policies towards
urban public transport and towards the private movement of goods and
people in cities will be analysed, as will the relationship between
transport policies and urban renewal policies.

(e) *Economic Policy.* This includes regional economic and industrial
location policies. Macro-economic monetary and fiscal policies are
referred to only as they have affected programmes of the functional
areas of urban policy, and these will be referred to under the
appropriate chapters.

(f) *Inner City Policies.* Government attempts to discriminate positively
in favour of certain disadvantaged areas will be analysed. Coverage will
be confined to disadvantage as it affects individuals in areas and
areas *per se.*

Chapters 2 to 7 will correspond to each of these broad policy areas.
In each case, an attempt will be made to trace the evolution of policy
since 1945 and to assess the extent to which national policy has been
shaped by political parties, interest groups and bureaucracies. The
changing nature of the policy agenda will also be placed in the broader
economic and social environment, and particular attention will be paid
to how ideas about urban form and urban change have influenced
policy over time. In addition, some reference will be made to what
broadly might be called protest movements, or attempts by citizens'

groups to advance their interests outside of the normal channels provided by political parties and established economic and professional interest groups. Our comments on protest movements will by necessity be brief. Little systematic research into the relationship between citizens' action groups and the policy process has been undertaken and most of our references will be confined to noting the level of activity undertaken by such groups.

Our study concentrates on the post-war period simply because it was during the 1945-50 Labour Government's tenure in office that substantial state involvement in urban society was established. As we are concerned with the evolution of policy, however, we do not treat 1945 as an arbitrary starting point, and reference to the state role prior to this date will be included in every chapter.

Chapter 8 has three main purposes. First, to summarise the particular configuration of influence in each of the areas covered and to discuss the consequences of this pattern for urban society. Our second objective, which is to explain this pattern, inevitably raises questions on the performance of government, and in particular the effectiveness of party in government. That this is an important exercise is obvious, for as we earlier implied, if party politics are failing, then the prospects for democracy are dim. In the urban context, the rise of protest movements may be linked to the failure of party, so what is at stake is not only the technical performance of government in urban society, but also the viability of liberal democracy itself.

In a context in which we are increasingly told that the vast complexity of modern society and its political interactions have rendered countries like Britain 'ungovernable',[24] it may be that there is little hope for a revitalised and responsive role for national government in urban society. Chapter 8's final aim, then, is to discuss whether such a renaissance is possible, or whether, as much current opinion would have it, new approaches and policies simply create new problems.

Notes

1. For a good review of Marxist and non-Marxist approaches to the study of urban society, see Michael Harloe (ed.), *Captive Cities: Studies in the Political Economy of Cities and Regions* (London, Wiley, 1977), and especially Harloe's 'Introduction' and R.E. Pahl's 'Managers, Technical Experts and the State'.

2. Ibid.; see also C.G. Pickvance (ed.), *Urban Sociology: Critical Essays* (London, Tavistock, 1976), and in particular the 'Introduction' and the essays by Manuel Castells.

3. The long (and continuing) community power debate is centrally concerned with this question, see Michael Aiken and Paul E. Mott (eds), *The Structure of Community Power* (New York, Random House, 1970), as is the debate within British sociology on housing classes and community conflict, see John Rex and Ray Moore, *Race, Community and Conflict* (London, Oxford University Press, 1967); J. Lambert and C. Filkin, 'Race Relations Research: Some Issues of Approach and Application', *Race*, vol.12, no.3 (1971), pp.329-35.

4. See Pickvance (ed.), *Urban Sociology*; also R.E. Pahl, *Whose City?* (Harmondsworth, Middx., Penguin, 1975).

5. See in particular, Douglas Ashford, 'The Effects of Central Finance on the British Local Government System', *British Journal of Political Science*, vol.4, Part 3, pp305-22; John Dearlove, *The Politics of Policy in Local Government* (London, Cambridge University Press, 1973); Kenneth Newton, *Second City Politics* (London, Oxford University Press, 1976). In addition, a growing literature on local government expenditure outputs and their correlates is centrally concerned with the relationship between structure and party at the local level. For a summary of research findings in this area, see Kenneth Newton, 'Community Performance in Britain', *Community Research*, vol.26 (1976), pp.49-86.

6. Manuel Castells, *The Urban Question* (Cambridge, Mass., MIT Press, 1977); C.G. Pickvance, 'On the Study of Urban Social Movements', in C.G. Pickvance (ed.), *Urban Sociology*, pp.198-218. There is, however, an increasing interest in central state structures among Marxist scholars at least at the level of theoretical discussion. Empirical work is rarer, but see Peter Dickens, 'Social Change, Housing and the State', paper before the CES Conference on Urban Change and Conflict, York University, January 1977.

7. Ibid.

8. R.E. Pahl, *Whose City?*; John Rex and Ray Moore, *Race, Community and Conflict.*

9. E.E. Schattsneider, *The Semi Sovereign People*, quoted by Jack Walker, 'Setting the Agenda in the U.S. Senate: A Theory of Problem Selection', *British Journal of Political Science*, vol.7, Part 4, p.423. See also Peter Bachrach and Morton Baratz, *Power and Poverty* (New York, Oxford University Press, 1972).

10. The literature on these general subjects is now vast. For a good sample and excellent bibliography, see Richard Rose (ed.), *Studies in British Politics* (London, Macmillan, 3rd edn., 1976), chs. IV and V and bibliography.

11. Of recent studies of the two major parties, two stand out, David Howell, *British Social Democracy* (London, Croom Helm, 1976), and Nigel Harris, *Competition and the Corporate Society* (London, Methuen, 1973).

12. David Robertson, *A Theory of Party Competition* (London, Wiley, 1976), p.1. In the United States, at least, there has been a resurgence of interest in the impact of political parties and institutions on policy. For example, Douglas A. Hibbs's 'Political Parties and Macro Economic Policy', *American Political Science Review*, vol.LXXI, no.4 (December 1977), pp.1467-81, attempts to assess the role of party incumbency on macro-economic policy in Britain, the US and other western countries.

13. Walter Dean Burnham, 'American Political Parties in the 1970s: Beyond Party', in William Nisbet Chambers and Walter Dean Burnham (eds), *The American Party Systems* (New York, Oxford University Press, 2nd edn., 1975); Richard Rose, *The Problem of Party Government* (Harmondsworth, Middx., Penguin, 1976); Jean Blondel, *Political Parties: A Genuine Case for Discontent?* (London, Wildwood House, 1977).

14. See in particular, Alan Cawson, 'Pluralism, Corporatism and the Role of the State', *Government and Opposition*, vol. 13, no.12 (Spring 1978); J.T. Winkler, 'The Corporate Economy: Theory and Administration', in R. Scase

(ed.), *Industrial Society: Class, Cleavage and Control* (London, Allen and Unwin, 1977); also, Nigel Harris, *Competition and the Corporate Society* (London, Methuen, 1972).

15. See J.A.G. Griffith, *Central Departments and Local Authorities* (London, George Allen and Unwin, 1966).

16. Kenneth Newton, 'Community Performance' and sources cited.

17. Particularly in housing. See Pat Niner, *Local Authority Housing Policy and Practice*, University of Birmingham, Centre for Urban and Regional Studies, Occasional Paper No.31 (Birmingham, 1975); Alan Murie *et al.*, *Housing Policy and the Housing System* (London, George Allen and Unwin, 1976), ch.7.

18. Douglas Ashford, 'Central Finance', pp.320-2. See also, O. Hartley, 'The Relationship Between Central Government and Local Authorities', *Public Administration*, vol.49 (1971), pp.439-56.

19. For a good overview of different sociological perspectives on the city and urbanism, see Leonard Reissman, *The Urban Process* (New York, The Free Press, 1970); also R.E. Pahl, *Whose City?*

20. For a discussion of migration theory, see Brian J.L. Berry, *The Human Consequences of Urbanization* (New York, St. Martin's Press, 1973), pp.80-3.

21. Manuel Castells, *The Urban Question*.

22. Ibid.

23. See James L. Sundquist, *Dispersing Population: What America Can Learn from Europe* (Washington, DC., The Brookings Institution, 1975), chs. 3 and 5; *Successes Abroad: What Foreign Cities Can Teach American Cities*. Hearings before the Subcommittee on the City of the Committee on Banking, Finance and Urban Affairs, House of Representatives, Washington, DC, 4, 5 and 6 April 1977, testimony of Peter Hall.

24. On ungovernability in Britain, see Anthony King, 'Overload: Problems of Governing in the 1970s', *Political Studies*, vol.23, nos.2-3 (1975); and in the US, see Daniel Bell, 'The Revolution of Rising Entitlements', *Fortune*, April 1975, pp.98-103; Aaron Wildavsky, 'Government and the People', *Commentary*, August 1973, pp.25-32.

2 LAND-USE PLANNING AND ADMINISTRATION

> When it turned out to have been an illusion that the need for
> a particular intervention was only temporary; when the acts
> of intervention proved to have disturbing effects, often far
> outside the field where they were applied. . .; when their lack
> of compatibility with each other and with other aims and
> policies. . .stood out as irrational and damaging; and when they
> created serious administrative difficulties. . .[then]. . .attempts
> at coordination were forced on the State. . .This is the road we
> have travelled toward planning. (Gunnar Mydal, Beyond the Welfare
> State, 1960.)

In many respects land-use planning is the 'key' urban policy, for the
granting or withholding of planning permission for development
together with more positive land-use controls can fundamentally affect
population movements and patterns of industrial, commercial and
government investment. As such, land values, and housing and
employment opportunities can be directly affected by governments'
planning policies. In the present chapter, land-use planning policy will
be defined in terms of legislation affecting local plan making and
regulation of development, as well as land-use policies such as the
dispersal of population and investment to New Towns, which are
designed to control and direct the growth of development between
and within conurbations and regions. Specifically economic policies
designed to achieve similar objectives will be discussed in Chapter 6.
Because of the central importance of this policy area, the main changes
in central government administrative structure in the urban policy area
and in central/local relations will also be reviewed in this chapter.

As in all other areas of urban policy, different political parties and
governments have frequently adopted different positions in relation to
land-use planning, and a useful way of identifying these is to
characterise them in terms of four abstract models of the land-use
planning system. (By land-use planning system we mean simply an
administrative structure and process by which spatial forms in urban
areas are regulated, controlled or determined.) In the post-1945 period,
Britain has experienced a number of policy changes which can be
placed on a continuum ranging from positive to non land-use planning.

1			1
positive land-use planning	indicative land-use planning	regulative land-use planning	non land-use planning

Positive land-use planning requires the state to control all resource allocation in urban areas and to *dictate* future investment and population patterns according to centrally drawn up plans.[1] Naturally, such a system would require that the state had the administrative structures necessary to integrate all those variables which impinge on planning policies. Hence, closely co-ordinated local, regional and central agencies would be needed, as would a close liaison between physical and economic planning.

Indicative land-use planning implies that the state does not determine changes in spatial forms through the allocation of resources by central and local governments, but instead indicates the objectives towards which private and public resources should be harnessed. Under such a system forward planning is essential as is the sort of local-regional-central structure required under positive land-use planning. Indicative planning, then, is typical of planning within a mixed economy, with the state indicating likely trends and objectives on the basis of consultation between the public and private sectors.[2]

Regulative land-use planning implies that the state's role in physical planning policies is limited to the regulation of initiatives emanating primarily from the private sector. Hence the public sector does undertake some development, but this is minor compared with private development, the main public planning function being regulation rather than direction and control. Administrative structures with integrative functions are not required and state agencies' main job is the local oversight of private sector development plans and proposals. Obviously, under regulative planning, extensive state financial resources are not required.

Non land-use planning is fairly straightforward as it requires no state administrative structures for regulating or determining changes in urban form. This also means that a major input of financial resources is not necessary and the private sector is able to determine changes in spatial form at will.

These four models are idealised. At no time has any British Government adhered to any one of them in total. However, policies have approximated towards them. As we shall see, neither positive land-use planning nor non planning have been important since 1945 — although Labour Governments almost created positive planning systems in 1947 and 1975. Generally, indicative planning styles have dominated the period, but with Labour Governments advocating rather more interventionist policies than Conservative Governments. Before describing the differences in policy since the war, some reference to the 1945 period is necessary.

Government and Land-use Planning Until 1945

Pre-1945 policies in this issue area were basically aimed at the creation of a regulative planning system. In other words, legislation during the nineteenth and early twentieth centuries was aimed at giving local authorities powers to enable them to regulate — but not control and direct — urban development. So, factory and public health legislation in the 1840s gave local authorities powers and resources to intervene to ameliorate the social and physical conditions of populations[3] and although local authorities could provide sewerage, parks, lighting, public utilities and gas and electricity, they could not control development undertaken by the private sector.

By the turn of the century it was clear to some observers that the amelioration of social ills on this *ad hoc* basis could never solve the problems created as a consequence of urbanisation. For Ebenezer Howard the problem of inner city squalor and overcrowding was not caused by the inability of people to help themselves but by the urbanisation process itself.[4] If this was the case, local authority intervention could only be a piecemeal and limited response to more fundamental problems. Howard's solution was to argue for the creation of 'Garden Cities' to give the benefits of both the urban and rural life style. Self-contained towns would be created on green-field sites outside existing urban areas, and as they grew so they would draw population from existing urban areas. By this process of gradual dispersal it was hoped that the tide of urban congestion would be abated and the evils of overcrowding, squalor and potential revolution removed.

Howard's analysis argued clearly for the integration of economic, population and urban policies to solve the urban problem, and gradually during the late nineteenth century, sentiment in favour of some urban planning mounted in size and strength. In 1899 the Town and Country Planning Association (TCPA) was formed just before the creation of the first 'Garden City' at Letchworth in 1901. Soon afterwards, the Town Planning Institute (TPI) was formed in 1914 to foster higher standards in town planning.[5] Both of these bodies wanted more state intervention, but their aims were by no means identical. The bias of the TPI was for local authorities to regulate rather than initiate, while the TCPA advocated a more interventionist planning of urban development with a positive role taken by the state.

It is not surprising, however, that the 'Garden Cities' ideal was not realised in the pre-1945 period — in spite of the success of Letchworth and its sister development at Welwyn Garden. The idea of positive intervention by the state to disperse jobs and population was far too radical an idea for Conservative and Liberal Governments in the early years of the twentieth century. However, these Governments were not averse to intervention on a limited basis if they felt that it might serve some useful purpose. Thus in 1909, partly as a consequence of the poor condition and performance of urban recruits during the Boer War, the first Town Planning Act was passed which allowed local authorities to plan (on a regulative basis) their suburbs on the approval of the relevant Ministers.[6] This legislation was within the ameliorative, rather than positive interventionist, strand of earlier legislation. It was hoped that a better planned physical environment might enhance the condition of the populace and therefore produce a more efficient work force to assist Britain's competitiveness.

Enlightened self-interest has always played a role in government legislation and planning policies were no exception. Subsequent additions to this 1909 legislation in 1919 and 1935 were, however, more the result of the influence that the embryonic planning interest groups were able to bring to bear on policy-makers than of politicians seizing the 'main chance'.[7] Thus the 1919 Act made it obligatory for towns with populations of over 20,000 to plan their suburbs, and this was followed in 1935 by legislation to control ribbon developments outside urban areas.[8] The creation of regulative planning to ameliorate serious urban problems was the major objective of this legislation. No commitment to positive or indicative planning by the state existed — as is revealed by the fact that the Planning Acts did not really assist the local authorities to intervene in the development process, and private developers could build freely unless a local authority plan was in force. Even this latter caveat was often nonsensical since if local authorities refused to allow developments they were obliged to pay prohibitive compensation to developers.[9]

But pressure for a more interventionist/positive role for the state was mounting, and reaffirmed in a series of reports published during the Second World War which marked the rejection by all political parties of the regulative planning bias of the pre-war period. The reason for this change was basically twofold. On the one hand was the glaring internal problem of unemployment and regional imbalance in Britain. On the other hand was the growing acceptance of planning in the context of the major economic and political changes produced by the Second World War.

Along with other industrial countries, Britain had experienced chronic unemployment during the 1930s. However, it was clear to many that the world-wide depression which had hit Britain first in the Western World masked major structural and regional problems in the economy.[10] Serious regional imbalance existed with the traditional heavy engineering and coal-based industries of the North, Scotland, Northern Ireland and South Wales declining in relation to newer consumer oriented industries based in the Midlands and the South-East.[11] The resulting drift of investment and population to the South-East and Midlands was substantial and had effectively produced 'two nations', one rich and growing, the other poor and declining.[12]

To the embryonic planning professions, as well as to most Labour politicians – and also many within the Conservative Party – there seemed to be an obvious correlation between this drift and the depression of traditional industrial areas. As a result and in a drive to ensure that immobile workers would not suffer again the same levels of unemployment and debilitating living conditions, many politicians in the 1930s began to look to planning as a means of directing industry and employment to the areas which most required it.[13] At the same time, the planners hoped that this commitment would allow them to realise their own ambitions of co-ordinating urban with industrial and economic development. In addition, rural/agricultural interests saw this as an opportunity to launch an attack on the decline of agriculture and concomitant urban encroachments into rural areas via speculative ribbon development.[14]

These pressures by 1935 had already led to legislation to control ribbon development and a re-acceptance of Ebenezer Howard's call for green belts and dispersal to contain urban growth, and in 1937 the Barlow Commission on the Distribution of the Industrial Population was instituted.[15] The major importance of the Barlow Report, which appeared in 1940, was that it brought together as one integrated problem the growth of urban conurbations and the question of regional imbalance. It argued that there was a direct relationship between urbanisation and structural economic change which required joint solutions. Hence, government intervention should create a regional balance through the mechanisms of industrial location controls and urban dispersal and containment — the latter being the avowed goal of the planning interest groups.[16]

The Barlow Report was important in other respects, for not only did it lay the groundwork for immediate post-war industrial and regional policies, but it also delved into a range of centrally related issues. As a consequence, further government war-time studies were initiated including the Reith Report on New Towns, the Uthwatt Report on Compensation and Betterment, the Scott Report on land utilisation in rural areas and the Dower and Hobhouse Reports on national parks and national parks administration.[17] The Scott Report accepted the need for the community to control agriculture and agricultural uses in rural areas. But the full thrust of state planning was rejected with the conclusion that the 'onus of proof' for a change of use must rest with those wishing to change an agricultural or rural usage. Therefore, unless a clear case could be made out in favour of an urban or industrial development, then the land in question would be left as it was and accorded the benefit of the doubt. The Uthwatt Report proposed a solution to the compensation and betterment issue in favour of the public sector (see Chapter 3), a conclusion underscored by the Reith Report, which called for the dispersal of an expanding population to self-contained and planned New Towns with all development undertaken by the state. Of course, this implied positive planning, since it was intended that private development would be largely curtailed. The Dower and Hobhouse Reports called for central park agencies to protect areas of natural beauty and recreation.

Labour's Attempts at Positive Land-Use Planning, 1945-1951

In the wake of pre-war economic depression, regional imbalance and the cathartic experience of massive state intervention in the economy and society during the war, a general shift of sentiment in favour of planning had occurred by 1945. In some policy areas, in particular nationalisation, fierce political party controversy existed over the nature and extent of state intervention. In other areas, including land-use planning, a remarkable absence of party dispute or rancour existed. To politicians of all parties the main planning objectives outlined by the wartime reports — planned urban containment with the dispersal of population to New Towns — were accepted as absolutely necessary. An examination of the party manifestos and of the relevant Parliamentary debates of the time confirms this general consensus on planning policy.

While political consensus existed, the full logic of the Scott, Reith and Uthwatt Reports was not accepted in the subsequent 1946 New Towns Act and 1947 Town and Country Planning Act. Remember that the reports together with the findings of the Barlow Commission proposed the creation of positive land-use *and* industrial planning. What, in fact, transpired was a system which at the most went only half-way towards these goals. In sum, only the agricultural protectionist bias of the Scott Report and the creation of a Green Belt around London in line with the 1944 Greater London Development Plan were accepted in full. The operations of the market in land transactions were not totally ended,[18] and local authorities were denied powers to plan their own green belts or control new town developments as originally proposed. Instead, outside London, County Councils could create green belts — but they did not need Ministry approval for their plans.[19]

The 1946 New Towns Act did accept the need for urban dispersal to self-contained communities on green field sites outside the normal local government/central government system. But the New Towns would be built and planned by *ad hoc* 'Development Corporations' financed by the Exchequer. Also, the relevant Minister would appoint the Corporation chairman, his deputy and seven other members. The Corporations would be helped by being able to purchase any land they required at existing-use value under compulsory purchase orders. These powers were not accorded to local authorities except in areas of war damage and blight.[20] This positive role of the new Corporations was strengthened by their power to finance most housing and infrastructure services development, to select which industries they required, and recruit their new inhabitants on the basis of the skills they possessed. Between 1946 and 1950 the new Labour administration designated fourteen such New Towns in an attempt to encourage urban dispersal and to solve regional imbalance.[21]

As an adjunct to these positive development powers local authorities were given statutory powers to plan and regulate development within their boundaries under the 1947 Town and Country Planning Act. This Act also dealt centrally with the issue of compensation and betterment which is discussed in Chapter 3.

The important point to remember about the 1947 Act is that although it sought to penalise the private developer and landowner by levying a 100 per cent development charge on land transactions and development, this impost was not geared to giving the local authorities a positive role in the development process. As we have argued, their only positive powers to intervene and commence development were the limited Comprehensive Development powers for war blighted areas. The 1947 Act simply gave local authorities the obligation to control future developments by regulatory planning; it did not provide extra resources for the local authorities to intervene positively.

The major provisions of the 1947 Act — as they related to local authority planning — were therefore the statutory obligation for all county councils and county boroughs in England and Wales and all counties, cities and burghs in Scotland to plan changes in land use. In future no change in land use would be possible without first approaching the relevant local planning authority and obtaining planning permission. The local planning authorities were also obliged to create 20-year development plans showing likely changes in land use, and subject to quinquennial reviews given changes in population and industrial demands.[22] These powers were further formulated in London under the 1947 Act by the decision to create a Green Belt with effective local government day to day control being supplemented by central government veto of any local decision or appeal. But these powers were only specifically given to London under the 1947 legislation. Obviously, while these developments allowed, at the local level, the state to intervene much more effectively than previously, the involvement envisaged was essentially regulatory rather than initiatory. In future, the local authorities would be able to curtail unwanted development by the private sector, but without extra resources it was unlikely that they would be able to undertake the development *they* might deem essential if the private sector would not undertake it.

This lack of a major commitment to positive state direction of development and dispersal was underscored by the somewhat muted attempts at administrative co-ordination and reform in this period. A new central Ministry of Town and Country Planning was created in 1943 with responsibility for New Towns, local planning ratifications and planning appeals. There was, however, no central co-ordination of land-use, housing, economic and transport policies. Moreover, although the new Ministry did set up eleven Regional Planning Offices under Regional Controllers, the co-ordination among and between other regional offices of Whitehall Departments was limited. At the same time, the regional offices were more clearly the 'eyes and ears' of the new Ministry than agencies encouraging the local authorities to intervene positively in development. The scope of the regional offices work was largely confined to an advisory role should the embryonic local planning authorities run into difficulties.[23]

Clearly, therefore, the integrated and directive system of administration necessary for indicative or positive planning was lacking in the latter half of the 1940s. This said, the 1947 Act did commence the post-war rationalisation of planning responsibilities in government. Prior to 1947, county boroughs and county council districts had been responsible for the control of development. After the Act, only the county councils and county boroughs were responsible, which meant that the number of involved authorities fell immediately from 1,441 to 145. As of 1947, therefore, only larger local authorities were able to plan future changes in land use in their areas (subject to Ministerial approval and the right of appeal to the Minister by private individuals on the refusal of planning permission).[24]

The 1947 system did begin a process of administrative rationalisation therefore, but it did not create integrated bureaucratic structures, nor did it allow local authorities to plan positively for land use changes. The 1946 and 1947 legislation did create a self-contained system which *in theory* was supposed to enable positive public planning, but in practice Labour policies fell short of the creation of a positive planning and dispersal system. This asymmetry between theory and practice resulted mainly from unforeseen circumstances arising in implementation. The 1947 system was predicated on the assumption that population would be fairly static and that development could therefore be planned twenty years in advance. Future development was expected to take place in the autonomous New Towns or under local authority housing provisions. Through the use of building licences and planning permissions the state (at local and quasi-central levels) was to be given the major role in physical development. Private sector involvement in housing and other development was expected to be limited to minimal 'in-filling' and the development of industrial infrastructure. Even this latter role was to be controlled by the state through the system of industrial development certificates created under the 1945 Distribution of Industry Act.[25]

Clearly this self-contained approach was well on the way to the creation of a positive planning system. This was true even though it did not integrate physical or industrial development on a local-regional-central basis, or allow the state to determine industrial and economic policies other than by the means of location control.

As it turned out, these weaknesses were quickly revealed by demographic and social changes. In particular, the post-war baby boom undermined the static population assumptions of the legislation, and the rapid increase in demand for owner-occupied housing brought the regulative planning role of the local authorities into question. Rather than dealing with limited and piecemeal developments in the private sector, the local authorities, who were themselves only beginning to gain experience in their new role, found themselves inundated with a mass of work. This was not helped by the fact that local development plans did not look at broad socio-economic trends, nor did they indicate the likely future demands for land. As a result, land allocations in the initial development plans were quickly used up. To make matters worse, the 100 per cent development charge imposed by the Act effectively dried up the supply of land and made it unprofitable for landowners to develop.[26]

When attempting to explain why the Government decided on these particular policies, we should look first to the role of interest groups. At first sight, the influence of the TCPA and TPI looks crucial. Their policies were, after all, roughly those embodied in the 1946 and 1947 Acts, and they constituted an active lobby throughout this period. Moreover, planners are, at once, a profession, a sectional interest and government servants.[27] As such, planners and their professional associations have generally been viewed by governments as respectable and responsible.[28] One might conclude that since these bodies have been accorded the 'seals of approval' which all interest groups strive for, and because their policy aims seem to have been granted in the immediate post-war period, that they have been a major force shaping policy-making by the Labour Government.

But to accept such a claim would be to oversimplify greatly, for by 1945 the TCPA and TPI were operating in an environment which was much more favourable to their objectives. One simple explanation of the dramatic change in policy represented by the 1946 and 1947 Acts could be the election of a Labour Government committed to a planning and dispersal approach. At one level this is a sound analysis of the forces precipitating policy change, because the Party in its manifesto for the 1945 election did make a commitment to land-use planning and dispersal in the period of post-war reconstruction.[29] But this does not tell us *why* the party was so committed, and it should always be remembered that both the Coalition Government's White Paper 'The Control of Land Use' and the Conservative Party favoured the introduction of a land-use planning and dispersal system at this time. As J.B. Cullingworth has argued, it would probably have made little difference which party had been returned to office in 1945, since

Labour simply implemented policies which the Coalition Government had been finalising prior to the election.[30]

If this is the case, then other forces and actors must have been shaping policy making more directly than either the senior politicians and ministers, the concerned interest groups or the simple fact of a change of government. There are two major elements involved here. On the one hand there are the social and economic conditions which precipitated a reappraisal of policy making, and secondly — and crucially — there is the role of civil servants.

As earlier noted, the experience of the depression and the war was important in transforming attitudes towards the role of the state in the economy and society. Mass opinion moved sharply to the left and produced the Labour victory in 1945.[31] Among elites, the recommendations of the war time committees on the interrelated problems of unemployment, mobility of labour, land values, rural areas and planning and dispersal demonstrated that politicians and civil servants had also been radicalised by events. By 1945, a consensus on the need for centrally directed regional and employment policies as well as planning and dispersal policies existed,[32] and the greatly enhanced role for the state desired by so many had already been established during the war. Perhaps, given this sudden expansion of state power in a period when party politics were almost suspended, it is not surprising to learn that civil servants in the embryonic Ministry of Town and Country Planning had a major influence on policy.

Cullingworth's extensive history of planning policy in this period reveals this,[33] and also points to other reasons why civil service advice was so central. The policy area was, first of all, highly technical, and in the absence of party division, expert opinion was critical. Second, a truly positive land-use planning system requires both central co-ordination and public ownership of land. Land nationalisation was rejected by Labour in line with the expert Uthwatt Report. As will be shown in the next chapter, this was largely because Labour lacked the political resources to push through a measure which could have been electorally damaging. But without land nationalisation or the resolution of the compensation and betterment conundrum it was difficult to give local authorities the resources to plan positively or to create a centrally administered economic and land-use planning system.

Once it had been decided that the state would not intervene to take over all land, then it was probable that the debate over the actual shape of policy would be conditioned by internal bureaucratic debates dominated by departmental demarcation disputes over existing operating procedures and boundaries.

Thus the relatively weak role of the new Ministry of Town and Country Planning which lacked co-ordinating functions over land-use, housing and economic developments, transpired largely because the Treasury viewed any such tendencies with a mixture of alarm and apprehension. This uncertainty was mirrored by the Ministry of Health which was responsible at that time for housing and local government functions. Both these agencies were concerned to ensure that their own roles in government would not be usurped by an embryonic planning ministry. For this reason the last minute decision to name the new Ministry 'Town and Country Planning' rather than 'Planning' was something more than symbolic.[34] This defeat was also presumably of interest to the Board of Trade, the Ministry of Agriculture and the Ministry of Transport who would be concerned respectively with the maintenance of their economic, agricultural land and highway planning roles in government. So, after existing departmental responsibilities had been protected, the lowest common denominator was a Ministry with negative controls over the use and development of land. It was this, given Labour's failure to force through any coherent policy on positive planning, that led to the creation of the new ministry with its limited brief for state intervention.

Therefore, the Labour legislation of 1946 and 1947 owes more to socio-economic circumstances impinging on general and bureaucratic attitudes towards state intervention, than to consciously drawn up policy plans by the government, or to the manipulations and machinations of interest groups. When interest groups were of importance it was usually at the level of their ideas being utilised by civil servants intent on defending their own roles in government. Thus while the failure of the government to reorganise local government may have owed something to local authority associations defending their interests, it seems more likely that the Ministry of Health, fearing for its own autonomy, worked hard to prevent reorganisation. The dominant role of civil servants in this period is amply demonstrated by the Whiskard Committee's decision to abandon its brief from the politicians to review the proposals for land use and national planning in Whitehall and to substitute a brief of its own![35]

Regulative Planning Conservative Style: 1951-60

As we have seen, by the beginning of the 1950s it was clear that the 1947 system had not worked in practice and this had been accepted by the Labour Government. Indeed, before the 1951 election, legislation was being drafted within the Ministry of Town and Country Planning to give local authorities extra powers for positive development. These Labour plans were accepted by the new Government, and the 1952 Town Development Act gave local authorities powers to extend existing towns and villages. The Act allowed local authorities wanting to disperse their populations to work in co-operation with importing authorities wishing to expand. The logic of this arrangement was that if the state was to play a major role in a continuous dispersal programme, then existing local government structures should be utilised since the scope for a continuing increase in semi-autonomous New Towns was limited.[36] Apart from this and the further extension of local powers in the 1955 Circular on Green Belts, the rationale of Conservative policies between 1951 and 1960 was to undermine the logic of Labour's attempts at positive land-use planning and return to regulative planning. The emphasis on limiting any positive role to local authorities rather than central agencies when additional powers were needed was basic to the Conservative desire to reduce the level of state intervention in society on their return to power.[37]

Thus while the new Government did not dismantle the New Towns already designated, they were to designate only one more (at Cumbernauld) between 1951 and 1961. Indeed, in 1957 they went so far as to argue that there would be no more New Towns under future Conservative Governments. As the next chapter will show, Conservative rejection of Labour's interventionist posture was also evident in land values policy as the free market in land was partially restored in 1953 and 1954. So, Labour's movements towards a positive state role after 1945 were further eroded — a fact reinforced by the dismantling of the separate Ministry of Town and Country Planning in 1951. The regional offices (the first embryonic movement towards integrated administrative structures) were also abolished, as the functions of the old Ministry passed within the new Ministry of Housing and Local Government. Although this was an attack on the integrated planning ideal, in the long term it was probably beneficial. For while it initially meant that Housing and local government issues would predominate over those of planning, it *did* bring housing and local government functions under the same roof as those of land-use planning, and the long-term development of integrated planning was probably assisted since all these functions are inherently inter-related.

It should be added, however, that this was not the Conservative Government's primary intention. The fact that the local authorities were now left with a regulative land-use planning role shows this. The desire to limit the public role, both centrally and locally, was underscored by the constraints placed on local authority borrowing through the Public Works Loan Board and by the 1959 Town and Country Planning Act.[38] Not only did the 1959 Act re-establish the free market in land, it also introduced certificates of alternative development. Under this new system anyone refused planning permission, or having their land compulsorily purchased, could serve the relevant local authority with a certificate stating the alternative development which would have been allowed on the land if the local authority had not purchased it or refused planning permission. Generally, the certificates assumed the land would have been used at least for residential development which would then be the basis for compensation. Obviously, this arrangement inhibited effective planning as the potential costs involved were enormous. It is no surprise that in this period local authorities felt themselves prey to the whims and fancies of the private sector and were grateful for recording minimal planning gains in predominantly private schemes.[39]

The Conservative Government between 1951 and 1960 therefore looked primarily to the private sector to meet the physical development needs of the populace. Given the wartime belief in planning and the desire to allow the state at all levels to play a much more positive role, the return to a solely negative, regulatory local government role in 1951 was a major reversal of policy. As a consequence, the broad socio-economic trends of a rapid increase in population, the continuing drift to the South-East, the growing impact of the motor-car on urban areas and the continuing regional economic and unemployment imbalance went largely unabated, unplanned and unchecked. As we shall see, the internal logic of these developments could not be resisted indefinitely by the Conservative Government and between 1960 and 1964 there were major shifts in emphasis towards a more interventionist state role.

When attempting to explain policy in this period we must look first to ideological changes within the Conservative Party. Nigel Harris has argued that after 1947, the Party moved significantly to the right on industrial policy, and as we have shown, a parallel move occurred in land-use planning.[40] In addition, Conservative housing and land values policies increasingly emphasised market solutions after 1951. If the return to a regulative planning role owes much to this general shift in sentiment against state intervention, does this relegate civil service advice and interest group activity to a residual role? Not entirely. It could be argued that although this was an anti-planning decade, the planning interest groups (TCPA and TPI) and professions were

successful in maintaining planning on a regulative basis. After all, the
Conservatives did not return to a totally free market solution
immediately, for until 1959, local authorities and New Towns were
able to purchase land at existing rather than full market values.
Moreover, while the Tories designated only one additional New Town,
the existing ones continued with their development programmes. There
is also evidence that the TCPA, through its President's contacts with
Duncan Sandys, was successful in encouraging the Green Belt policy of
the mid-1950s.[41] In fact, by the late 1950s most of the larger towns in
Britain were operating within the constraints imposed by green belts.
With populations increasing and controls on land prices and building
eased, this encouraged a uniquely British form of urbanisation. Cities
became increasingly working class, while the middle class and upwardly
mobile tended to move not to suburbs contiguous with metropolitan
areas, but to smaller towns, cities and New Towns beyond the Green
Belts.[42] But these events should be kept in perspective. The fact remains
that the Conservatives, rather than modifying Labour policy so as to
iron out some of inconsistencies and anomalies in the 1946 and 1947
Acts, sought to undermine the whole system by undoing key financial
arrangements, and by abolishing the autonomous planning ministry and
its regional offices.

If the TCPA and TPI were finding their stock with government at a
low ebb at this time, it was an encouraging time for several new groups.
In particular, the Civic Trust, formed in 1957 with the aid of a
government grant and the Council for the Protection of Rural England
(CPRE) were to witness a general agreement between their objectives
and government policy. Both accepted the limited dispersal, rural
protectionism and high density urban development which were the
main results of Conservative policy.[43] Also in broad agreement with
the Government was the Society for the Promotion of Urban Renewal
which was created at this time.[44] These groups did not, of course,
dictate policy. Rather, they found themselves operating in a climate
more favourable to their objectives than probably would have prevailed
under a Labour Government.

Neither could it be claimed that civil servants moulded policy
during these years. However, the Treasury and the Ministry of Health
probably encouraged the abolition of the Ministry of Town and
Country Planning in 1951. As was emphasised earlier, an autonomous
planning ministry with a brief which potentially overlapped with those
of existing ministries had always been opposed by the civil service
establishment. The Conservatives' ideological opposition to such a

ministry was, therefore, no doubt helped by civil service opposition. Moreover, the administrative solution arrived at – the creation of the Ministry of Housing and Local Government combining planning with the housing and local government functions of the Ministry of Health – satisfied both the anti-planning sentiments of the Conservatives and protected existing departments from potential interference from a 'super' ministry. But this bureaucratic 'in fighting' with the resulting demise of the planning ministry cannot be separated from the fact of a new Government in 1951. For without the Conservative victory it would have been highly unlikely that the reorganisation would have occurred.

The Conservatives and Indicative Planning 1960-4

By 1960 it was becoming increasingly clear to the Government and to officials in the Ministry of Housing and Local Government that planning and dispersal policies would need to be amended if the problems besetting local authorities were to be solved. As we shall see, this new perception was largely brought about by interest group demands, but it was also a consequence of the dawning realisation in Conservative circles in the 1960s that the British economy was not performing as successfully as its international competitors.[45] Indeed, by the early 1960s there were a range of pressures being felt by government which were to precipitate major changes in policy in the land-use planning and dispersal fields. The Conservative response was to move, somewhat haltingly, towards an acceptance of an indicative planning framework. In other words, the Conservative response was not to give the state (at any level) major resources to intervene positively, but rather to encourage 'tripartite' forms of consultation and advice between local, central and private actors in the planning sphere. From these consultative arrangements would come studies and plans to indicate the likely economic, population, transport and land-use trends which would be used as the basis for forward planning on an indicative basis in each area being studied. At the same time, reforms were to be attempted in plan making, the supply of land for development and in dispersal policies.

The first evidence of this modification in policy was the decision to designate more New Towns – six between 1961 and 1965 – in an attempt to enhance the Government's commitment to the containment of existing urban areas and to solve problems associated with the continuing demand for land.[46] But this was not the only reason for the Conservative policy reappraisal. In addition to aiding dispersal, the

newly designated towns would be part and parcel of the growing
Conservative commitment to solving regional problems. The New
Towns at Skelmersdale, Washington and Livingstone were conceived
as centres to accommodate population growth and to encourage
regional development, rather than simply as centres designed to halt
massive urban growth – the intention of the earlier generation of New
Towns.[47]

A classic example of the new indicative planning was the creation
of Washington New Town which followed the recommendation of the
North-East Study, *A Programme for Regional Development and
Growth*, published in 1963. This plan had been drawn up quickly
after the economic recession of 1962/3, as had a similar plan for
Central Scotland – an area also regarded by the Government as
distressed. The rationale of these plans and their importance will be
dealt with elsewhere (pp.206-7); however, it is clear that they
were *pari passu* with developments in the land-use planning
sphere at this time. By the beginning of the 1960s it was obvious to
many planners that local planning offices lacked any precise idea of
which trends might affect their individual local plans. The closure of
regional offices by the Conservatives had not assisted the local planners
who, by the end of the 1950s, were without any means of co-ordination
or overview. This failing coincided with continuing population
increases and rising prosperity which intensified the pressures for land
and development in many areas – particularly the South-East and
Midlands. It was not surprising, therefore, that in line with reappraisals
on the economic front a new path would be followed in land-use
planning.

In 1961, regional studies were instituted in a number of population
and housing 'pressure' areas under the auspices of the Ministry of
Housing and Local Government. Formulated by *ad hoc* teams of central
and local government officials, these studies undertook to cover large
areas of the country to give local planning officers and their authorities
a basic idea of the broad trends likely to affect their own specific areas
and plan-making exercises.[48] The first of these studies was undertaken
in the South-East, with two more in the West Midlands and North-West
following immediately. The South-East Study completed in 1964
called for the extension of dispersal to existing large towns at
Southampton-Portsmouth, Bletchley, Northampton, Peterborough and
Ipswich. This emphasis on continuing dispersal and overspill policies
was also evident in the North-West and West Midland Studies which
reported in 1965, and all the reports called for the extension of the

New Town idea to their own areas.[49]

While the Government's acceptance of these recommendations implies a return to the planning system of the 1940s, developments on two fronts demonstrate that Conservative indicative planning was a very long way indeed from even the limited form of positive planning pioneered by Labour in the post-war years. First and foremost, the Conservatives were not prepared to see private sector development relegated to the in-filling and marginal construction originally envisaged by Labour. At least from 1954, Conservative housing policy was geared primarily to private sector solutions, with the public sector assigned a residual role. With only minor modifications, this position was maintained until 1964. Even the move back to public sector development on a more positive scale in New Towns did not significantly undermine this objective, for the New Towns were viewed as 'special cases' rather than the primary source of new development. Most local authorities, far from being viewed as the main actors in development, were actually being put under pressure from the Government to build at higher densities – often resulting in high rise developments.[50] This residual and largely unprofitable role for the public sector was reinforced by changes in land values policy which required that local authorities purchase land at current market rather than existing use values, while the private sector was able to reap all the profits of development unhindered. The Conservative commitment to indicative planning was premised primarily on helping private rather than public development, therefore.[51]

Second, the Conservatives failed to create the administrative structure necessary for an effective and integrated indicative planning system. It is true that there were developments in economic planning in the North-East and Central Scotland, but these were not related in a coherent way to land-use planning regionally, locally or nationally. Neither were the South-East, North-East and West Midlands Planning Studies integrated into economic and industrial policy making. So, in spite of the initiation of regional planning studies, the general picture emerging in this period is one of failure to integrate the various aspects of planning policy. By 1963 indeed, the Buchanan Report was able to claim that a major reason for Britain's increasingly chaotic traffic situation, was the almost complete absence of integrated land-use and transport planning.[52]

In local government reform too, Conservative policies were hesitant. Throughout their thirteen years in office, only the reform of local government in London can be seen as a step towards positive planning.

Other than this, the Conservatives did little. Hence, the 1958 Local Government Act failed to set up a Royal Commission in Local Government. But the Government could not delay reform for long. Their own regional studies seriously questioned local government responsibilities and boundaries, and in many urban areas, the inefficiency and inconsistency of existing arrangements was obvious. Cities such as Birmingham, for example, had the same powers and responsibilities as much smaller towns such as Canterbury, and the planning responsibilities for the Greater London conurbation were split between the unco-ordinated twenty-eight Metropolitan Boroughs, the Middlesex County Council and the Croydon, East Ham and West Ham County Boroughs amongst others. Clearly these anomalies could not be allowed to continue indefinitely.[53] As far as London was concerned things moved quite quickly. Following the publication of the 1959 Herbert Report, it was inevitable that some reform would come, and in 1963 the London Government Act rationalised the old local government system.[54] From 1963 an overall co-ordinating authority, the Greater London Council would be responsible for overall planning, main roads, fire and ambulance and some housing and education functions in an area covering 620 square miles and a population of approximately 8 million. The old conflicts of interest between county council and borough authorities were, in theory at least, to be swept away by the creation of thirty-two new London Boroughs and the City of London Authority who would work in conjunction with the GLC. These authorities would be responsible in co-operation with the GLC for housing, education and planning policies as well as being responsible for a wide array of local services and functions.[55]

This reform was undoubtedly one of the more radical developments under the Conservative Government in the 1960s and once more marked the gradual rejection of the regulative planning approach adopted during the 1950s. Again, however, it should be stressed that the Conservative approach, even in 1963-4, can hardly be characterised as a positive commitment to an enhanced state role. Reviewing the major developments in this period it is clear that the Conservative Government was being forced to accept a more interventionist state role in the development process *while at the same time* attempting to hold as much ground as possible for the private sector to fulfil the major role assigned to it in the 1950s. The commitment to a form of indicative planning was growing; it was not, as we shall see, a central article of party policy and faith as was Labour's commitment in the 1960s.

If the attitudes of Conservative leaders and politicians were crucial in explaining policy between 1951 and 1960, the same cannot be said of any explanation of policy in the 1960-4 period. These years saw the gradual reversal of the anti-intervention role of the Government until the groundwork for an indicative planning system had been laid. The major factor involved here was the deleterious consequences (experienced by actors in the planning and property market) of Conservative policies in the 1950s. Though it would be unfair to lay all the blame at the feet of the Government — there were unforeseen developments like the rapid rise in population and increasing pressure of demand for housing precipitated in part by rising prosperity — it is probable that these were aggravated by Government policies. The freeing of the speculative builder in the 1950s encouraged capital to enter the property market and resulted in higher land and housing prices. Price inflation was further encouraged by the inability of many local authorities to extend into green belts and peripheral rural areas. This, together with the ending of financial aid to local authorities' land purchases under the 1959 act, obliged them to concentrate on low-cost high density development and to encourage private commercial development on expensive city centre sites.

Ironically, this failure of planning did not satisfy the private sector either. With potentially large profits to be reaped from the property boom, builders were increasingly demanding from government extensions of what was a very limited land supply. By the end of the 1950s, therefore, the Conservative Government was being pressured on all sides to modify its policies.[56]

Local government and building industry concern was joined by that of the TCPA and TPI who wanted extensions to planning of the physical and economic environment. On the specific question of urban renewal, the architects and surveyors favoured wholesale redevelopment and a limited extension of land supply. The only discordant note in these varied (and by no means always compatible)[57] demands for more development land and more extensive planning came from the protectionist CPRE and Civic Trust who were concerned that more development and urban renewal would destroy Britain's architectural heritage as well as threaten existing agricultural land.

Disquiet at the passive policies of the 1950s was also evident within the civil service. There is evidence that the Permanent Secretary at the Ministry of Housing and Local Government, Evelyn Sharp, and the Ministry's Chief Planner, J.R. James, were generally in favour of more indicative planning and of extending the New Towns concept.[58]

The initiation of advisory/trend plans and the creation of a number of advisory, planning and research groups within the MHLG was almost certainly in response to the wishes of these senior civil servants.[59]

It would be easy to claim that the Government policies actually pursued during these years – the creation of further New Towns, hesitant attempts at regional planning and administrative reform and the encouragement of urban renewal by private developers – were designed to appease the variety of groups and interests 'pressuring' the Government for change. No doubt this is partly true – certainly the Conservatives were not so centrally in control of policy making as they appeared to be in the 1951-60 period. However, the changes in policy were not fundamental, and the moves towards indicative planning were probably influenced as much by personalities as by the combined pressures of external actors and civil servants. Prime Minister Macmillan had long been sympathetic to some variety of indicative planning – especially in relation to regional imbalance[60] – and Keith Joseph who replaced Lord Hill at the MHLG in 1962 was less prone to preserve ineffectual policies in the face of advice to the contrary.[61]

Labour and Indicative Planning, 1964-70

On coming to power in 1964, the Labour Government did not attempt to return to the positive land use planning framework of the 1940s. Instead, the Wilson Government, effectively institutionalising the indicative planning system begun by the Conservatives, sought to extend planning to include economic as well as land use problems. Espousing the ethos of the mixed economy, the Government believed that an effective planning system could harness both public and private resources towards maximising economic growth and producing a socially just society. In such areas as housing and land values, any monopoly role for the state was rejected. Richard Crossman, the Minister of Housing and Local Government, accepted the role of the private sector in housing production even as he sought to enhance the public role (see pp.130-31). Also, the Government ignored its Manifesto commitments to nationalise all development land in a Land Commission and instead created an institution in 1967 whose aim was to intervene in the planning system to enable the *private* sector to fulfil its development role.[62]

The commitment to indicative planning was demonstrated in Labour's acceptance of the Conservative inspired regional studies which called for further extensions to the dispersal principle. Thus, Dawley, designated in 1963 was increased in size and renamed Telford in 1965, *k*

and Warrington (1968) and Central Lancashire (1970) were designated
as New Towns to accommodate Manchester and Merseyside overspill.[63]
Similar policies were accepted for Glasgow overspill (Irvine New Town
designated in 1966) and London (Northampton, Peterborough and Milton
Keynes, 1967/8) in line with the recommendations of the South-East
Study. Originally, it was hoped to extend this logic to include Ipswich
and Southampton/Portsmouth, but revisions in population and
employment projections together with continuing economic crisis led
the Government to abandon these plans.[64]

Party politics played virtually no role in producing these initiatives
which, incidentally, would produce much larger New Towns than the
30,000 to 50,000 optimum population envisaged by Reith. Third
generation New Towns would rise from this level to anything between
250,000 (Milton Keynes) and 500,000 (Central Lancashire). At the
same time, by creating new regional centres as counterweights to
existing cities and by building the new cities around existing small
towns and cities, the third generation New Towns abandoned the
'virgin green field sites' approach of the original New Towns.[65]

One interesting institutional change in the period was the creation
of a Department of Economic Affairs (DEA) with responsibility for
drawing up regional strategies under the Regional Economic Councils
and Boards which had been created to assist the experiment in national
indicative planning.[66] On the face of it, the DEA's new responsibilities
with their partial integration — if only on a voluntary basis — of
land-use and regional planning under the regional planning bodies,
seemed to herald a new era of integrated planning long awaited by the
planning professions.[67] Such an integration was not intended, as the
DEA's original brief was confined to economic planning. But on
commencing their work, the DEA regional bodies soon found
themselves concerned with spatial as well as economic planning.[68]

Labour was not at this time committed to local government reform
without which the ambivalent position of the DEA would remain.
Nonetheless, aware of the need to rationalise a system in which local
authorities had the requisite powers but no regional vision, and the
regional bodies had the vision but no powers, Labour did create a further
ad hoc advisory team of central/local officials for the South East region.
On reporting in 1970, this team argued for a regional approach to
future physical and economic planning.[69]

These hesitant steps towards the rationalised and integrated planning
structure needed for a truly comprehensive indicative planning system
were not taken without opposition from existing bureaucratic interests

and organisational relationships. The Labour Government initially
alienated the old Ministry of Housing and Local Government by hiving
off the land values element of its responsibilities to an autonomous
Ministry of Land and Natural Resources. This body was not wanted
even by the officials who were seconded there, and by 1966 its
functions were transferred back into the Ministry of Housing. Similarly,
the creation of the DEA, while alienating the Treasury, also had the
effect (as we have argued) of questioning existing central and local
powers and functions.[70] Since these functions were represented in
government by the Ministry of Housing, it is not surprising that the
creation of a more integrated planning system had to wait until 1968
when the DEA was largely defunct and its regional planning
responsibilities had passed back to the Housing Ministry. After 1968,
the Labour Government was on firmer administrative ground in its
attempt to create an overlord Ministry of Local Government and
Regional Planning under Anthony Crosland. The minister was given the
job of co-ordinating the autonomous Ministries of Housing and Local
Government, Transport and the regional economic planning bodies of
the DEA.[71] Further rationalisation occurred in 1968 through the
creation of the Scottish Development Department under the Scottish
Office with responsibility for co-ordinating all Scottish local
government, planning, environmental, housing, transport and industries
policies.[72] Labour also accepted the recommendations of the
Conservative initiated Planning Advisory Groups (PAG) on local
planning authorities' development plans. Generally, the PAG report
criticised the exclusive emphasis on spatial/physical planning of land
use embodied in the 1947 system, and called for the integration of
land-use planning with trend planning of population, employment, and
other socio-economic changes.[73]

Such an approach clearly required some regional or area perspective,
and the two tier city/regional system proposed by the Report was
accepted by the Government and embodied in the subsequent 1968
Town and Country Planning Act. In future, there would be Structure
and Local plans. Structure plans would be based on trend analysis and
broad indicative projections of transport, land use, demographic,
economic and environmental trends in county areas (*not* regions) and
major towns, and would be subject to central approval by the relevant
Minister or Secretary of State. Local plans would be concerned with
the detail of physical/spatial arrangements for local areas and would
not be subject to ministerial approval unless an appeal against a local
authority decision was to be heard. No element of party controversy

was involved in these changes – the PAG had, after all, been initiated by the Conservatives. Nor did the new planning structures involve major changes in local authority powers. The only exception was the power given to local authorities under the Act to designate certain localities as 'Action Areas', or areas considered ripe for major development, improvement or redevelopment. Once the structure plans had been accepted by the Minister, the relevant local authorities were free to use compulsory purchase powers in these areas without recourse at all times to Ministerial approval.[74]

A further interesting and novel development in this period was Labour's commitment to public participation. In the words of the 1968 Act, the public were to be given 'adequate opportunity' to make representations on structure plans, the content of which must in future be 'adequately publicised'. The public were also given the right for objections to be heard by the relevant Minister. In the same way, objections could be raised to local plans and lodged with the local authority who were bound to institute an inquiry under an independent inspector. While these provisions were hardly revolutionary – only the well informed were likely to take advantage of inquiries – they do represent an important innovation in the planning field. Moreover, also in 1968 the Government instituted a committee to look into the general problem of public participation in the preparation of plans. When the report (*People and Plans* or the Skeffington Report[75]) was published in 1969 it did not take the legislative commitments of the 1968 Act much further, but it did strongly support the view that public participation was in the interest of sound planning.

Labour's flirtation with participation was almost certainly a response to the growing disenchantment with the wholesale redevelopment which was characteristic of planning in the 1960s. Slowly but surely, community groups were being formed specifically to oppose some redevelopments, and while information on such groups is scant, their increasing visibility did demand some response on the part of government.[76]

Public participation *per se* was generally not an issue of party controversy, but the final innovation of Labour's period in office, local government reform, certainly was. We have indicated elsewhere that the desire for a rationalisation of local government boundaries and responsibilities was increasingly necessary with the rapid growth of urban areas and the resulting impact on urban hinterlands. This tendency was also encouraged by the move to indicative planning as it became clear that there might be a need for some form of regional planning and government. Obviously this would be a highly contentious subject since it would question existing local authority boundaries and in particular the jurisdictions of the politically conservative county councils. But reform could not be eschewed forever, as the experience of Greater London in the early 1960s had revealed. Indeed, in addition to the existing jurisdictional anomalies caused by archaic administrative arrangements, the continuing flood of new legislation made matters even worse. For example, in order to implement the 1968 Act, with its distinction between local and structure plans, it was necessary to create yet more *ad hoc* planning bodies.

In response to earlier pressures, in 1966 the Government had set up the Redcliffe-Maud Commission into the future of local government in England and Wales. In 1969, amid a flurry of activity on administrative and constitutional reform — the Kilbrandon Commission on Constitutional Reform was also set up at this time[77] — the Redcliffe-Maud Report was finally completed. It recommended a two tier approach (similar to the approach adopted in Greater London) for the metropolitan areas of Manchester, Birmingham and Liverpool. Single tier unitary authorities were to be created to administer the existing areas of the country on the broad city-region approach much favoured by the planning professions.[78] This recommendation for England and Wales differed significantly from the recommendations made in the same year by the separate Wheatley Report on Scottish local government. Wheatley argued for a two tier system of large regional authorities and smaller local authorities for the whole of Scotland.[79]

These recommendations were bound to arouse opposition — especially in England and Wales where the firmly entrenched county councils would resist any attempt to sweep them away in regional reform. At the national level also, the Conservatives would hardly regard with benevolence any measure which undermined the Conservative dominated counties. However, before action on the Report could be taken, Labour was defeated in the 1970 general election — although there is some evidence that Labour would have accepted the main recommendations of the Maud Report.[80]

By 1970, therefore, party consensus on planning and related fields was beginning to break down. The specific disagreements on local government reform were, moreover, reinforced by a growing disillusionment in the Conservative Party with indicative planning. At the much publicised meeting of the Conservative Shadow Cabinet at Selsdon Park in January 1970, the Conservatives stated their devotion to market principles and selectivist social policies. Little reference was made to planning with all that it implied for the role of the state.[81] One point however cannot be ignored. Though it is clear that the major factor leading to the convergence of policy during the 1960s was the reappraisal of the Conservative Government in the 1960-64 period, the Labour Government of 1964 had also changed its policy emphasis significantly. The Labour Government was not in 1964 prepared to move towards the institution of the positive planning and land-use system which had almost been created in the 1940s. This was revealed in the failure to recoup all betterment for the state, the acceptance of an equal share for the private sector in housing development, the use of New Towns as only one means of development, and the failure to extend the resources and powers of local authorities other than in the framework of plan-making. The emphasis of the Labour Government was quite clearly on negative, regulatory land-use planning and the creation of the requisite institutional bodies — by administrative reform when necessary — to allow indicative and integrated planning to proceed. It was essentially a commitment to 'mixed' economic and land-use planning in which both the public and private sectors would be encouraged to maximise their respective and clearly defined roles to the full. There was no vision of a dominant state role in this period.

When attempting to explain the essentially incrementalist policies adopted by Labour in the 1964-70 period, we can identify three main influences.

(a) *Changes Within the Labour Party.* Labour politics — as well as the social and educational background of many of its leaders — had changed drastically under Gaitskill and Wilson.[82] Electoral failure in 1951, 1955 and 1959 had led to a fundamental reappraisal within the Party. The well documented debate on nationalisation culminating in the effective rejection of clause 4 of the Party Constitution demonstrates most dramatically the Party's retreat from massive state intervention.[83] At the 1963 Scarborough Conference, Harold Wilson's 'white hot heat of technology' speech revealed a belief instead in technocratic solutions to the country's ills. Hence, administrative reform together with indicative planning would be the wave of the future — and would also, so it was thought, help Britain's laggardly economic growth rate. We have already noted the widespread disillusion with the 1947 planning system which by 1951 many Labour politicians and professional planners felt.[84] By 1964, there was little support for a positive land-use system and the 1964 Manifesto instead advocated extensions to New Towns and extra resources for local authorities outside an integrated state dominated land-use planning system.[85] This disillusion, together with intra-party changes, helped assure the adoption of administrative reforms to aid a new indicative planning structure.

(b) *The Role of Professional Interests.* During this period, the approach of most planning professionals and groups — The Royal Institution of Chartered Surveyors (RICS), The Royal Institute of British Architects (RIBA), the TPI and TCPA accorded well with the policies adopted by the Labour Government. The TCPA and TPI were generally in favour of extensions to existing New Towns and the rationalisation of existing planning procedures.[86] This was also the basic position of the RICS and RIBA who both, presumably, saw procedural reforms as means of easing the problems of planning delays and bureaucratic overload without further extending the role of the state.[87] In part, it is probably true that Labour's commitment to New Town extensions and extra aid for local authorities, plus planning procedure reforms and administrative co-ordination and integration in regional economic planning boards and councils, was a consequence of the Party accepting expert opinions in this period. Indeed, in 1961 the Party introduced a major policy review exercise under Peter Shore to tap professional opinion and to identify likely developments in the area over the next few years.[88] This was obviously an exercise in pragmatic policy making aimed at discovering winning electoral positions. It was hardly policy based on party principle or ideological commitment. It also accorded well with the Wilsonian image of an expertly informed government operating on an administrative/rationalising basis. A more cynical view is that during the early 1960s the Party was eager to latch on to any issue where informed opinion could be said to coincide with Party opinion. By so doing, the Party could rebuff any charge that they represented only narrow class interests, and were therefore unfit to govern.

(c) *The Role of Civil Servants.* At the same time, the perpetuation of policies which had been gradually forced on the previous Conservative Government owed something to bureaucratic developments and the tendency towards incrementalism within administrative structures. Thus the acceptance of second and third generation New Towns owed a great deal to the influence of J.R. James as chief planner in the MHLG and to the general support for the New Towns in this Ministry.[89]

The creation of agencies to research the problems of urban renewal and basic design and development techniques after 1960 was also likely to lead to continuing commitments in this direction, as was the work of the Planning Advisory Group which was set up to look at the problems of planning procedures and delays. Bureaucratic demarcation disputes and squabbles were also significant — especially with regard to the Ministry of Land and Natural Resources whose demise owed much to opposition from within the MHLG.[90]

In sum, the period 1964-70 was one principally of policy incrementalism rather than major change. Labour was able to extend policies initiated by the Conservatives (such as indicative planning and procedural reform) and to introduce legislation which the previous government had found difficult to countenance (such as land values and local government reform). However, apart from the emphasis on public participation, none of the policies between 1964 and 1970 were significantly different from the earlier period. Generally, the reasons for this can be found in changes within the leadership of the Labour Party — although as we argued, interest group and bureaucratic influences almost certainly reinforced Labour's incrementalist commitment to indicative planning.

The Culmination of Administrative Rationalisation: Conservative Policy, 1970-74

One of the first acts of the new Conservative Government was to continue the rationalisation of planning functions begun by Labour by creating the Department of the Environment (DOE) in 1970. Truly a comprehensive department, the DOE embraced transport, housing, local government, environmental, land-use and regional planning as well as the responsibilities of the former Ministry of Public Buildings and Works.[91] The DOE did *not*, however, include the main *economic* planning functions. Nonetheless, the integration of most government responsibilities impinging on land use was a bold step.

In order to accommodate the regional economic planning councils and boards of the DEA within the DOE, a new regional structure was created. So, each of the eight new economic planning regions of England (East Midlands, Northern, East Anglia, North-West, Yorkshire and Humberside, West Midlands, South-East and South-West) was assigned a regional office whose director also sat as chairman of the DEA regional economic boards. As under the DEA, however, these boards and offices had few powers, their main function being advisory. In Scotland, until the reform of local government, these arrangements

were to remain very much *ad hoc* in nature. A similar problem arose
with regard to responsibilities for local and structure plans under the
1968 Act. The Conservatives therefore continued the previous
government's practice of commissioning *ad hoc* teams of related local
authorities and advisory central and regional officials to draw up
structure plans, leaving local plans to existing local authorities.[92]

The creation of the DOE apart, the Conservatives continued few
Labour initiatives in the 1970-74 period. Perhaps the most dramatic
example of their break with past policies and initiatives was their
rejection of the Redcliffe-Maud recommendations for a regional-unitary
local government system. Instead, the 1972 Local Government Act
reprieved the traditionally Conservative County Councils which would
have been swept away if the Redcliffe-Maud proposals had been
accepted. Therefore, instead of four metropolitan conurbations with
two-tier systems of administration and unitary single tier authorities
throughout England, the Conservative Government produced six
metropolitan areas (counties) on a two-tier basis plus a two-tier system
of county councils and district councils. Even the extension of
metropolitan status to Tyne and Wear and to parts of South and West
Yorkshire was not a major concession to the now rejected regional-
unitary approach desired by Labour and most professional planners.
The degree to which political considerations intervened in this policy
approach is revealed by the fact that in 1972 it was not the
Conservative dominated county councils who would lose their powers,
but instead many of the Labour dominated county boroughs. A similar
pattern emerged in Wales with the creation of 8 county councils and
37 district authorities.

While there was little agreement over the Kilbrandon Commission
which reported in 1973, with some people arguing for legislative
authority in Scottish and Welsh Councils and others arguing for regional
devolution in England, the broad outlines of the Wheatley Report on
Local Government reform in Scotland were accepted by both parties.[93]
Wheatley had argued for a two-tier system with large regional
authorities and smaller local authorities. The 1973 Local Government
(Scotland) Act instituted such a system based on slight modifications
to the Wheatley recommendations. Instead of 7 regions and 37 district
authorities, the Act instituted 8 regions, 3 quasi-regions and 47 district
authorities.[94]

The one major benefit of these reforms, irrespective of the damage
done to any degree of regional government for another two decades,
was that they did rationalise and finalise the effective planning

responsibilities outstanding since the passing of the 1968 Town and
Country Planning Act. Under the 1972 Act, structure plan
responsibilities in England and Wales passed to the county councils
and metropolitan areas. In Scotland, these powers were given to the
regional authorities though with three major amendments.[95] District
and Metropolitan authorities in England and Wales were therefore
given the local plan-making responsibilities with county councils
having certain default powers in these matters as well as in major
development control which was a second-tier responsibility.[96]

So, by 1972, administrative rationalisation and reform had been
completed by the Conservative Government and not without some
loss of existing powers by local government.[97] While generally, the
Conservatives maintained the indicative planning system created
between 1960 and 1970, they did retreat from the increased state
role established by the 1964 and 1966 Labour Governments. Thus
the Land Commission which had been attempting to perform a
positive state role by loosening the supply of land for development
was scrapped largely because of Conservative opposition to the
Commission's 40 per cent betterment levy on development. Moreover,
the central government role in this area was not replaced with a
revitalised local role. Rather, the Conservatives sought to limit central
and local state roles and instead instituted a review of the possibilities
of streamlining the local planning applications system to allow private
developers to obtain planning permission and the land they desired for
development more quickly (the Dobry Report).[98]

Labour's revitalised role for New Towns was also reduced. Only two
New Towns were designated in this period at Stonehouse near Glasgow
and Llantrisant in South Wales, and these were *ad hoc* additions
designed to alleviate specific problems in Central Scotland and South
Wales, rather than part of a grand design for further dispersal. Whether,
however, the decision not to continue systematic dispersal was a result
of Conservative antipathy towards an enhanced state role, or of other
factors, is difficult to say. Certainly, downwardly revised population
projections for the year 2000 were reducing the need for further
dispersal. Also, increasing economic difficulties (especially after
mid-1973) militated against schemes involving great government
expenditure. Finally, Peter Walker, Secretary of State for the
Environment for much of the period, was probably affected by general
shifts in sentiment against grand redevelopment schemes and in favour
of improvement and rehabilitation in inner city areas.

Conservative land-use policies between 1970 and 1974 were, then, inconsistent. On the one hand, they appeared to want a reduction in the state's role and a return to a regulative system. On the other hand, they were streamlining and updating the administrative framework which had the inherent logic of assisting the interventionist role of the state at the local and central levels. This contradiction was epitomised by the 1972 Town and Country Planning (Amendment) Act which both gave the public the right to be consulted and involved in local plan-making, yet also abolished their right to be heard at inquiries into structure plans. The mechanism of an 'Examination in Public' meant that only those issues which the Secretary of State felt were relevant to his/her consideration of the structure plan would be heard by an independent chairman and panel.[99]

When explaining these changes, political party factors appear once more to be relevant, if not always crucial. Between 1966 and 1970, the Conservative Party in opposition undertook major policy reviews most of which involved a retreat from state intervention and a 'return' to market principles.[100] On the face of it, many of the policy innovations after 1970 look like a response to those reviews. The abolition of the Land Commission, withdrawal from New Town expansion, and the abandoning of a regional element in local government reform in England and Wales are all consistent with a reorientation of party principles towards reduced state involvement in society.

But in many of these areas the Government position was buttressed by socio-economic trends and/or the views and advice of interested groups. Both new evidence on demographic change and professional planners questioned the need for more New Towns.[101] Also, policies for land supply extensions by local authorities and procedural planning reforms received a generally sympathetic response from such groups as the builders' organisations, the RICS, RIBA and the local authority associations.[102] Moreover, as the next chapter will show in some detail, in an area such as land values, external forces — in particular the property boom — obliged the Government to return to solutions with well tried pedigrees (such as taxation based betterment solutions) which were acceptable to interested groups and civil service advisors.

Only in local government reform did the Conservatives appear to execute a major policy reversal which rode roughshod over informed opinion and interested groups. But some groups — notably the Country Councils Associations and the Rural District Councils Association — strongly supported the Conservative position.[103] More importantly, a consensus on the need for sweeping local government reform existed, and this alone gave the Government very much more freedom to act than otherwise would have been the case.

Labour's Prevarication over Positive Planning, 1974-78

If, between 1970 and February 1974, the Conservative Government was unsure of the direction it wished to take on policy, the record of the Labour Government in the years 1974 to 1977 was similarly confused and lacking in direction. Events would appear to fall into two distinct periods coinciding with the tenures at the DOE of Anthony Crosland (until September 1976) and Peter Shore (since September 1976).

Under Crosland the major aim of Government policy was, at least in theory, a move towards positive land-use planning. The vehicle for this change was the 1975 Community Land Act which not only reintroduced the heavier betterment taxes traditionally associated with Labour, but also imposed a statutory obligation on local authorities to purchase any land required for development at existing use values.

To achieve this, the local authorities were obliged to create Land Acquisition and Management Schemes on the basis of agreements between county and district authorities on ten year rolling programmes of land needs. They also have the right either to undertake any development for their areas themselves or to allow private developers and builders to undertake the development on a tender basis. Hence, the Act gave local authorities the power to plan positively by intervention in the development process both directly and on a regulatory basis. Indeed, between 1974 and 1975 it looked as though Labour was returning to a more interventionist state role than at any time since the war. The Community Land Act, together with the 1975 Industry Act which created the National Enterprise Board and the Planning Agreements Systems, seemed to signal a new era of state planning in economy and society.[104]

But the period between 1974 and 1977 was hardly the time for such a transformation. Above all, serious economic problems plagued the Government and critically affected many of its social programmes. Neither Anthony Crosland nor John Silkin the Minister for Planning and Local Government until September 1976, nor Peter Shore who replaced Crosland after this date, were able to provide the resources necessary for a successful beginning to the Community Land Act.[105] On the contrary, the cuts in Government spending introduced by the Heath Government in 1973 and which fell particularly heavily on local

authorities, rather than being restored by Crosland were maintained
and accompanied by dire warnings from the DOE to authorities to
contain spending – especially on staffing. DOE circulars also
advised local planning authorities to undertake only *profitable*
development – particularly on virgin green field sites – which hardly
encouraged the pursuit of positive planning policies.[106]

Moreover, in the 1976/7 period, British urban policy underwent
what could arguably be called the first major departure from the
post-war 'decrowding' and dispersal principles. Chapter 7 will document
this transition in some detail, but for now it is important to stress that
pressure for a policy reappraisal had been building for some time. Inner
city decay had persisted – and in some areas increased – in spite of
slum clearance and redevelopment, and a variety of government and
private research reports had pointed to the need for additional resources
for the inner cities. In fact, as early as 1974, the Government had
adjusted the needs element in the Rate Support Grant in order to give
more money to metropolitan authorities and less to the counties.

With the replacement of Anthony Crosland by Peter Shore in
September 1976, inner city directed policies were given a further
boost, for it was known that Crosland and John Silkin favoured a
maintenance (and even a strengthening) of dispersal whereas Shore
supported a redirection of resources towards the inner city. But the
first change to result from the cabinet reshuffle was the demise of an
integrated administrative structure in urban policy, for transport was
hived off from the DOE and resumed most of the status of a separate
ministry. In addition, John Silkin's functions for local government and
planning were transferred directly to the overlord Secretary of State
for the Environment (Silkin himself was promoted to head of
Agriculture, Fisheries and Food). One of Peter Shore's first actions was
to scrap the Stonehouse New Town and instead to channel the freed
expenditure into an inner-urban renewal project in East Glasgow.[107]
The retreat from the New Town ideal was revealed in further statements
during 1977, promising a revitalisation of the inner cities and a cut-back
in the optimal population of the third generation New Towns.[108] Few
additional resources had been allocated to the inner areas by early 1978,
however, and the new policy looks as though it is more an *ad hoc*
reaction to the worsening political and economic situation in many
inner cities, than a carefully worked out urban strategy adapting past
policies and achievements to a new urban context. This is not to say,
it should hastily be added, that the New Towns ideal has been
completely abandoned. But for the first time since the war, a Labour

Government is consciously diverting resources from New Town expansion into the inner cities, and appears to be doing so without any clear conception of what form urban growth should take over the next several decades.

The period between 1974 and 1977 also was notable for heightened debate and controversy over local government finance. It is perhaps extraordinary that while party disputes over categorical grants for housing, transport and so on have been legion in the post-war period — and these will be itemised in later chapters — there has been virtually no party debate at the central level on the central/local finance system and in particular on the operation of the rate support grant (RSG). Over the years, the RSG, which is a central government subsidy towards local authority current (revenue) expenditure, has increased steadily and reached 65.5 per cent in 1976/7. In fact, this increase together with a rapid increase in all local government expenditure has been precipitated by the need to finance and staff ever proliferating centrally initiated programmes.[109] With productivity increases difficult to achieve in this service area, and given the problems of improving income from authorities' main independent revenue source, property taxes, this increasing dependence on central government is not surprising.[110]

As was noted earlier, in 1974/5 the Labour Government used the RSG as an instrument of planning policy by redistributing the needs element in the grant away from the counties and towards metropolitan authorities. This act assured a rise in the political salience of the system, which aroused further controversy with the publicaton of the Layfield Report on Local Government Finance.[111] Layfield's recommendation that local authorities should be given power to levy local income taxes and therefore have more control over resources, was not received with great enthusiasm by either party.[112] Such an innovation would be electorally unpopular and would, of course, involve the surrender of powers by central departments — not a policy likely to inspire support among Ministers and their civil servants.

Layfield apart, further debate and party controversy on this issue is likely, for central governments have begun to use the RSG not only as an incremental disbursement to myriad local authorities, but also as an instrument of planning policy. It may, in fact also have become an instrument of macro-economic policy. After years of steady increase, in 1976 the RSG was reduced to 61 per cent at a stroke, thus forcing on local governments considerable cutbacks in programmes and staffing.

A final characteristic of this period was the growing number of permanent and *ad hoc* groups formed to protest against central and local government planning, urban renewal and transport policies. As Anthony Barker has emphasised, it is not easy to categorise all those activities which come under the general rubric of public participation. But in Britain, at least, public participation is usually used as a description of political activity conducted outside of the established political party and interest group framework.[113] During the 1970s two aspects of such activity are worthy of note. First, as public participation (especially in the form of protest) increased, so the scale and volume of government inspired changes in the physical environment tended to decrease. That the one caused the other is not so easy to demonstrate, however. The relationship between protest and the policy process is complex and requires more research. This period was, after all, one where the external pressures on government to reduce expenditure were great, and this may explain the retreat from large scale projects. Second, at the national level at least, public antipathy towards grand schemes did not become a *party* issue. It is probably true that governments are now more circumscribed than before in the area of physical planning simply because of the potential for protest that many developments can produce. However, unlike some countries (notably France) political parties in Britain have not become the defenders of the 'community' or the champions of planning conservation.

It is probably too early to provide adequate explanations for Labour land-use planning policies between 1974 and 1978. These years do, however, fall into two distinct periods. Until September 1976, the Labour Governments maintained the basic policy directions laid down in earlier years, and, via the Community Land Act and the embryonic NEB, even moved towards positive planning. Since September 1976, the denial of resources for state land development and the rather haphazard reappraisal of basic post-war principles suggest a return to the *ad hoc* style of the 1964-74 period. Labour's apparent radicalism on planning between 1974 and 1976 can probably be attributed to changes within the Party following the 1970 election defeat. Unlike the defeat of 1959 which was seen by many Labour leaders as a result of the *embourgeoisement* of a working class whose interests were increasingly at odds with traditional Labour policies,[114] the 1970 defeat was analysed in terms of a traditional working class reacting against the non-radical policies of a Labour Government.[115] Perhaps in reaction to this, the Labour Party sought a closer relationship with the trade union movement after 1970.[116] Certainly, by the time of the publication of *The Labour Programme, 1973* the Party appeared to have moved to the left. Indeed, this document (which was to become the basis of the election Manifesto in February 1974) with its references to economic planning, nationalisation and public ownership of land read more like something from the early 1940s than from the early 1970s.[117]

As the next chapter will show, the Community Land Act faltered in a hostile economic and bureaucratic environment, and hopes for an integrated planning structure were reduced when Transport was hived off from the DOE in September 1976. Therefore, while talk of co-ordinated economic and land-use planning with regard to the inner cities continues,[118] and while the Community Land Act retains the potential for radical change, the immediate prospects for a return to positive land use planning are slight. There seems little doubt that Labour's retreat from the promises of 1973 owes a great deal to the national economic crisis which has persisted throughout the period — although the tenure of James Callaghan as Prime Minister, who has proved rather more conservative than Harold Wilson, could also be relevant.

Conclusions

As Figure 2.1 shows, land-use planning policy in the post-war period can be quite clearly divided into two periods. Down to 1961, political party differences were great. Indeed, the contrast between the 1947 system and that introduced by the Conservatives after 1953 and 1959 was extreme, with policy fluctuating from a near positive to a regulative planning system. Since 1961, party and government policies have been much closer, and a general consensus on the need for some form of

Figure 2.1: Governments and Land-use Planning, 1945-78

	1945-1951	1952-1960	1961-1970	1971-1974	1975-8
Positive land-use planning	Labour				
Indicative land-use planning			Conservative/ Labour		Labour
Regulative land-use planning		Conservative		Conservative	
Non land-use planning					

indicative planning has existed. In some areas critically important to land use planning such as land values (and to a lesser extent local government reform) party rancour has, however, been great. As the next chapter will demonstrate, the reasons for this relate to the two main political parties' quite distinct positions on the question of property rights. Since the 1950s, land-use planning proper has not however, been a subject of great party controversy – and this in spite of the many major changes which have been wrought on British towns and cities as a result of dispersal, New Town and Green Belt policies. It is true, of course, that during the 1960s and 1970s grass roots opposition to many redevelopment schemes (especially transport redevelopment as Chapter 5 will show) increased perceptibly. However, this opposition was not translated into party controversy at the national level – in spite of the obvious fact that the costs and benefits resulting from planning policies by no means fell equally on different social groups. Peter Ambrose has noted that the low political salience of land-use planning is both surprising and unjustified:

> . . .whereas the conflict about the price of labour is visible, well understood and acceptably political, the conflict about planning-induced wealth transference is, to most people, invisible, mysterious and non-political. Yet it is reasonable to suppose that in terms of the total weight, the latter conflict may well be as significant as the former.[119]

Even during the period between 1947 and 1960 when objective differences between the parties were great, land-use planning did not cause great party controversy in the same way as did nationalisation, housing or industrial relations. The columns of Hansard can be searched in vain for evidence of frequent clashes over land use, with each side arguing from the sort of well rehearsed and relatively coherent positions characteristic of nationalisation or housing policy. Four factors seem relevant to this relative absence of political conflict:

(a) The esoteric nature of planning problems leads to a situation in which land-use regulation and development control policies are left to experts. The vagaries of debate over the need for three dimensional rather than two dimensional plans during the PAG deliberations were of this nature, as were discussions over the need for trend (structure) and spatial/physical (local) plans in the 1968 Town and Country Planning Act. In these situations, policy making tends to pass by default to expert civil servants and interest groups.[120] Thus the technical nature of many planning policies leads to a situation in which politicians are largely unable by training, skills or bias, to comprehend the political importance of planning issues.[121]

(b) No doubt reliance on expert advice has been aggravated by the inherent tendency in bureaucracies towards inertia and incrementalism.[122] Hence the important innovations represented by the creation of a Ministry of Land and the integration of Transport into the DOE was reversed in part because of opposition from existing bureaucratic structures with interests and jurisdictions to defend. The unquestioned acceptance of dispersal until the mid-1970s also must owe something to bureaucratic inertia.

(c) For most of the period, a generalised belief has prevailed that if local authorities have planning permission and development control powers, then effective planning is being undertaken. Both the public and politicians share this belief — even though local governments simply do not have the powers needed for effective planning. Even the ambitious system of structure planning has helped little. For apart from the serious delays in formulating and approving plans, counties have few independent powers to control the pattern of development which derives from the functional division of powers in the central/local system.

(d) Finally, as Peter Hall has argued, certain ideas and values about urban society have dominated official thinking in the post-war period.[123] In particular, the notion that urban containment and rural protection are important over and above welfare criteria has dominated. Questions such as the effect of dispersal policies on different social groups have not, until very recently, been on the policy agenda. Indeed, such concepts as equality and social justice, bandied around so freely in some policy areas, have figured rarely in land-use planning. Of course the original impetus to the post-war system came from a perception that overcrowding and social injustice were rife in Britain's industrial cities. However, little effort has been made to relate the actual policies pursued to spatial, income or class inequalities.

None of these explanations of the relatively apolitical status of planning since the war is completely adequate — especially when we attempt to explain why some other areas of urban policy, equally technical and bureaucratic in nature, have been highly political. For answers to this problem we will have to look to the peculiar nature of party ideology in Britain which is the subject of Chapter 8.

It would be wrong to leave this chapter without some acknowledgement of the success of post-war policy. Unlike some modern industrial countries, local authorities in Britain do have regulatory and plan-making powers to deal with all urban related development. Through the use of Green Belts, New Towns and dispersal, urban sprawl has at least in part been avoided, and a more balanced employment and urban environment created. By 1970 some 5,595 square miles in England (or 11 per cent of the land area) were covered by Green Belts.[124] British New Towns were, and remain, bold experiments in urban planning which are rightly admired throughout the world. Almost two million people now live in designated New Towns, and of these more than one million represent new population.[125] But British planning policy has also had its failures, some of which are serious. Urban sprawl *has* occurred in many locales — and especially in suburban 'growth towns' near large population centres. We also do not know for sure *exactly* how land is used in Green Belts. Perhaps typically, given the tendency in Britain not to evaluate policies, land surveys in this area have been few and far between.[126] Moreover, as implied earlier, land-use policies may have encouraged high-density high-rise inner urban solutions to the living space needs of city and town dwellers. New Towns have tended (not) to take economically disadvantaged sections of the population and the siphoning off of productive populations may have aggravated inner city problems. Essential administrative reforms, especially of local government, have occurred, but Britain still lacks the sort of central/regional/local structure which most planners and interested academics agree is necessary for responsive and effective planning.[127] Since 1953, local authorities have lacked the power to *direct* and *implement* rather than merely draw up and regulate plans and development. Finally, government policies have failed to control property and land prices which have often risen at a rate above and beyond inflation rates.

Notes

1. On this approach generally, see Peter Ambrose, 'The British Land-use Non-Planning System', a paper given to the inaugural meeting of the Conference of Socialist Planning (London, 19 February 1977).

2. J.E. Meade, *The Theory of Indicative Planning* (Manchester, Manchester University Press, 1970).

3. J. Parker, *Local Health and Welfare Services* (London, Allen and Unwin, 1965), pp.15-36.

4. Ebenezer Howard, *Garden Cities of Tomorrow* (London, Faber, 1965).

5. For further details of these bodies' formation, see D. Foley, 'Idea and Influence; The Town and Country Planning Association', *Journal of the American Institute of Planners* (1959), pp.10-17, and Gordon E. Cherry, *The Evolution of British Town Planning* (London, Leonard Hill, 1974), pp.33-43.

6. Cherry, ibid., pp.64-71.

7. Ibid., pp.44-64.

8. Ibid., pp.83-92 and 98-106.

9. Peter Hall *et al.*, *The Containment of Urban England* (London, Allen and Unwin, 1973), vol.1, pp.104-7.

10. Peter Hall, *Urban and Regional Planning* (London, Pelican, 1976), pp.81-98.

11. Ibid.

12. For more details, see *Report of the Royal Commission on the Distribution of the Industrial Population* (Barlow Report) (Cmd. 6153, HMSO, 1940).

13. Nigel Harris, *Competition and the Corporate Society* (London, Methuen, 1972), pp.48-61.

14. Cherry, *Town Planning*, pp.120-35, and on the problems of agricultural land loss, see G. Wibberley, 'Land Scarcity in Britain', *Journal of Town Planning Institute* (April 1967), vol.53, Part 4, pp.129-36, and P. Self and H.J. Storing, *The State and the Farmer* (London, Allen and Unwin, 1971), pp.15-61.

15. Ibid.

16. Cherry, *Town Planning*, pp.120-35, and Foley, 'Idea and Influence', pp.11-12.

17. Hall, *Urban England*, pp.91-112.

18. J.B. Cullingworth, *Environmental Planning 1939-1969, Volume 1: Reconstruction and Land-Use Planning: 1939-1947* (London, HMSO, 1975), especially pp.251-8.

19. Hall, *Urban England*, 91-112.

20. For an inclusive presentation and discussion of these powers, see Frank Schaffer, *The New Town Story* (London, Paladin, 1972), pp.19-32, and J.B. Cullingworth, *Town and Country Planning in Britain* (London, Allen and Unwin, 5th edn., 1974), pp.78-80.

21. Shaffer, ibid., pp.278-325.

22. Hall, *Urban England*, vol.2, pp.37-71.

23. Cullingworth, *Planning in Britain*, pp.44-5.

24. County councils were, however, expected to share many of their powers with smaller district authorities, ibid., pp.41-4.

25. Hall, *Urban England*, vol.2, pp.37-71.

26. On these problems see Peter Hall (ed.), *Land Values*, Report on the Proceedings of a London Colloqium, March 1965, under the auspices of the Acton Society Trust (London, Sweet and Maxwell, 1965), vol.2, pp.390-405; H.R. Parker, *Paying for Urban Development* (London, Fabian Society, 1959).

27. See Foley, 'Idea and Influence'.

28. See Cherry, *Town Planning*.

29. Cullingworth, *Environmental Planning*, p.183.

30. Ibid., pp.251-8.

31. On this general change, see David Butler and Donald Stokes, *Political Change in Britain* (Harmondsworth, Middx., Penguin, 1971), pp.321-33.

32. On these general conclusions as outlined by the major wartime reports, see Hall, *Urban England*, vol.1, pp.85-92.

33. Cullingworth, *Environmental Planning*, pp.251-8.

34. Ibid., p.253.

35. Ibid., pp.191-225.

36. These powers were also given to Scotland in the 1957 Housing and Town Development (Scotland) Act.

37. Generally on Conservative thinking, see Harris, *Corporate Society*, pp.249-73, and R.D. Hoffman, *The Conservative Party in Opposition* (London, Routledge and Kegan Paul, 1977).

38. Peter Ambrose and Bob Colenutt, *The Property Machine* (Harmondsworth, Middx., Penguin, 1975), pp.68-73.

39. See, O. Marriot, *The Property Boom* (London, Hamish Hamilton, 1969), pp.263-6; S. Jenkins, *Landlords to London* (London, Constable, 1975), p.215.

40. Harris, *Corporate Society*, pp.77-154.

41. Interview with Wyndham Thomas, Past Director of the TCPA.

42. Hall, *Urban England*, pp.78-9.

43. On the growth of these organisations, see, respectively, *The First Three Years*, Report by the Civic Trust Trustees, 1960; and L. Allison, *Environmental Planning* (London, Allen and Unwin, 1975), pp.115-121.

44. See '1960 Report: Framework for Urban Renewal', *Official Architecture and Planning* (January 1961), pp.14-16.

45. On this general subject, see Samuel Brittan, *Steering the Economy* (London, Penguin, 1971), pp.171-270.

46. See Schaffer, op.cit., pp.278-328.

47. Cullingworth, *Planning in Britain*, pp.234-6.

48. Ibid., pp.275-6.

49. See *South East Study, 1961-1981* (London, HMSO, 1964); Ministry of Housing and Local Government, *The North-West: A Regional Study* (London, HMSO, 1965); Department of Economic Affairs, *The West Midlands: A Regional Study* (London, HMSO, 1965).

50. See Circular 37/60/MHLG (1960), and 'The Minister is Converted', *Architect and Building News*, 7 September 1960, vol.218, p.289, and *Housing* (Cmnd.1290, HMSO, 1961).

51. See A.W. Cox, *British Land Values Policies*, 1959-70, unpublished manuscript, University of Essex, 1979, chs. 4 and 5.

52. *Traffic in Towns* (Buchanan Report) (London, HMSO, 1963).

53. See Gerald Rhodes, *The Government of London: The Struggle for Reform* (London, Weidenfeld and Nicolson, 1970), pp.1-85.

54. Ibid., pp.1-23.

55. Ibid., pp.171-96.

56. See Cox, *Land Values*, chs. 4 and 5.

57. Ibid.,

58. Private interviews.

59. See, 'The Urban Planning Group of the MHLG', *Official Architecture and Planning*, vol.26 (June 1963), pp.541-3; 'The Work of the Research and Development Groups', *Official Architecture and Planning*, vol.29 (August, 1966), pp.378-401; Derek Senior 'The PAG Report', *Architects Journal* (4 August 1965), pp.234-5.

60. See Harold Macmillan, *The Middle Way* (London, Macmillan, 1966).

61. See 'The Minister is Converted', *Architecture and Building News*, vol.210 (September 1960), p.239; 'Land for Houses: Conservatives Debate Review of the Planning Acts', *The Builder*, 21 October 1960, p.748.

62. See ch.3.

63. Hall, *Planning*, p.170.

64. See R.H.S. Crossman, *The Diaries of a Cabinet Minister, Vol.1: Minister of Housing, 1964-1966* (London, Hamilton and Cape, 1976), p.617.

65. Hall, *Planning*, pp.175-85.

66. Eric Roll, 'The Machinery of Economic Planning', *Public Administration*, vo
(1966), pp.1-11.

67. For examples of the planning professions' support of such changes, see
'The Buchanan Report: A Statement of RIBA Views', *RIBA Journal* (May 1964),
pp.186-90; 'The South East Study (Memorandum to the MHLG)', *Town and
Country Planning* (August/September 1964), pp.341-9; 'Report of the TPI
Conference', *Architects Journal*, 15 July 1964, pp.144-6.

68. Hall, *Planning*, pp.172-4.

69. *Strategic Plan for the South East* (London, HMSO, 1970).

70. On the demise of the DEA, see Hugh Heclo and Aaron Wildavsky, *The
Private Government of Public Money* (Berkeley, California, University of
California Press, 1974), pp.209-10.

71. E. Jacobs, 'Chief of Staff/Environment', *The Sunday Times*, 19 October
1969; Nora Beloff, 'Wilson Plans Super Ministry', *Observer*, 21 September 1969.

72. See Brenda White, *The Literature and Study of Urban and Regional
Planning* (London, Routledge and Kegan Paul, 1974), pp.7-9.

73. *The Future of Development Plans*, Report of the Planning Advisory
Group (London, HMSO, 1965).

74. For further details, see Cullingworth, *Planning in Britain*, pp.71-92.

75. For details of the Skeffington proposals see Cullingworth, ibid.,
pp.293-316, and for a critical appraisal of the results see W. Hampton, N. Boaden,
M. Goldsmith, and P. Stringer, 'Public Participation in Planning within a
Representative Local Democracy', Paper presented to the Political Studies
Association Annual Conference, April 1977, Liverpool University.

76. Cullingworth, ibid. For a comprehensive and annotated bibliography of
public participation in planning, see Anthony Barker, *Public Participation in
Planning: A British Review* (Interim Version), paper before the ECPR Workshop
on Public Participation, Grenoble, April 1978. See also, John Ferris, *Participation
in Urban Planning*, Bell Occasional Papers in Social Administration, No.48, 1972;
Norman Dennis, *Public Administration and Planners' Blight* (London, Faber and
Faber, 1972).

77. *Royal Commission on the Constitution* (Cmnd.5460, London, HMSO,
1973).

78. Jack Brand, *Local Government Reform in England* (London, Croom
Helm, 1974), pp.59-87.

79. *Royal Commission on Local Government in Scotland* (Edinburgh,
Scotland, 1969).

80. Brand, *Local Government Reform*, pp.77-8.

81. On the Conservative Selsdon ethos see Grant Jordan, 'Hiving-Off and
Departmental Agencies', *Public Administration Bulletin* (August 1976), pp.37-51,
and J. Bruce-Gardyne, *Whatever Happened to the Quiet Revolution?* (London,
Knight, 1974).

82. See Jean Blondel, *Voters, Parties and Leaders* (Harmondsworth, Middx.,
Penguin, 1975), pp.87-157.

83. David Howell, *British Social Democracy* (London, Croom Helm, 1976),
pp.203-44.

84. For the reconstructed view, see Parker, *Urban Development*.

85. *Let's Go With Labour* (Labour Party, London, 1964), pp.14-15.

86. TCPA views were outlined in the pre-1964 election policy document and
party policy discussion booklet: *The Intelligent Voter's Guide* (London, TCPA,
April 1964); TPI views were expressed in a number of memoranda at this time.
One of the more important being *The South-East Study* (Memo to MHLG, 29
June 1964).

87. For RIBA views see 'The New Planning Procedures', *RIBA Journal* (December 1965, No.12), pp.570-1. The limited RICS view was witnessed most starkly in their view on land values policies cf. Land Values Policies chapter.

88. Howell, *Social Democracy*, pp.230-6.

89. Private interviews.

90. This view was underscored by the officials in a television programme during the summer of 1976 entitled *Labour and Land*. This programme was in the series *State of the Nation* (Granada TV; transcript available from Brian Lapping, Granada TV, Gordon Square, London).

91. For further details, see *Town and Country Planning in Britain* (London, Central Office of Information Reference Pamphlet 9, 1975); *The DOE and its Work: A Factual Note* (London, DOE, April 1975).

92. Hall, *Planning*, pp.172-85.

93. T. Kellas, *The Scottish Political System* (London, Cambridge University Press, 1973).

94. Ibid., p.155.

95. The three major changes are the introduction of regional reports, amendments to the mandatory regulations involved in structure planning, and powers to prepare local plans prior to the structure plans. For further details, see Cullingworth, *Planning in Britain*, pp.329-31.

96. Ibid., pp.324-9.

97. For example the loss of health service and water and sewage and river responsibilities to new and autonomous regional authorities.

98. *Review of the Development Control System: Interim Report* (London, HMSO, 1974), Dobry Report.

99. Cullingworth, *Planning in Britain*, pp.327-8.

100. See Robin Blackburn, 'The Heath Government – A New Course for British Capitalism', *New Left Review*, No. 70 (November/December 1971), pp.3-26.

101. See in particular, David Eversley, *The Planner in Society* (London, Fabian, 1973), and *Planning Without Growth* (Fabian Research Series, 321, July 1975).

102. 'Evidence submitted to the Royal Commission on Local Government', *RIBA Journal* (December 1966), pp.540-42, but in particular see Brand, *Local Government Reform*, pp.88-128, and *Land for Housing* (House Builders Federation, July 1977).

103. Brand, *Local Government Reform*, pp.114-30.

104. For a review of the new law, see Sir Frederick Corfield, 'The Community Land Act: An Assessment', *Journal of Planning and Property Law* (July 1975), pp.385-91.

105. See Rosemary Righter, 'All at Sea with the Land Act', *The Sunday Times*, 29 February 1976, p.62; M. Jones and R. Righter, 'Land Act: Shore Pulls Out', *The Sunday Times*, 6 March 1977, p.53.

106. Judy Hillman, 'Labour Acts to Curb Land Grabs', *Guardian*, (14 February 1977), p.5.

107. Rosemary Righter, 'Glasgow Wakes the Wasteland', *The Sunday Times*, 30 January 1977.

108. Judy Hillman, 'Expansion of New Towns in Doubt', *Guardian*, 4 February 1977, p.6; *Policy for the Inner Cities* (Cmnd.6845, HMSO, 1977).

109. See Department of the Environment, *Local Authority Expenditures*, Circ.51/75 (HMSO, London, 1975); Robin Simpson, 'For Richer for Poorer' (Rate Support Grant Guide), *New Society*, 10 November 1977, pp.299-302.

110. Robin Simpson, ibid.

111. *Local Government Finance: Report of the Committee of Enquiry*

(Cmnd.6453, London, HMSO, 1976), Layfield Report.

112. See *The Times*, 9 May 1976, p.1.

113. Barker, *Public Participation*, pp.3-5.

114. See Mark Abrams and Richard Rose, *Must Labour Lose?* (Harmondsworth, Middx., Penguin, 1960).

115. Howell, *Social Democracy*, pp.287-302.

116. See R. Taylor, 'The Uneasy Alliance: Labour and the Unions', *Political Quarterly*, vol.47, October/December 1976, pp.398-407; also *The Labour Programme 1973*.

117. Ibid.

118. See *Policy for the Inner Cities*.

119. Peter Ambrose, p.6.

120. See Derek Senior, 'The PAG Report'; and Walter Bar, 'The Future of Development Plans', *RIBA Journal* (October 1965), pp.488-96, 'The Town and Country Planning Act', *The Planner* (May 1974), pp.699-702.

121. This is a common assertion about an implied failing of the British Cabinet system, see Bruce Heady, *British Cabinet Ministers* (London, George Allen and Unwin, 1974); M. Gordon 'Civil Servants, Politicians and Parties: Shortcomings in the British Policy Process', *Comparative Politics*, vol.4, (October 1971), pp.28-58.

122. For an overview, see Peter Self, *Administrative Theories and Politics* (London, Allen and Unwin, 1972), pp.19-54 and 247-301, and sources cited.

123. Hall, *Urban England*, vol.2, pp.329-63 and 406-8.

124. J.B. Cullingworth, *Problems of an Urban Society, Vol.1, The Social Framework of Planning* (London, George Allen and Unwin, 1973), p.105.

125. Pat Blake, 'Britain's New Towns: Facts and Figures', *Town and Country Planning*, February 1977, p.94.

126. See Cullingworth, *Urban Society*, pp.101-5.

127. Alice Coleman, 'Is Planning Really Necessary?' The text of a lecture to the Royal Geographical Society, 3 May 1976.

3 LAND VALUES POLICIES

One symptom of the contradictions in the cities of the rich is the essential paradox that the very desire to control or destroy the property speculator in the name of the public good could, in the developed economy, jeopardise those vast savings funds which, through banks and insurance companies, have been invested in property. The irony is that these institutions are in turn the guarantors of the pensions and life insurance schemes of the stable middle classes. The heart of the paradox is that the very forces which prevent a middle-class citizen from buying his house in the cities of Western Europe and Tokyo, in Manhattan or Chicago's North Side, are those on which his security depends. (Peter Wilsher, *The Exploding Cities*, 1977.)

As was emphasised in the last chapter, land values fundamentally affect land use, housing, transport and other aspects of urban life. High land values can create problems for local authorities when they attempt to plan and regulate growth, and the need to compensate landowners for highly priced land can act as a deterrent to necessary industrial and residential development. In sum, land values can determine land use, and some of the most serious spatial inequalities characteristic of British cities have been caused at least in part by high — many would say unfairly high — land values. The decline of many inner city areas, for example, is inextricably entwined with high land values which make the cost of clearance and purchase prohibitive. Indisputably, then, the role of the state in relation to land values and prices is of fundamental importance to all other urban policies. Two issues have dominated land values policy is Britain since 1945: at what level should the state *compensate* land owners whose land is acquired (either by agreement or compulsion) for public or community purposes; and whether or not, and at what level, the state should seek to collect increases (*betterment*) in land values created by private capital or government action. Unfortunately, as is the case with all issues of relative justice, the two concepts are prey to varying interpretations — often as a result of prior political judgements and prejudice which serve to leave the formulation of equitable policy as much to the vagaries of political expediency as to any clearly studied and well thought out policy prescription. The land values question is highly complex, and before proceeding to an analysis of policy, a short introduction to the basic issues involved will be useful.

The Compensation and Betterment Problem

Contrasting party policies on land values relate closely to general views on the right of the state to interfere with individual property rights and the free operation of the land and property market. As is normal when individuals and parties disagree on the role of the state in social and economic life, the complexity and intractability of these twin problems has grown as the state's involvement in the land-use planning and development systems has increased.

Traditionally, it has been argued that the owner should be treated fairly whoever purchases his land and that the state should pay market values (the price that would be obtained in the open market in a transaction between willing sellers and buyers) for any land which it decides is necessary for public use. This view can be defended on grounds of natural justice and also because without the use of market valuations the only recourse is to utilise an administrative/quasi-political and potentially arbitrary valuation based upon the social value of the land, rather than the value the owner might obtain in the market if he was left to his own devices. Consequently, it is argued that corruption or unfairness between different owners might well result, and that the only fair solution is to allow the owner to be compensated for the loss of his land at market value for its most potentially profitable use – even though there is no guarantee that such a use would have been obtained.[1] Indeed, others have taken this even further arguing that the state should pay an additional amount above market value to cover any disturbance or loss of option felt by the owner as a result of state purchase.[2]

This might well be regarded as the *Free Market* solution to the problem of compensation since it enshrines the belief that the sanctity of property rights should be maintained in the face of all state actions in the land and property markets. As such, the argument appears fairly logical and defensible and implies a view of the betterment problem which holds that any increase in land values rightly belongs to the owner of the land, and that the state should not recoup at all. Hence, when any development takes place, the actual development (e.g. the provision of houses) is considered a sufficient gain to the community, and any subsequent tax or state recoupment of betterment is therefore an unwarranted and punitive impost on development and individual rights.[3] It is a view that is questioned by those who have argued that the state and society at large play a major role in increasing land values over and above the activities of the property owner or developer.

In one of the earliest formulations of this position, Henry George argued that the rent from land was an unjust impost by landowners because land values and therefore rents were created by the natural growth of industrial society and its consequent developments.[4] John Stuart Mill had argued in a similar vein when he claimed that increases in land values were an 'unearned increment' and that as the profits so gained were unproductive ('they spin not neither do they weave') they could be taxed away without any detrimental effect on the state of the productive economy.[5]

This, then, might be seen as the *classic* statement of the problem, since the view is taken that owners do not enhance their land values by their own actions and therefore they should not be able to keep any realised or unrealised gains in the land they own. On the contrary, since the community at large creates all betterment then the community should recoup most, if not all, of it. Obviously this view of the betterment problem has important implications for the question of compensation rights under state purchase. If the state is to recoup all betterment then the need to compensate owners at market values is less compelling.

Clearly this position is closely related to the arguments that have been put forward to support land nationalisation.[6] If land values are created by the community and not by the actions of owners, then it would appear unjust not only to allow them to earn unwarranted profits but also unnecessary to have private ownership. This position, accepted by most land nationalisers, has been reinforced by the view that since 1066 the British Crown has been the superior landowner and that individuals and other private property rights have not been vested in land itself, but in rights to use land. Thus land nationalisers have argued that the owner should not be allowed to recoup betterment, and if he is also not the superior landowner then it only makes sense to allow land to revert to the Crown, or the state, in modern conditions.

This *classic* view is not, however, the only interventionist position that has been taken on the problem of compensation and betterment. There has been a history of limited acceptance of the fact that the state can create betterment by its own actions and that when this is so the state should recoup these increases in value. Thus in 1427 an Act of Parliament sought to recover increases in the values of property which were attributable to public expenditures on projects of sea defence. Similarly a levy was imposed upon owners of property who benefited from street widening in London in a 1662 Act, and in 1670 the tradition was maintained in the Acts passed to assist the rebuilding of London after the Great Fire.[7] However, these traditions were not maintained and extended in the eighteenth and nineteenth centuries — even though the central governments of the day imposed obligations on local authorities to provide public utilities, and also to assist in the development of the burgeoning railway system.

Obviously, the provision of services like gas, water and roadworks may enhance the value of contiguous land. Thus, if a local authority provides what may be termed infrastructure services to land in the interest of the community, this will enhance the development potential of land that was not previously developable. In this way it was recognised that the state may indeed create values and that it should recoup those incidences of betterment directly attributable to its own activities. This view of the betterment side of the double headed coin of compensation and betterment has also resulted in a developing reappraisal of compensation rights over and above the arguments in the *classic* formulation.

The state may well be purchasing land for non-remunerative purposes; in other words for the provision of essential services which are in themselves non-profit making but necessary. One can think quite easily of the majority of local authority statutory undertakings such as the provision of land for schools, open spaces, roads and waterworks and sewerage as examples of these non-profitable undertakings. However, provision of such services may result in land values rising and this adds a further dimension to the problem of whether the state should collect more betterment than it traditionally did under specified legislation or state schemes. On the other hand, it raises the question of whether or not the state should compensate the landowner at the full market rate for the land at its highest potential use when in fact that use is not to be accorded to this particular site. To argue that it should not, creates an additional problem because if the state compensates the owner only at the existing use value of the land then a dual market in land is created, with owners being treated differently depending on whether the state purchases their land, or whether they are left to dispose of it freely and obtain the prevailing market price.

That this issue is complex is obvious, yet it is further complicated by the position taken by those who seek to defend the sanctity of property rights and ensure equity of treatment among owners. The argument is posited that whereas the state may create values it may also diminish them (*worsenment*) by placing restrictions on land use or by placing undesirable projects on land adjacent to the owner. Thus, the siting of a sewerage works next to a piece of property may have a marked effect in lowering values. It is logical to assume then, that if the state collects the betterment it creates it should also provide for compensation for worsenment of land and property.

This argument appears logical and not particularly difficult at first sight, yet it becomes so when the state begins to play a major role in controlling and planning competitive land uses, purportedly in the interests of the community at large. Once the state controls development, owners who are refused planning permission to develop can argue that but for this refusal they might have developed their land to its most profitable use, and that the state has heavily penalised them in the interest of sound planning while allowing other owners to make large profits. As a result of this worsenment, the owner can argue that he should be compensated at the most profitable use for either refusal of planning permission or state purchase of his land for non-profitable uses. But all landowners can make the same argument and demand full compensation. However, as the 1942 Uthwatt Report argued, this ignores a major problem for the state, for although it may *shift* values around in the country by planning, it does not as such create values. Rather, these values are a consequence of the total demand for profitable development in society, and if the state restricts development in one area it will *float* around the potential sites until a suitable site is found. There is, after all, only a limited amount of development that can take place. Unfortunately, if every owner who is refused planning permission or whose land suffers worsenment has his claims met in full, then the total sum that the state would have to pay would be far in excess of the real amount of development that would have or had actually taken place. Not every owner who is compensated would in the real world of market transactions have development coming to rest on his land, yet he can argue it could, and this can produce immense financial problems for the state.[8]

The issue therefore develops into one of how to allow for state purchase and planning while being fair to all owners, and at the same time not creating an enormous expense into the bargain. Unfortunately, these problems are aggravated when the state comes to control *all* land-use planning as has been the case in Britain since 1947. Although the Uthwatt Report had argued that the state only shifts values into competing uses, it is clear, as Balchin and Kieve have argued, that the granting of planning permissions in a market where demand is high is bound to create values — values furthermore which tend to be privately realised.[9] Thus the problem is further clouded because a solution has to be found that is equitable for all owners, but given that the state creates values and also plays a major role in the provision of unremunerative facilities, any solution must also be seen to be fair to the general community.

Historically, there have been numerous attempts to solve the problems of compensation and betterment, all of which have sought to arrive at a workable compromise between the rights of the owner and the needs of the community. As we shall see, the modern history of party policies reveals fairly wide disagreement on possible solutions to these twin problems. In very general terms, this disagreement has tended to be the result of the different views that the parties have taken about the role of the state, not only in the land market, but also in the planning and development systems.

Land Values Policies: 1909-47

Up to 1909 the emphasis of legislation and party policy had been confined more or less to the compensation side of the problem. The main questions involved seem to have been the level at which compensation should be set so that it was not extortionate for the state, and whether or not individual property rights were adequately protected. The fact that the property owner *was* more than adequately protected is ample testimony to the power of land and property interests in eighteenth and nineteenth-century British politics. Protection of the rights of owners as against the needs of the state was emphasised most emphatically by the 1845 Land Clauses Consolidation Act. Under this Act, land purchased by the state under compulsory purchase powers was to be compensated for at the value to the owner, plus any potential use value foregone, with the addition of a ten per cent solatium to offset the loss of option due to compulsion by the state. It would be hard indeed to think of more beneficial provisions for property owners — particularly as they were free to collect any betterment arising on their land irrespective of who created the increased value, and were also eligible for compensation for any injurious effect on any land remaining after compulsory purchase.[10]

This situation was maintained more or less intact until after the First World War when the Coalition Government in the 1919

Acquisition of Land (Assessment of Compensation) Act repealed the
ten per cent solatium and left compensation at open market value as
between willing seller or buyer. This reform in itself might have
appeared as an attack on individual property rights, but given
developments earlier under the Liberal Government it cannot be seen
as such. Also, it is fairly clear that the Coalition's reform of
compensation was predicated more on the desire to limit state
expenditure than on any desire to attack property rights head on.[11]

A more concerted attack on property rights had been contained in
the Liberal Budgets of 1909 and 1910. However, the land taxes imposed
under these measures yielded very little and they were repealed by 1920.
The most successful and lasting increase in state intervention in the
early twentieth century was embodied in Liberal measures to extend
the collection of betterment when it was directly attributable to state
actions, and also to give local authorities powers to commence
regulatory planning of changes in land use. That this should be so was
not surprising given that the Party was the heir to the tradition of
J.S. Mill and the theory of 'unearned increment'. However, perhaps
more pertinent was the slow increase in the statutory powers of local
authorities, including compulsory purchase powers during the
nineteenth century. But, as has been stressed, they were forced to pay
market-value compensation for any land purchased and were able to
recoup any betterment that might arise from their improvement
activities. These obvious restrictions placed upon local authorities
were attacked strenuously by the London County Council at the turn
of the century. None the less, from 1895 to 1902, nine LCC
Improvement Acts successfully passed through Parliament allowing for
recoupment when action by the LCC increased the values of
surrounding sites.[12]

That betterment resulting from specific state activities should be
recouped by the state came to be generally accepted by 1902, and the
Liberal Government's 1909 Housing and Town Planning Act gave those
local authorities desiring them powers to plan developments on urban
periphery sites and to raise a levy of 50 per cent on any site value rises
due to their planning schemes. Under a further Act in 1932, the levy
was raised to 75 per cent and in 1935 powers to control urban sprawl
were added.[13] Obviously, Liberal measures had all the hallmarks of the
'unearned increment' tax proposals postulated by Henry George and
J.S. Mill. However, they did not envisage anything more than limited
state intervention of a regulatory and partially fiscal nature. Liberal
and Lloyd-George Governments did not consider any direct attacks on

property rights nor any dominant state role in development. Hence, although the state was to be given limited regulatory powers of planning control and betterment collection (but only in urban areas) when any such scheme was initiated those whose land values fell as a result of worsenment were to be entitled to compensation under the 1919 Act at full market rates. This was also to be claimable by owners who were refused planning permission. It is not surprising, therefore, that commentators have argued that the protection of owners' rights in this fashion was enough to make sound planning by local authorities unworkable because of the exorbitant compensation bill likely as a result of any local authority scheme.[14]

The period up to the Second World War is, therefore, one in which successive Conservative Governments sought to 'hold the line' against attacks on private property rights in the face of the gradual acceptance by all parties of the need for some betterment collection and planning controls on changes in land use. The Liberal Party laid the ground work for the larger planning powers and attacks on the problem of betterment that were to come. However, at no time did they seek to attack the sanctity of property rights or the existing relationships between individual owners, local authorities and central government. Their vision was essentially one of an acceptance of the need for some betterment collection by the state when the state could be seen to be directly increasing values (for all other increases the owners' rights were sacrosanct) within a framework of limited local planning intervention in urban areas. The only major party with a radical vision was the Labour Party which throughout this period was committed to land nationalisation — a policy which fundamentally challenged existing relationships between property owners, local authorities and the central government. Perhaps not surprisingly, Labour did not work out a coherent policy on land nationalisation between the wars. Unlike industrial ownership, land ownership involves a 'bundle of rights' and 'nationalisation' can mean anything from confiscation and abolition of all private property rights to state ownership of land with compensation and exemption from state takeover for certain groups such as owner-occupiers. With just two short and stormy minority periods in office in 1924 and 1929, Labour had little opportunity to pursue the complex and highly radical course of land nationalisation.[15]

Land Values Policies Since 1945

(i) 1947-1959: From State Intervention to a Free Market in Land

After the Second World War, a majority Labour Government had the parliamentary resources to embark on some sort of land nationalisation but as we shall see, the political will to take this momentous decision was lacking. However, the 1947 Town and Country Planning Act did shift the emphasis of land policy firmly towards a more dominant state role, in which, though individual rights as they stood were to be adequately protected, owners' rights in land and the maintenance of profits were to be seriously curtailed — at least in theory. This was to be achieved by the purchase by the state of all rights to development in land with compensation to owners from a global fund of £300 million — a payment that was to be once for all and which, it was hoped, would end the compensation problem permanently. Such a payment was necessary because the Government had decided that any future development or change in land use would first of all require the granting of planning permission by a local planning authority in both urban and rural areas across the country. The payment was by way of compensation for the loss of freedom to develop at will which the state was now taking from owners.

In theory, then, the 1947 Act solved the compensation problem. Betterment, however, was potentially a more difficult matter because in the future *all* development would be subject to state regulation via planning approvals. If the state is controlling all development then it could be argued that the state does create increases or decreases in land values for owners by granting or refusing consent for land to be turned to a more profitable use. Not surprisingly, proponents of the view that owners in fact do very little to create betterment (the *classic* formulation) were after 1947 on stronger ground. In particular, they were supported by the recommendations of the war-time Uthwatt Committee on Compensation and Betterment and the policy implemented by the Labour Government. Under the 1947 Act, the Government sought to recoup *all* betterment created by state actions for the state by imposing a development charge of 100 per cent (the difference between the existing use value of the land and its new development value) on the granting of planning permission. The charge was to be paid by the prospective developer to a Central Land Board. To end the final problem of the level of compensation to be paid when the state has compulsorily to purchase land for its own purposes (to be fair to owners and to ensure that the state recouped all betterment attributable to its own actions) existing use value was agreed upon. Thus, no betterment would be paid over to owners when the state purchased land, and no betterment would be received by owners when it was created by the state granting a change of use through planning permission.

These measures were taken to be necessary so that a dual market in land would not be created. However, it was not regarded as likely to be a permanently contentious problem primarily because it was not envisaged that the private sector would play a major role in post-war development and redevelopment. The 1947 Act, the 1946 New Towns Act, the controls on industrial development and building created a dominant role for the state in this period — not only in land values policies but also in planning and development. Thus, most post-war development would be completed either by local authority building or by the creation of self-contained New Towns by *ad hoc* Development Corporations financed by and responsible to the Ministry in Whitehall. Agencies of the state would play the leading role — a role assisted by the ability of local authorities and New Towns to purchase land without betterment being paid to owners. Moreover, when the limited amount of private development that was envisaged did take place, the coffers of central government would be further replenished by the betterment that would flow to the Central Land Board on the granting of planning permission.[16]

Therefore, while the Labour Government did not nationalise land in 1947, their approach must be seen as a coherent attack on the problems of compensation and betterment. But it must be emphasised that Labour were not prepared to clash head-on with existing structures and relationships. The ownership of land was not directly changed in favour of the state and the state's planning role was confined to regulation rather than redistribution. Landowners still decided on whether or not their land should come forward for development — unless, that is, the state decided to purchase by compulsion all land deemed worthy of development. Similarly, although the financial benefits of development were to be curtailed for the landowners, profits could still be made by the rise in land and property values in line with inflationary pressures or the natural growth of the economy. The development charge only affected the betterment values realised when land went through a change of use; land already developed or undeveloped could rise in value without being penalised. Finally, while the state was to be given a dominant planning role, with the exception

of a few *ad hoc* New Town Development Corporations, the major
thrust would be towards utilising existing local authority structures
and central and local relationships.

The 1947 system therefore marks the first major shift to a coherent
state role in controlling and regulating the problems of compensation
and betterment in an essentially 'mixed' economy. The failure to go
further may well indicate a lack of political will, but it also reveals how
Labour came up against the same constraints which led the Uthwatt
Committee to conclude that though land nationalisation with
compensation and the protection of the rights of owner-occupiers
was perhaps the only logical solution to the problem, it was politically
'impractical'. In other words, the committee recognised the electorate's
antagonism to outright nationalisation with its *implied* attack on the
right of the individual to own housing. As such, the 1947 system
probably represents the furthest a reformist political party can go in
this field in giving the state a major interventionist role *without*
threatening existing structures and relationships in a fundamental way.
The 1947 Act allowed the state to intervene; it did not allow the state
to control planning, development or land values — whatever the pious
hopes and expectations. In many respects this limited solution to the
land question was predictable. The political and economic costs of
nationalisation would be very high, and unlike housing and the
nationalisation of basic industries, the electorate was largely
uninterested in the apparently complex and technical questions of
betterment and compensation. Even within the Labour Party, although
left and right diverged on the issue, this policy disagreement was rarely
manifest in important political contexts. In sum, given the greatly
expanded role of the state in economic and social life in this period, it
was understandable both that land nationalisation would be seen to be
less essential than in some other eras, and that the Labour Government
should shy away from an issue with potentially high political and
economic costs, but of relatively low political salience.

Although the Conservative Party had toyed with the idea of an
increased state role in planning and betterment in the Coaltion
Government's 1944 White Paper (*Control of Land Use*) and at the
1945 General Election, by the time they returned to office in 1951
such sentiments had virtually dissipated.[17] By 1947, the Party had, in
fact, undergone a major shift of emphasis in its erstwhile commitment
to heightened state intervention which had been evident during and just
after the war. At the same time there was mounting feeling within the
Party that the 1947 system had, in expecting the state to dominate all

planning and development, gone too far.[18]

One of the major problems with the 1947 Act was that because of the 100 per cent charge on development, landowners refused to bring land forward for development unless they could obtain a price in excess of the existing use value allowed to them. In other words, they were unwilling to part with their land unless there was a financial incentive to do so. This resulted in land being withheld from the market — a serious problem by 1949 since the Labour 'bonfire of controls' had meant they expected the private sector to play a larger role in development than had been intended initially, and developers found that they had to pay the development charge twice over (often out of profits) which was an added burden on postwar reconstruction.[19]

These facts were presented by the Conservative Government in a White Paper in November 1952, and in two Acts in 1953 and 1954 the financial provisions of the 1947 system were repealed and the free market was allowed to operate once more with limited protection for the state.[20] Thus the development charge was abolished along with all but unexpended claims on the Global Compensation Fund, and owners were free to collect betterment once more. However, while these measures mark the return of the Conservative Party to its traditional defence of property rights in the face of the needs of the state, the repeal of the 1947 Act's financial provisions was curious in that it did not move totally to a rejection of any and all betterment collection by the state. On the contrary, when local authorities or public agencies used compulsory purchase powers, compensation was to be based not on market value but on existing use value or 1947 values, whichever was the greater. Similarly, the state regulatory planning role on a statutory basis was maintained intact, as were the New Towns which had been designated under Labour. It would be misleading, however, to imply that these changes indicated an acceptance by the Government of a major role for the state. In all of the provisions which favoured the state's role *vis-a-vis* the property owner, obvious precedents existed. The maintenance of planning powers for local authorities was hardly surprising given that the regulation of development by planning permission in no sense can be seen as giving the state a controlling role in development. At the same time, earlier Conservative measures had accepted the need for some planning in urban areas provided that it was administered by existing local authorities, and the 1947 Act had merely extended this principle to the country as a whole. In no way, therefore, was Conservative acceptance a break with precedent, especially as these measures had also been accepted as necessary by the expert Uthwatt

Committee. The same was true of the acceptance of compulsory purchase at existing use value since the Uthwatt report had argued that the excessive compensation burden on local authorities before the war had been the major impediment to sound planning.[21]

The Conservative measures can be seen then as a compromise biased in favour of property interests who could not only collect betterment again, but would also receive compensation for refusal of planning permission. Therefore, only in cases when the state had definite statutory obligations to fulfil in the community's interest was the private owner to be penalised. Unfortunately, the compromise did not work out in practice, for with the state purchasing at existing use rather than at market value a dual market in land was created. Thus owners who sold their land on the open market obtained their full share of betterment value while those whose land was taken for public use did not. Many considered this an unjust arrangement, and during the 1950s Parliamentary and public sentiment against the Act slowly mounted. Parliamentary pressure for the reform of compensation law received further impetus following the suicide of a Mr Pilgrim who had been made bankrupt in part because under the 1954 Act his land had been compulsorily purchased at existing use value by a local authority. In the wake of this and in the context of growing disenchantment among Conservatives with planning law generally, with the passage of the 1959 Town and Country Planning Act, the Government returned to full market value as the basis for compensation for compulsory purchase.

Thus, by 1959, apart from one or two concessions to New Town, Town and Comprehensive Development schemes, the owner of property was free to collect and keep all betterment in his land and the state was in future to pay for all land at full market rates. The Conservative Government had come almost full circle to reject *any* state share in betterment collection and to uphold the sanctity of property rights in a free market in land values, if not in land use. Indeed, the defence of property rights was taken further in the 1959 Act since owners who were refused planning permission could now claim 'certificates of alternative development'. This provision meant that when land was being purchased for a non-profitable use by the state the owner could serve a certificate on the relevant authority claiming compensation on the alternative use that the land could be put to — usually residential development — even though the land was not to be so used. Similarly, owners whose land had been blighted by a planning decision so that their land became unmarketable were allowed to serve 'blight notices' on local authorities claiming market value under the compulsory purchase provisions indicated above.[22]

Clearly, therefore, the 1959 Act marked the lowest point to which the state's role in controlling land values and development planning had fallen since before the 1919 Act. Owners were allowed to keep all betterment however it was created, and the compensation provisions of the Act mirrored the 1919 Act to all intents and purposes. Compounding this, Labour Party policy was more or less bankrupt in this period. The Party had a vague commitment to land nationalisation but failed to take the second reading of the 1959 Bill to a division in Parliament and offered no real defence of the state's role or rights.[23]

However, between 1959 and 1970 both political parties were to reappraise seriously their policies and move back towards the recreation of a larger state role in these matters. Yet, and this is perhaps more important, while both parties came to accept very different commitments to a state role (in the degree of intervention and its nature) between 1964 and 1967 both were substantially to modify these very different commitments.

(ii) 1959-1970: The Free Market Questioned and the Return to Limited State Intervention

The period between 1959 and 1970 can be seen essentially as one of return to first principles for the Labour Party, and continuing turmoil and soul searching by the Conservative Party, given that they had by 1959 committed themselves more or less to a free market solution.

Perhaps the most important factor in this period was the massive boom in land prices (Chart 3.1), which was set in motion by the 1959 Act's freeing of the development market and also by continuing economic and population growth. These forces produced a high level of demand for housing, particularly in the South-East.[24] Not surprisingly, by the time the index of land prices had reached a peak in 1961, the Labour Party had presented in *Signpost for the Sixties*, a scheme to nationalise 'dead ripe' development land via state purchase through a central agency called the Land Commission.[25] Although this scheme differed in many respects from the earlier 1947 system — particularly as no development could take place without prior purchase and subsequent 'lease back' by the Land Commission, which implied a more positive role in development for the state than under the earlier legislation — it did represent a return by the Party to the *principle* of state recoupment of betterment and intervention in the planning system which the Conservative policies of the 1950s had successfully ended.

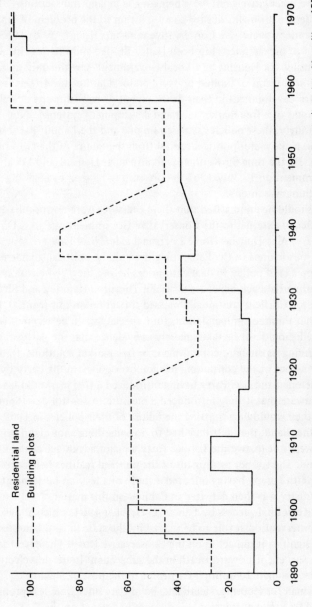

Chart 3.1: Prices of Residential Land and Building Plots in Relation to Retail Prices, England, 1890-1969

Residential land
Building plots

Source: Reproduced from Graham Hallett, *Housing and Land Prices in West Germany and Britain* (London, Macmillan, 1977), p.100. Until the 1960s there was little data collected on land prices in Britain. The few sources (mostly non-official) quoted by Hallett are all that are available.

However, the Conservative Party was not immune to the effects of rising land and house prices, especially as the press was arguing that massive speculative gains were being made in land transactions.[26] Faced with demands on all sides for some solution to the problem of land and house prices, successive Conservative ministers from 1959 to 1963 tended to prevaricate. Thus both Henry Brooke and Charles Hill, while responsible for Housing and Local Government, saw the only possible solution in terms of limited pressure on local authorities to release more land for development in their development plans within the overall constraint of a free-market land and development system.[27] Not surprisingly, these policies satisfied no one and the Labour Party was able to make major political capital from the failure of the Government to act. By the time Sir Keith Joseph arrived at Housing and Local Government on 13 July 1962 the pressure to be seen to be doing something was intense.

It should be emphasised that these pressures were not peculiarly or specifically external to the Conservative Government or Party. On the contrary, Alec Douglas-Home's personal aide, Nigel Lawson, sent numerous memos to the PM arguing it would be political suicide not to develop a land policy to deal with prices before the 1964 election, and the influential back-benchers Sir Colin Thornton-Kemsley and Sir Frederick Corfield continually pressed for action on this front.[28] The fact that these recommendations for a special tax on betterment were rejected should not be taken merely as evidence that the party was reaffirming its die-hard commitment to free market solutions. Rather it is evidence of the continuing turmoil over policy in the Party by 1964. On the one hand, the Party having introduced a free market in land had to be aware that if they introduced a measure to control development gains they would be admitting the failure of their policies in 1959. On the other hand, they felt they had to do something about land prices if they were not to give the Labour Party a major advantage at the next election. The former assessment of the political realities helps explain why Keith Joseph having initiated a study of a levy on betterment in his Ministry was then defeated in Cabinet on this matter.[29]

The electoral success by Labour in October 1964, which allowed a more interventionist role to be played by the state in land issues, also had a significant impact upon the Conservative Party. The defeat led to the success of Edward Heath in the subsequent leadership election and also brought John Boyd-Carpenter to the post of Shadow spokesman for Housing. Heath and Boyd-Carpenter were less prone to defend free market solutions — or, more important, in the face of obvious political and public opinion realities. Indeed, at the time, Boyd-Carpenter was, like Thornton-Kemsley, committed to enshrining a betterment tax or levy in party policy. Accordingly, Heath instituted a Land Study Group in 1964/5 under Reginald Maudling's Chairmanship, and Conservative policy was spelt out by Boyd-Carpenter in February 1965 to Conservative Central Council and later at Conference in October. By 1965, therefore, the Conservatives were committed to a special tax or levy on betterment and speculative gains in land.[30]

Surprisingly, this acceptance of the need to treat betterment as a special case coincided with a movement by the Labour Government from their more extreme proposal for total nationalisation of development land to a much more constrained policy for a Land Commission, which was to collect a 'betterment levy'; a proposal which had not been in the Manifesto at all.[31] It is probably true to say that in the period between 1964 and the beginning of 1966 Conservative and Labour Party policies were as close to one another as they had ever been. Of course, this is not to argue that the Conservative Party supported the idea of even a limited and permissive Land Commission. This they certainly did not do since their approach was to search for a fiscal solution. However, they did accept that the betterment element in land values was in part created by the state and was therefore eligible for *special* state recoupment. This was ample testament of a return to the Party's general minimalist interventionist attitude of the immediate post-war period, in contrast to the more *laissez-faire* nostrums of the 1950s.

The drift away from free market solutions was, however, to prove short lived. Geoffrey Rippon's transfer to the Shadow Housing post, and the appointment of Graham Page and Margaret Thatcher to head the Opposition's handling of the Land Commission Bill in Committee, coincided with a growing acceptance within the Party that a special levy was unnecessary to solve the land question and that it could be handled adequately through normal capital gains and income tax measures. This reappraisal was undoubtedly aided by a number of factors; in particular by the perceived arbitrary workings of the Land Commission in practice, and the influence of the 'Selsdon' spirit of free enterprise which was gaining momentum at the time.[32]

(iii) 1970-1977: From the Free Market to Intervention

So by 1970 the Conservative Party had undergone yet another reversal of policy. Minimalist intervention was now to be a thing of the past as

the Party came to reject not only the role played by the Land
Commission and the technical machinery of the levy (as it had always
done), but the idea of any separate levy at all to deal with betterment
as a special case. This policy was to be enshrined in the Land
Commission Dissolution Act in 1971 and the Finance Act of the same
year. In future, there would be no Land Commission and the level of
tax on gains in land values would be assessed under capital gains
provisions at the lower level of approximately 32 per cent as compared
to 40 per cent under the 1967 Act. On top of this, those liable to levy
would be eligible for the extra allowances available under capital gains
legislation as compared to those written in to the Land Commission Act.

The Labour Party in Opposition did not oppose the dissolution
measure in any major way, and indeed Richard Crossman admitted that
the Commission had to all intents and purposes been a failure.[33]
However, the perceived failure of the 1967 Act did not, as it had in the
1950s, send the Labour Party into quiescent opposition. On the
contrary, the Party quickly instituted a further study group to look
into the land question. The Party made speedy progress and in the 1973
document *Labour Party Programme*, a policy committing a future
government to legislation was unveiled; a policy which would give local
authorities similar powers to those of the now defunct Land
Commission.[34] This commitment to local authority purchase within ten
year rolling programmes of future development needs at current use
value, plus a small and declining percentage of the development value
for the landowner or developer, highlights two important tendencies
in Labour policy formulation after 1959.

First of all, the Labour Party has since 1959 maintained a continuing
commitment to state intervention in order to iron out the perceived
deleterious consequences of the mixed market and a locally controlled
planning and development system. This commitment can only be regarded
as enshrined within Party doctrine after 1959, for between 1951 and this
date it is difficult to see what policy if any the Party had on the land
values and development issues. Second, Labour policies in this field have
shown a fair degree of continuity. The failures of the 1947 system (the
100 per cent tax and lack of positive state involvement in development
and land supply) were avoided in the 1967 Act. Similarly, the perceived
failure of the 1967 Act (massive opposition by local authorities to a
central state land trading agency usurping their role) was avoided relig-
iously in the Community Land Act which might be seen as an attempt by
the Labour Party indirectly to subvert local authorities by giving them
many financial benefits in exchange for taking on a more positive develop-

ment and interventionist land supply role.[35]

On the other hand, Conservative policy has never shown a firm commitment to any one view of the role of the state in this issue-area. As we have seen, other than a complete rejection of direct, physical intervention, party policy has tended to drift between the minimalist interventionist role of a special betterment tax through capital gains taxation, and the belief that the state has no right to be involved in this area of society at all because the building of houses in itself is a gain to the community and any further taxation or impost is a punitive measure. This continuing debate has been apparent throughout the early 1970s and would seem to be still with us if we trace recent developments.

Throughout the period 1971 to 1973 the Conservative Party did little to minimise the impact of very rapidly increasing land and house prices (see Chapter 4, Table 4.7) for either the public sector on the private house buyer. Peter Walker at the Department of the Environment did encourage the Sheef Report, which looked to public and private consortia as the answer to redevelopment, and extra finance was found for local authorities for the provision of sewers and some services.[36] However, this was hardly a significant contribution to a problem which had been largely caused by the indiscriminate cheap money policies of the Government.[37] Neither the Minister's statements on the possibility of his solving the problem by directing local authorities to increase land supply, nor the White Paper on the same lines directing authorities to do just that by his successor at the DOE, Geoffrey Rippon, was an adequate answer to the problem.[38]

Indeed, by 1973 the continuing attempt by the Conservative Government to maintain a non-interventionist role was seen to be a failure. Thus in the general statement on the 1973 Budget the Chancellor introduced the idea of a land hoarding charge on undeveloped land with planning permission. The subsequent White Paper on this also introduced the idea of a contribution to local authority 'infrastructure' costs from relevant developers and builders.[39] However, the Government did not want to introduce a general impost on betterment, as it had said it would not do so prior to 1970. But the desire selectively to penalise builders and developers in an attempt to solve the problems of rising land prices was a nonsense, because these groups were not responsible for the general monetary and investment decisions which were largely the cause of price inflation.[40]

These confused ideas were not translated into policy, however, and when, in December 1973, the Chancellor introduced the idea of a

Development Gains Tax, which would bring the capital gains on the sale of buildings and land into line with income and corporation tax, the Government seemed to be returning to a more conventional solution. At the same time a scheme to introduce a first letting charge on empty office blocks was unveiled.[41] Clearly, by 1973/4 the Conservative Government had reversed its policy quite drastically since its non-interventionist position in 1970. But it must be emphasised that though the Government had changed its policy, it did so by a resort to a fiscal solution, a minimal interventionist role. No major interventionist role which would see the state, locally or nationally, intervening in a positive way in the land supply and development market, was ever considered seriously by Conservative politicians during this period or throughout the post-war years.

Having pointed to this one irreducible strand in Conservative policy since 1945, it is still the case that the Party has witnessed far more internal turmoil in this policy area than has the Labour Party. Even the rise of Margaret Thatcher to leadership and her supposed commitment to more *laissez-faire* policies does not seem to have solved this problem. Although there is no clear evidence as yet, it is probable that the degree of state intervention in the land market is the major stumbling block facing the recent Conservative Land Study Group initiated by Thatcher and Hugh Rossi, the spokesman on Land and Housing. When it reports in 1978, the Group will probably recommend the repeal of the Community Land Act, but will almost certainly advise that the Development Land Tax be maintained at a lower level than at present, and that additional powers or resources be given to local authorities to assist their development programmes without giving them monopoly or statutory powers as under the Labour Act.[42] Obviously much of this is guesswork, but it looks as though the Thatcher tenure, for all its rhetoric on the free market, will not lead to particularly *laissez-faire* solutions in land policy. Indeed, the policies are striking in that they seem to follow the general trend of minimal interventionism as laid down by John Boyd-Carpenter and Sir Colin Thornton-Kemsley, and as such are far less *laissez-faire* than those pursued by the Heath government up to 1973.

(iv) Summary: 1947-1977

As we have seen, there has been a marked difference in both the doctrinal positions of the two parties over land policies and their willingness to modify these policies since 1945. While the Labour Party has maintained a stronger commitment to major state intervention than the Conservative Party, this commitment has been a fairly permanent feature of party policy. However, the Party has accepted important changes in policy; most notably the reversal of draconian measures between the Manifesto commitment to a Land Commission in 1961 and the eventual enactment of the legislation in April 1967. At the same time this decision to try a Land Commission and not the failed 1947 system, and later to try local authority intervention rather than a central state agency in 1975, represent important modifications of party policy which require explanation. On the other hand, the history of Conservative policies reveals a far greater degree of disagreement on the requisite legislation and the role of the state in these matters. As . such we can pinpoint periods: 1947 to 1964, 1964 to 1966, 1967 to 1973 and 1973 to 1977, when Conservative Party views were modified along a continuum stretching from free market solutions through income tax proposals to specified taxation measures. These policy adjustments or reversals also require explanation and it is the purpose of the next two sections to assess the role of those professions, interest groups and party and bureaucratic actors most centrally involved in land questions. In doing so, it will also be important to describe the changing nature of group activities and whether their influence on policy has waxed or waned over the years.

The Interest Group and Professional Policy Role, 1947-77

If one surveys developments in planning and land use it is striking how in recent years the groups and professions involved have taken an increasingly active interest in the question of compensation, betterment and land values. Thus the Town and Country Planning Association (TCPA) published a *Statement on Development Values and Land Assembly* in May 1972 and the Royal Town Planning Institute (RTPI) and the Royal Institution of Chartered Surveyors (RICS) both reported their respective views on the question in 1974. More recently the House Builders Federation (HBF) has initiated its own study of the problems of land.[43] At the same time, groups which might have been seen as opposed to state intervention in the land market have increasingly shown a willingness to accept some limited intervention — as well as a desire to influence the way that recent governments have attempted to solve the problem.[44]

These developments are in contrast to group activities in earlier times when, as late as the 1960s, the RTPI was unwilling to commit itself in a major way to any position on land values issues, and the RICS and HBF disagreed with Labour Party policy between 1964 and 1967 without undertaking any major study to indicate which way government policy should be directed. Activity, such as it was, tended to be reactive rather than initiatory, negative and technical rather than positive and principle oriented. Although it would be misleading to claim that these groups now see themselves as policy formulators, concerned as much with principles as technical details, it does seem to be the case that they are now increasingly active and visible in terms of their concern to arrive at a once-for-all equitable solution to this highly contentious problem.

Given that the group/professional views on this issue have tended to emphasise the necessity of facing realities and instituting only workable solutions, and that recent party policies have tended to mirror this generalised view, one might conclude that external groups had exerted a not insignificant influence on policy. However, on closer analysis this interpretation would seem to be an oversimplification.

(i) 1947-4959: Group Re-Activism

Although one or two groups had been unhappy with the 1947 system and the impact that it was said to have on their members, it was generally the case that external groups did not play a major role in influencing the return of the Conservative Governments of the 1950s to free market solutions.

While the builders' associations had railed against the planning controls imposed on their members and the 100 per cent development charge, and the land-owning fraternity represented by the Country Landowners Association (CLA), had attacked the 1947 Act for its similarity to back-door nationalisation, their influence on Conservative policy making in Opposition was at that time limited.[45] These organisations were particularly small bodies with limited financial and staff resources in the immediate post-war period. Given these limitations and the constraints imposed by having to deal with massive amounts of new and unfamiliar legislation after 1945, the role of these organisations was one of bemoaning the loss of freedoms and hoping that subsequent administrations might repeal the 1947 Act — but they had no clear perception of what in fact might replace it.

This attitude tended to be mirrored by the RICS, the dominant valuation profession in land affairs. The RICS position in these years was to minimise its involvement with government on what were regarded as non-professional matters. In other words, they tended to protect their members' interests in terms of pay and demarcation and educational policy disputes while maintaining a low profile on public policy matters which they regarded as political.[46] Thus they suffered from the same constraints as the CLA and the housebuilders, as well as the added impediment that their membership worked for both the landowner and the local authorities, and could not as a result appear to be taking sides.

Perhaps the most that one can say concerning these bodies is that they contributed to the environment in which Conservative Governments had to operate. That they desired the ending of the 1947 system and its draconian complexity is not in doubt, but given their combined resource limitations, their desire to avoid active political involvement and their willingness to make the 1947 system work, it is unlikely that they would have had a major influence on Conservative policy. Of more obvious relevance to the Conservative Governments of the 1950s was the perception that the 1947 system had failed, the obvious inequity of a dual market and the machinations in Parliament of Frederick Corfield.

Nor, therefore, is it surprising to discover the Labour Party in Opposition maintaining a low profile, in what had become an anti-planning decade, as the Party strove to come to terms with its perceived policy failures. In the same way, the two major planning interest groups, from having been influential in encouraging the acceptance of planning and a solution to the land-values problem in 1947, had limited influence on policy in this period. The TCPA and the TPI had enough to do defending further erosions of the planning system rather than working out viable solutions to compensation and betterment problems, or modifying Conservative or Labour policies. Indeed, it might not be very far off the mark to argue that the planning professions and planning interest groups were witnessing cumulative disillusion with the planning system as it failed to achieve their highest expectations. In this light it is not surprising that they maintained a non-interventionist role throughout the 1950s in so far as policy initiatives were concerned.

In conclusion, then, it would seem that public policy towards the compensation and betterment problem was not the result of group activities and influence on Conservative or Labour policy between 1947 and 1959. Groups seem to have spent this period reacting to government legislation rather than initiating it. They were a long way from shaping or directing party policy even if they did contribute to the environment in which party and government policy choices had to be made. To explain party policy initiatives and modifications we have to look elsewhere: the changing needs of the economy by 1951, the resurrection of neo-liberal/free enterprise values in the Conservative

Party in this period, a generalised belief that the 1947 system had failed on the part of the professions, politicians and civil servants, and the growing sentiment that government was intervening altogether too much in the social and economic life on the nation.

(ii) 1959-1970: The Arousal of Group Professionalism and Responsibility

Between 1959 and 1970, when policy in both parties moved first in one direction and then in the other, changes were also discernible in the role of interested groups. With most, a reorientation occurred that one might assume heralded not only a more active and publicly visible role for these groups, but also a more influential voice in party and government policy making.

Thus in the period between 1958 and 1964, the TCPA instituted a number of new committees on compensation and betterment, urban renewal and regional development. Their increasing activism was underscored by a novel decision in February 1964 to publish a pamphlet setting out the policies the TCPA supported, which indirectly indicated which party might best fulfil these aims at the coming election.[47] At the same time, the National Federation of Building Trade Employers and the Federation of Registered Housebuilders (NFBTE/FRHB) had become more active, setting up a study group to look into the combined problems of land supply and land values and pressing the government for speedy action in forcing local authorities to allocate additional building land in their development plans.[48] Finally, the RICS had begun to question its traditional attitudes. In June 1959 the junior organisations had initiated a research group on the compensation and betterment issue which reported in 1961 calling for further government legislation.[49] Later in 1964 an independent RICS group under Sir Colin Thornton-Kemsley, and a follow-up official study group, also reiterated this demand for further action.[50]

As we can see, a significant change in the attitudes of the major groups had taken place. No longer would they simply react to government initiatives, they now saw their role as one of attempting to clarify issues and problems so as to be that much more informed in influencing government legislative proposals. However, although these groups became increasingly active and visible, it appears that this did not result in increasing influence on government legislation.

Thus, while the RICS, TCPA and the builders had become involved in calling on the Conservative Government for action to solve the problems of rising land prices and a paucity of land supply, policy did not change appreciably between 1959 and 1964. There was immense debate in the Government over whether anything should be done but the free market in land was maintained.

Similarly, even though the policy outlined by the TCPA bears a surprising similarity to Labour legislation in 1967 and the Land Commission White Paper of 1965, it would seem to be the case that the groups involved here did not have a major influence in shaping Labour policy. This is not surprising since many of these organisations did not set up specific study groups until the White Paper was published, and even those that did, like the TCPA and RICS, were not officially consulted until after publication. Labour's policy, although perhaps influenced marginally by the fact that all but two of the groups questioned the proposals, was essentially a political decision taken by Ministers on the basis of civil service advice.[51]

Similar relationships apply to Conservative policy positions up to 1970. The Conservative Party was obviously influenced by the fact that the RICS, TCPA and TPI had come to accept that state recoupment of betterment was justifiable, and that the NFBTE/FRHB and CLA were hardly strident in their opposition to such a solution to this problem. However, it appears that the decision to change policy was not primarily a result of group influence. On the contrary, the decision to develop a commitment owed more to the influence of personalities (such as Colin Thornton-Kemsley, John Boyd Carpenter and Nigel Lawson) to the perception that having no policy might have been electorally damaging in 1964, and to the belief that as Labour had only a small majority it would be sensible to defuse this issue by developing a policy before the next election.

The final policy reversal in this period, when the Conservatives returned to simple taxation measures, perhaps of all the modifications discussed so far, may have owed something to professional advice. There is some evidence that the continuing disaffection of many surveyors, landowners and builders, as revealed in the debates on the Land Commission in Parliament, convinced Geoffrey Rippon and Graham Page that a special tax was both unnecessary and an unwanted impost on the land and building market.[52] However, rather than assume that the politicians were led by external groups, it would be more accurate to argue that group activity created an environment in which some Conservatives could reassert their hold on Party policy after the apparent reversal of their influence under Boyd-Carpenter's tenure of the Shadow Housing portfolio.

In summary then, while the period up to 1970 did witness the awakening of the slumbering giant of interest group involvement with government, this embryonic interdependence was still predicated more on reaction to party and government initiatives than the other way round. Thus if we want to account for party policy changes in this period we would have to look more to the general effect of socio-economic trends such as the rapid increase in house and land prices throughout the 1960s, which clashed with existing legislation and thereby necessitated party policy reappraisal in the light of electoral necessities and party ideology, than to the innovation or directives of external groups or interests.

(iii) 1970-1977: Group Activism without Policy Influence

Changes in party policy during this period coincided with ever increasing activity on the part of the major professions and groups involved with land and building. Indeed, these bodies have gone beyond their self-imposed limitations of 'internal' problem analysis to the publication of what they regard as the basis of sound and workable schemes to solve the continuing problem of land values being a political football.

The TCPA was the first body in this period to initiate a study of the land problem, and its 1972 Statement mirrored in many ways the findings of the somewhat similar Labour study group, which committed the Party to local authority land assembly and purchase at existing use value. Although the Party's attitude may well have been influenced by the TCPA's continuing commitment to public land assembly at roughly existing use value, it is unlikely that the TCPA did more than confirm the policy commitment for their proposals were more in line with the repealed Land Commission than the subsequent Community Land Act. The only major discernible influence may well have been the idea of having a limited period for advance public acquisition.[53]

Heightened activism does not seem to have had very much effect on Conservative policies either. While we might conclude that the RICS, CLA and the builders were happier with the neo-free market approach of the Conservative Government between 1970 and 1973 than they had been under the previous Labour administration, we cannot conclude that these policies were due specifically to their activities. Indeed there is evidence that there was some disagreement amongst the bodies. The builders had some members who regretted the demise of the Commission and the RICS was shortly to argue that some special tax might be necessary to stop property speculation.[54] If these bodies were not influencing Conservative policy up to 1973, and it goes without saying that the more interventionist inclined RTPI and TCPA were not, there is scant evidence that these bodies precipitated the change in policy in 1973. It is probably true to argue that the bodies were responding, in their reports, to the same pressures (the property price boom of 1971-3) which forced the Conservative Government to act.

But this is not to argue that these bodies did not have an influence on Government policy once it had been outlined. Thus the pressure brought to bear on the Conservative Government by the builders over their 1973 proposals may well have been influential in overturning the White Paper of 9 April which intended placing a land hoarding charge on builders. However, the decision to introduce a special fiscal solution in 1973/4, via a Development Gains Tax, though in line with earlier RICS recommendations, smacks more of the political expediency of 1964/5 than a coherent policy with well thought out goals. Indeed, this conclusion would seem to be underscored by the fact that the Cabinet was being pilloried by the Opposition, its own backbench, and the press over Centre Point — the 30 storey unlet speculative office block in central London — and continually rising property shares. Once again, the external groups and professions were influencing the environment of choice — they do not however appear to have been guiding that choice.

Thus we may conclude that even in this period of heightened professional and interest group activity, the dominant impact of groups would seem to be in reacting to party and governmental policy initiatives. If one takes the period as a whole, they have become increasingly active, visible and concerned with policy prescription, without any really discernible impact on party or government policies. All too often interest group and professional successes have come in 'ironing-out' technical problems associated with policies — the principles of which they have not directly influenced or shaped. While it would be rash to denigrate this role, it is still surprising that given the increasing input of working hours by officers and members of these bodies that they have not had more influence on policy output.

The Influence of Party Politics and Civil Service Advice

As we have seen, the impact and influence of interest groups on land-values policies has not been particularly marked. In general terms their influence has been limited and reactive, not dominant and directive. If this is true then the effective locus of policy formulation on land values issues must be situated not with interested external groups but within the party and civil service/governmental policy-making structures.

The adversary politics characteristic of the political parties must be a major explanation of changes in land policy during this period. Hence, as a result of the fundamental differences in the political parties over their perceptions of the role of public ownership and state intervention in the economy, contrasting policies for land-values problems have been formulated.[55] Thus the position taken by the Conservative Government after it was returned to office in 1951, later in 1959 and subsequently in 1970, when Labour legislation was repealed and the private sector was accorded a more central role than under more interventionist Labour Governments, is largely explainable in terms of the impact of ideological precepts held within the Party. In 1951, 1959 and 1970 legislative proposals attempted to minimise the role of the state at central and local levels in the land and property markets. The only other significant non-governmental Conservative policy reversal in this period occurred in Opposition during 1965 when the Party accepted a fairly interventionist role in these matters. This policy position was adopted largely because it was thought to be necessary for the Party to have a commitment to solve land-values problems with an election likely by 1966.[56] So, the one major reversal of Conservative post-war policy was a clear example of electoral expediency — a tactic which was to be rejected categorically when the policy appeared to have no influence on the fortunes of the party in 1966.

On the other side of the political coin, the Labour Party in 1947, 1967 and 1975 introduced policy options which were characterised by a desire to extend the role of the public sector in the planning and property markets while at the same time placing imposts of varying degrees of severity (100 per cent, 40 per cent and 80 per cent), on private transactions in land. Labour policies have also varied in the locus of their involvement, with the primarily centrally based solution of a Land Commission replacing a mixed central and local system in 1967, and this in turn being replaced by the local government dominated Community Land Act of 1975. Whatever the primary locus of control and intervention in the two parties, there can be little dispute over Labour's much stronger commitment to state involvement in land, and their desire to see a substantial share of betterment returning to the state.

These facts point to two conclusions. First, the Labour Party has shown a continuing commitment to intervention and this is explainable in terms of the ideological basis of the Party. Similarly the Conservative Party has maintained its desire to minimise the state's role as a consequence of the mixture of ideologies which underpin Conservative thinking.[57] Second, at one level at least, party policies have often become government policies − even if the parties have not always persevered with policies which have been perceived as failures or have been repealed in the past. Thus, although both parties (Labour in 1967 and 1975 and Conservative in recent policy statements and in 1965) have apparently learnt from past mistakes, they have attempted fairly consistently to implement Manifesto commitments when in office. This implies that the parties have been a major focus of policy choice and, as we have seen earlier, a focus which has not been strongly marked by interest group or other external, non-governmental pressures. But a cautionary note is in order here, for although land value policies are not intelligible without an awareness of party perceptions and discussions about electoral possibilities and ideological precepts, to conclude that the party alone has been the major and only important source of policy initiative on land values would be misleading.

That this is so is revealed most emphatically by the number of policy reversals which have taken place whilst parties were in government. The Labour Party in 1945 did not really have a coherent land-values policy other than a vague commitment to nationalise all land, and the basis for the 1947 Town and Country Planning Act's land-values clauses was determined within government and not within Party headquarters. Similarly, the Labour Party in 1961 had committed itself to the nationalisation/municipalisation of all development land. By the time of the publication of the Labour Government's White Paper on the Land Commission in 1965, however, this commitment had been diluted to a policy of piecemeal land purchase and assembly for the public *and* private sectors, with full scale purchase of all land for development purposes consigned to a second appointed day which as it turned out, was not to arrive. This policy reversal took place in office not in Opposition.[58] Finally, in the period between Labour coming into office in 1974 and the drafting of the details of the Community Land Bill, the commitment to a policy of allowing all land for development to be nationalised on the basis of local authority purchase had been altered into a Bill which would take some land into council ownership over a long period, and, together with the Development Land Tax, place an impost on betterment arising from private development.[59] Development would then be allowed by the private sector by lease-back from the public sector on reasonable terms. This was arguably not the intention of the drafters of the *1973 Labour Programme* when a commitment to state, rather than private monopoly of development was postulated.[60]

These Labour policy reversals point to the important role of civil service advice in the British political system which has not been confined to influencing Labour policy. Significant pressures were also being exerted on Conservative Governments in the early 1960s when the Government maintained its defence of the private sector, and also in 1973 when the anti-interventionist role of the Conservatives was rescinded in favour of a tax on betterment and other mooted policy options such as an impost on undeveloped builders' land and the levying of 'infrastructure' charges to assist the development role of the public sector.

The central role of civil servants in the formulation of land values policies has been adequately documented in the 1939-45 period by J.B. Cullingworth who pinpointed the effect that departmental responsibilities and advice to Ministers may have on the perceptions of relevant party politicians when in office. Thus in 1945, Bevan, as Minister of Health, argued for a much simpler local authority housing department Bill for speedy land purchase as opposed to the much more complex and draconian central purchase Bill being developed by Lewis Silkin as Minister of Town and Country Planning.[61] Bevan alone did not overturn the Silkin initiative — which in itself was an attempt to fulfil in part the Manifesto commitment to nationalise land — he was aided by the fact that his civil servants were working on counter policy proposals and also by the support he was to receive from the Treasury as it fought to limit the potential cost to the Exchequer of a central land purchasing agency.[62] In the long term Silkin had to accept that as a result of inter-departmental rivalries and the need for any policy to be 'administratively practicable' the central purchase scheme he preferred had to be waived in favour of the development charge and the granting of reserve powers to the Central Land Board which was eventually decided upon in 1947.[63]

Notwithstanding the traditional argument that this type of thing is normal practice when party aspirations confront the reality of their operational environment as represented by Ministerial Departmental responsibilities, it does seem to have been the case that the basic outline of the 1947 Town and Country Planning Act was one which was laid down in terms of a compromise between the civil servants responsible for this policy issue in the Treasury, and the Ministries of Health and Town and Country Planning. At the time, this was highlighted by the fact that any issues which proved unintelligible to Cabinet or could not be decided, were generally consigned to an official

committee — the Whiskard Committee — for resolution.[64] As
Cullingworth has argued:

> In the circumstances, a very large measure of initiative fell to
> officials. Ministers might discuss, debate and compromise but, in
> this extraordinary war-time period, the lines of debate were largely
> settled by civil servants. The effective opposition was not a political
> party, but the Treasury and a host of Departments who saw threats
> to their traditional areas of responsibility.[65]

Civil servants were therefore obviously very much in control, especially
in the light of Cullingworth's further comment: 'In this field as in few
others (at least in the nineteen 'forties), those who had the time to
master the subject had considerable tactical advantage.'[66]

However, Cullingworth's view need not be confined to the 1945-7
period; the same forces were at work in the early 1960s and presumably
in the 1970s. It is now fairly clear that the lineal descendant of the
Ministry of Health, the Ministry of Housing and Local Government,
together with the Treasury, were the major actors bringing pressure on
the new Ministers of Land and Economic Affairs in the first Wilson
Government to change the Labour Manifesto promise of a draconian
once-for-all Land Commission purchase of development land. The 1967
Land Commission Act may well have suffered from the continued
attacks in Cabinet of Richard Crossman, but his attacks were window-
dressing compared to the major onslaught on the Manifesto
commitment which was perpetrated by the Ministry of Housing and
the Treasury with the help of civil servants who were seconded to the
nominally responsible Ministry of Land from the Housing Ministry. It is
true that the Ministers responsible were unspecialised in this policy area
and, consequently, were relatively easily dominated by their advisers.
This point was brought home most emphatically by Crossman's later
view that he may have been somewhat misled by his officials over the
nature, purposes and potential of the proposed Land Commission.[67]

That this type of thing occurs in government may surprise few
people. But it is remarkable that the views and proclivities of civil
servants should have a continuing impact on Labour policy-making.
As we have said, while there is as yet no clear evidence, it is likely that
in 1974 John Silkin's somewhat inclusive interventionist proposals for
a Community Land Bill were rejected and rewritten by Anthony
Crosland. This might appear to counter the general view of the civil
service in relation to Labour policies being presented here. Yet on closer

analysis it does not, because Silkin's role and position in the Department of the Environment was not dissimilar to that of Fred Willey at the Ministry of Land when he faced Crossman and the combined wisdom of the Ministry of Housing. Instead of Crossman, Silkin had to face the Secretary of State and the dominating wisdom of the housing and local government branches of the DOE.[68] On balance then, it is clear that the reversal of Labour Manifesto commitment owed a great deal to the influence of civil servants. The experience of Conservative Governments in relation to civil service advice questions, however, the view that civil servants have dominated all land policies.

Conservative policy towards land values has, apart from the changes evidenced in 1965, 1973 and to some extent today, been largely non-interventionist and concerned with minimising the role of the state in the development process. Only during the 1965 period under Boyd-Carpenter and during the Heath Government's U-turn in 1973 has the Party accepted the need for the state to control and constrain private profitability by placing an impost on betterment. The Conservative Party has generally sought to undo interventionist Labour policies whenever it has come into office − often in the face of professional and no doubt civil service advice to the contrary. Rather than Conservative Ministers being influenced by their civil servants they have tended to go very much their own way in office. This fact is underscored by the evidence that civil servants were bringing substantial pressure to bear on Ministers after 1959 to make them aware of the deleterious consequences of their decision to restore the free market in land.[69] However, the Conservative Cabinet, on a number of occasions at this time, rejected the view that betterment should be taxed on any basis whatever.

Thus the civil service was not particularly able to influence Conservative policies when those policies (as appeared to be the case in 1959 and 1970) seemed likely to have serious and potentially disastrous economic and political consequences. Interestingly enough, of the two major reversals of Conservative policy, one has been in Opposition, in 1965, and the other in office, in 1970. Both these decisions would seem to have been the result of the Conservative Party's perception of electoral necessities rather than civil service influence on policy choice. The 1965 decision to tax betterment resulted in immediate rejection once this exercise in expediency had been seen as a failure in electoral terms in 1966. The 1973 reversal of policy was arguably a direct pragmatic response to the phenomenal increase in land and house prices. The involvement of the civil service was presumably important in terms of the delineation of the technicalities of the subsequent legislation, but interest groups were also involved at this stage of the policy process.

We can conclude, then, that while civil servants responsible for land values policy have played a major role in reversing party policies, they have only been able to play this role when Ministers were prepared to let them and/or, when external factors (such as financial crisis), made the *status quo* in land policy look more attractive. Labour's particular failure to pursue its election pledges in 1945, 1966 and 1974 must be attributable in part to this combination of bureaucratic opinion and external pressure. The more radical solution of land nationalisation has not been on the policy agenda in recent years — in part because Labour Governments have shied away from a measure which could be electorally damaging, and in part because of the potential political opposition from vested interests to a measure (or variety of measures) the implications of which are largely unknown.

In one sense, then, Labour has lacked the political will to fulfil its election pledges in land-values policies. Faced with an often hostile civil service and perceiving the high costs of carrying out their commitments, Labour politicians have opted for lower cost compromise policies.

It is important to add, of course, that ministerial responsibilities have not always overlapped with particular personal specialisms in this field, and consequently non-expert ministers have often faced expert civil service advisers on unequal ground. However, political parties with a commitment to radical change should be aware of the potential for opposition among civil servants. On entering office the parties should, therefore, have undertaken the necessary research to enable them to implement a coherent and logical policy on the lines intended. As civil servants tend to be trained in destructive rather than constructive argument, it is especially important that parties intent on change prepare well before coming into office. If they do not (and Labour experience on this matter is apposite) then the civil service will dominate by default — not because of any conspiracy against radical government.

The Conservative Party has been at an advantage not only because its land policies have been much less radical than Labour's, but also because it seems to have been more determined to carry out policies once in office. Future Labour Governments need, therefore, both to prepare more thoroughly in Opposition and to muster a greater commitment to carry out policies once in office. To be fair, political parties in Opposition cannot be expected to anticipate the sort of major economic crisis which, through cuts in government expenditure, has seriously weakened the Community Land Act. However, in 1974 economic crisis was not a new phenomenon in British government, and Labour should have anticipated the harmful effects (such as the constraint of development and the dislocation of the construction industry) which were likely to follow from an underfunded Community Land Act.

Conclusions

Reviewing the main directions of post-war land-values policy, it is clear that political party factors have been of greater influence than the efforts of external interest groups forcing unworkable and undesirable policies on weak governments. This said, it cannot be denied that the policies pursued by different governments have tended to favour some interests more than others. Generally, Conservative policies have favoured the free movement of capital in the land market and profits for the private builder and developer, while Labour policies have, at least in theory, been designed to prevent the accumulation of excess profits from land transactions and instead to redistribute betterment to the community as a whole. It would be wrong to infer from this, however, either that the parties have had a clear idea of which specific interests their policies have been designed to help, or that, in practice, policies have had the broad consequences intended by their framers.

Conservative Governments have made policy a compromise between party ideology and socio-economic necessity, which has usually resulted in the freeing of the market. Generally, private developers and builders have benefited, but this does not mean to say that Conservative Governments have always worked directly or exclusively to assist these interests. It means, rather, that these interests are able to maximise their role in the land and property market when Conservative Governments have attempted to implement free market policies. Often, Conservatives have deplored the consequences of their policies. Excess profits from land speculation and rapidly increasing land prices are *not* objectives of Conservative policy, yet both have occurred under successive Conservative administrations.

The broad aim of Labour policy has been to minimise the role of private actors in the land market in the belief that private profit from land is not in the best interests of the community, and in particular of the disadvantaged. However, how precisely the various Labour schemes would or could have aided the disadvantaged we cannot tell. For one thing, the schemes have never been implemented in full. Even if they had been (including nationalisation) we have no way of knowing what their effects would have been. Indeed, quite apart from the obvious fact that policies in practice usually differ from policies in theory, the absence of research in the Labour Party or in Labour Governments into the distributional and welfare consequences of particular land policies makes this whole question one of speculation. Labour Governments and politicians have almost certainly been right in thinking that public ownership of land has the *potential* for controlling prices and redistributing resources from the advantaged to the disadvantaged. But without very careful research and preparation before entering office, there is certainly no *guarantee* that these effects will result.

But as we demonstrated, quite apart from the question of technical proficiency, successive Labour Governments have found the political constraints of civil service advice and electoral opposition to public ownership major stumbling blocks in their efforts to achieve stated goals. Indeed, we have no reason to suppose that any new technically proficient policy would be able to overcome the fundamental *political* dilemma of ownership rights which is at the root of the continuing conflict over land-values policies in British politics.

Notes

1. P.N. Balchin and J.L. Kieve, *Urban Land Economics* (London, Macmillan, 1977), pp.109-36.
2. This view is represented in the 1845 Land Clauses Consolidation Act which gave the landowner market value compensation and disturbance and interference allowances.
3. D.R. Denman, *Land: Labour's Land Nationalisation Proposals Re-examined* (London, Aims of Industry, 1965); D.R. Denman, *Land in the Market*, Hobart Paper, no.30 (London, Institute of Economic Affairs, 1964).
4. Henry George, *Progress and Poverty* (London, Kegan, Paul Trench, Truber and Co., 1879), pp.231-387; Henry George, *Justice the object – Tax the means* (London, United Committee for the Taxation of Land Values, 1931).
5. J.S. Mill, *Principles of Political Economy* (Part V) (London, Green, Reader and Dyer, 1873), Book V, pp.479-590.
6. Balchin and Kieve, *Urban Land Economics*, pp.122-7; Nathaniel Lichfield, 'Land Nationalisation', in Peter Hall (ed.), *Land Values* (London, Sweet and Maxwell, 1965).
7. 'The Land Problem', *Local Government Chronicle*, no.5148 (30 October 1965), pp.1669, and (13 November 1965), no.5150, pp.1793 and 1794.
8. See the *Report of the Expert Committee on Compensation and Betterment* (Uthwatt Report), Cmnd.6386 (HMSO 1944); J.B. Cullingworth, *Town and Country Planning in Britain* (London, Allen and Unwin, 5th edn., 1974),

104   *Land Values Policies*

pp.144-51; Peter Hall *et al.*, *The Containment of Urban England*, vol.2 (London, Allen and Unwin, 1973), pp.35-70 and 195-245.

9. Balchin and Kieve, *Urban Land Economics*, pp.109-11.

10. 'The Land Problem'.

11. Ibid.

12. H.R. Parker, 'The History of Compensation and Betterment since 1900', in P. Hall, *Land Values*, pp.53-74.

13. Ibid., pp.60-1.

14. Uthwatt Report, and H.R. Parker, ibid., pp.60-6.

15. The failure to pursue party commitments generally in 1924 and 1929 is documented in David Howell, *British Social Democracy* (London, Croom Helm, 1976), pp.9-11.

16. Peter Hall, *Urban and Regional Planning* (Harmondsworth, Middx., Pelican, 1976), pp.99-125, and J.B. Cullingworth, *Town and Country Planning.*

17. J.B. Cullingworth, *Environmental Planning: Reconstruction and Land-Use Planning (1939-1947)*, (London, HMSO, 1975).

18. Nigel Harris, *Competition and the Corporate Society* (London, Methuen, 1972), pp.131-45.

19. Alan Day, 'The Land Boom and the Community', *National Westminster Bank Review*, May 1964 , p.7.

20. H.R. Parker, *Compensation and Betterment*, pp.66-70.

21. Uthwatt Report.

22. For an extended discussion of this problem, see Wyndham Thomas, 'Compensation and Land Values', Peterborough Development Corporation, Paper no.110, 1972.

23. J. Mackie, *Land Nationalisation: For and Against* (London, Fabian Tract, no.312, 1959).

24. Peter Hall (1976), *Urban and Regional Planning*; Malcolm MacEwin, *Crisis in Architecture* (London, RIBA publications, 1974).

25. Labour Party, *Signpost for the Sixties* (London, Labour Party, July 1961).

26. *The People*, 18 October 1959; *Westminster Review*, 18 October 1959; *Guardian*, 16 October 1959.

27. *Hansard*, 18 July 1960, vol.627, col.50-170, and *Hansard*, 20 July 1961, col.1477 ff.

28. The views of these members were discerned in private interviews and correspondence with the authors. See also: Sir Colin Thornton-Kemsley, 'Planning in Britain: some next steps', *Journal of the Town Planning Institute* (January 1962).

29. This view was expressed in private interviews by civil servants in the former Ministry of Housing and Local Government.

30. John Boyd-Carpenter, 'The Conservative Land Policy', *The Stock Exchange Gazette*, 17 December 1965, pp.5-6.

31. Compare 'Signpost', pp.20-22 with *The Land Commission* White Paper, Cmnd.2771 (September 1965).

32. On the arbitrary nature of the Commission and the amendments the Labour Government had to make see: Bryan Harris, 'The Land Commission: Two Years After', Occasional Bulletin, no.90, Co-operative Permanent Building Society (June 1969), pp.1-4; Desmond Heap, *Verbatim Report on the Land Commission*, Paper presented at the Conference on Land, Department of Professional Studies, Division of the School of Business Administration, Ashford, Kent, 9 March 1967.

33. R.H.S. Crossman appearing on TV, *This Week* (1 October 1970).

34. *Labour Party Programme: 1973* (London, Labour Party, 1973), pp.43-51.

35. On the problems facing the Land Commission in operation see: Peter Hall

et al., pp.232-42; Derek Senior, 'The Land Commission', *Official Architecture and Planning* (33), 1970, pp.349-53; John Silkin, 'Solving the Land Problem', *New Statesman* (23 July 1971), p.100.

36. *Conservative Party Campaign Guide: 1974* (London, Conservative Central Office, 1974), pp.269-80, and 1971 Town and Country Planning Act (London, HMSO, 1971).

37. John Myers, 'Why Property Fell', *Management Today* (August 1974), p.48; Peter Hillmore, 'More money, more sense', *Guardian* (19 May 1976).

38. *Widening the Choice: The Next Steps in Housing* (London, HMSO, April, 1973).

39. *Better Homes: The Next Priorities* (London, HMSO, 1973).

40. Myers, 'Why Property Fell', and Hillmore, 'More money, more sense'.

41. On this policy and its failure, see B. Colenutt and W. MacFadden, 'Behind the Property Lobby', *Street Research* (Summer 1974), pp.1-12.

42. There is no public expression of the Conservative position other than a speech by Margaret Thatcher and the interview with Hugh Rossi in *Land Letter* (1976), pp.2-14.

43. TCPA, 'Statement on Development Values and Land Assembly' (London, Town and Country Planning Association, May 1972); RTPI, 'The Land Question' (London, RTPI Planning Paper no.4, 1974); RICS, 'The Land Problem' (London, RICS, 1974); HBF, 'Land for Housing (London, Policy and Planning Group Report: HBF, March 1977).

44. Of the groups analysed here this argument applies to the (CLA) Country Landowners Association. In a private interview with their Parliamentary Secretary, F.G. Holland, it was stated that the CLA was involved in arguing that the recent Community Land Act should involve the following distribution of betterment tax: a third to the owner, a third to the Exchequer and a third to the local authorities. This implies an agreement that the state should recoup betterment which was not always apparent, although their own files reveal that this appraisal was developing in the 1960s over the Land Commission Bill. Interestingly enough this was a view with which the National Farmers Union has tended to agree; see 'The Land Commission: White Paper', *British Farmer* (24 September 1965).

45. F.G. Holland, 'The Property Revolution: 1947-1960' (CLA Paper, September 1959).

46. O. Marriott, *The Property Boom* (London, Gollancz, 1969), ch.2.

47. *The Intelligent Voter's Guide* (London, The Town and Country Planning Association, 1964).

48. NFBTE, *Land for Housing* (Report of a study group), reprinted in the NFBTE Annual Report, June 1960.

49. RICS Junior Organization, 'Report of the JO Compensation and Betterment Research Group', *Chartered Surveyor* (December 1961), pp.326-33.

50. For the independent scheme see, Sir Colin Thornton-Kemsley, 'Betterment scheme: some objections answered', *Town and Country Planning*, vol.32 (October 1964), pp.45-6, and for the official scheme, see RICS, 'Tax on planning consents suggested: RICS Working Party Report on Betterment', *Estates Gazette*, vol.192 (28 October 1964), p.846.

51. A.W. Cox, 'British Land Values Policies' (unpublished manuscript, University of Essex, 1979), chs. 4 and 5.

52. 'The Land Commission White Paper: Further initial reactions', *Estates Gazette*, vol.196 (2 October 1965).

53. TCPA, 'Development Values'.

54. RICS Report, 'The Land Problem', and NFBTE, *Annual Report, 1970* (London, NFBTE, 1970).

55. For an introduction to the general arguments, see S.E. Finer (ed.),

Electoral Reform and Adversary Politics (London, Macmillan, 1977).

56. Correspondence with Nigel Lawson (Personal advisor to Sir Alex Douglas-Home then PM). For further discussion of some of the issues, see R. Summerscales 'Division in Cabinet on Land Betterment Tax', *Daily Telegraph* (3 August 1964).

57. For an introduction to the ideological and philosophical basis of Conservatism, see N.K. O'Sullivan, *Conservatism* (London, Dent, 1976).

58. For details of the reversal of Labour policy see A.W. Cox, 'British Land Values Policies'.

59. For a critique of Labour's recent proposals see SCAT, *Lie of the Land* (London, SCAT, 1976).

60. *The Labour Programme, 1973* (London, Transport House, 1973). pp.48-51, and for an introduction to the Silkin-Crossland debate see 'A farce's third run', *Economist* (257), 14 September 1974, p.38.

61. J.B. Cullingworth, *Environmental Planning: 1939-1969*, vol.1 (London, HMSO, 1975), pp.184-5.

62. Ibid., pp.209-12.

63. The question of administrative practicability is one which recurs in discussions between civil servants in Whitehall in their attempts to determine an effective policy. The problem with this may be that the search for a workable policy within existing practical administrative arrangements may be understandable, yet at the same time seriously constrain policy choice. The issue was raised again in 1964 when Labour came back into office and was presumably raised over Labour's proposals in 1974. For a discussion and idea of the force of the arguments see *Labour and Land* (transcript of Granada TV 'State of the Nation' programme, summer 1976).

64. On the role of Whiskard, see Cullingworth, *Environmental Planning,* vol.1, pp.191-225.

65. Ibid., p.253.

66. Ibid., p.254.

67. See R.H.S. Crossman, *Diaries of a Cabinet Minister*, vol.1 (London, Hamilton and Cape, 1976), pp.260-1.

68. *Economist*, 14 September 1974.

69. See Cox, *Land Values Policies*, chs. 4 and 5.

4 HOUSING AND SLUM CLEARANCE

> I said that in my view. . .it was entirely undesirable that on
> modern housing estates only one type of citizen should live.
> I referred to them then as 'twilight towns', and said it was a
> reproach to our modern social planning that from one sort of
> township should come one income group. I said that if we are
> to enable citizens to lead a full life, if they are each to be
> aware of the problems of their neighbours, then they should
> be all drawn from the different sections of the community and
> we should try to introduce in our modern villages what was
> always the lovely feature of English and Welsh villages, where
> the doctor, the grocer, the butcher and farm labourer all lived
> in the same street. (Aneurin Bevan, House of Commons, 1949)

One fact stands out in any review of the housing situation in Britain:
the main period of urbanisation occurred in the nineteenth century and,
in spite of frequent housing construction drives after World War II, the
nature and quality of the housing inherited from the industrial
revolution and its aftermath continue to dominate discussion of housing
policy. Even by 1975, 56 per cent of all dwellings in Britain were built
before 1944 and a full 33 per cent were built before 1914.[1] The
problems of Britain's early industrialisation — which puts it at a distinct
disadvantage in relation to many other developed societies — have
probably been compounded by relatively low levels of investment in
housing in recent years. Hence, in 1975 Britain invested 4.4 per cent
of GDP in housing compared with 7.2 per cent in France, 5.3 per cent
in West Germany (1974), 6.7 per cent in Italy and 8.4 per cent in Japan
(1973).[2] Of the major industrial societies only the United States
invested less than the UK (2.7 per cent in 1975), but the American
housing stock is much newer than Britain's and *per capita* GDP is much
higher — as increasingly is the case with other industrial societies.[3]

  Given this context, it is not surprising that overcrowding, shortage
and poor housing conditions have been constant themes in British
housing policy for many years. As a political issue, the importance of
housing has fluctuated over the years, but at least since 1919 it has been
of sufficient importance to the electorate for political parties to have
adopted housing programmes. In more recent years, housing has become
an essential part of domestic policy, often outranking employment and

education in terms of significance.

As with other chapters, this chapter aims to assess the extent to which party political influences have been important in shaping the housing policy agenda. Specifically, to what extent have housing problems and solutions to those problems been defined by the political context of the time? And what has been the role of political factors in relation to other influences on policy? Surprisingly, this has not been a major focus of those academics concerned with the development of housing policy. Studies of the administration and economics of housing policy do, of course, refer to the differences in policy pursued by different governments. But rarely do they place differences in a framework which allows, however imprecisely, the analyst to gauge the significance of the political in relation to other factors. It is interesting, for example, that Murie, Niner and Watson's generally excellent and comprehensive review of housing policy does not attempt to assess the role of party politics in the housing policy system.[4] As the last two chapters demonstrated, the provision of housing is intimately related to planning and land-use values policies, and this interconnectedness will be referred to in the present chapter. However, in order to make the chapter manageable, the focus will be on legislation specifically concerned with housing and slum clearance. As a policy area, housing is, in fact, different from land-use planning and land values in at least one important respect. It is much more complex, involving as it does a vast array of interested parties: builders, architects, planners, estate agents, surveyors, building societies, local governments, poverty groups, landlords and tenants associations, a variety of central government departments and, not least, the public at large whose immediate interest in housing has few parallels in land-use planning and land values. Because of the size and complexity of the housing policy system, the present chapter cannot hope in any precise way to weigh all the various forces bearing on policy at every level. Instead, the particular focus will be on the role of party in affecting the national agenda as reflected in legislation. Relations between central governments, local authorities and relevant interest groups will also be referred to where relevant.

Historical Background

Government first became involved in housing in reaction to the appalling living conditions of Britain's new industrial cities. Following the publication in 1842 of the Inquiry into the *Sanitary Condition of the Labouring Population of Great Britain*, the first of many reports

into health and housing conditions in the nineteenth century, some
28 housing and health Acts were passed between 1851 and 1903,[5]
almost all of which were designed to improve sanitation and set
minimum standards of construction and amenity. None were sufficient
to do anything but dent serious overcrowding and slum conditions,
however, and by 1911 there remained a net shortage of at least 660,000
dwellings.[6] By the beginning of the century, it was obvious, indeed,
that the private housing sector could not cater adequately for the
working class.[7] The obvious alternative — local authority housing — had
been built in only very small numbers mainly in London and Liverpool
under Housing Acts which permitted local authorities to rehouse
slum dwellers, but without a subsidy.[8] That this was the
obvious alternative is explained by the fact that local authorities had
long been the agents for administering the poor laws and public health
regulations, and during the latter half of the nineteenth century the
slums were increasingly seen as a cause of social instability and breeding
grounds for epidemic disease. Any effort made by local authorities to
provide housing was not, therefore, inspired mainly by sentiments of
social reform, so much as a realisation that municipal housing might
serve the important function of providing the working class with
sanitary living conditions conducive to a stable family life and maximum
work effort.

   At the national level this 'sanitary' tradition also prevailed. The
main political parties did not perceive housing as an area where the
state should become involved — except where regulation of the private
market might serve to improve basic housing standards and reduce
health risks. Even as late as the general elections of 1908 and those of
1910, the Liberal Manifestos made no mention of housing.[9] Social
policy *was* very much a part of the political agenda during these years,
with the Liberals championing the cause of old age pensions and
unemployment insurance. Only the emerging Labour Party considered
that housing should be provided by the state as a social service and
before the First World War its impact on national politics was small.

   The war radically altered both public perceptions of the housing
problem and the relationship between the state and housing. Housing
production fell away almost completely, prices and interest rates rose,
and the private provision of working class housing which before the
war was becoming uneconomic, became even less so. As a result rents
increased and many private landlords sold out to tenants. These events
had two main consequences. First, the Government felt obliged via the
1915 Rent Restriction Act to intervene in the housing market to

control rents. Rents on houses below £35 rateable value in London, £30 in Scotland and £25 in the rest of England and Wales were controlled. Riots and rent strikes in Glasgow undoubtedly influenced the government's action,[10] and the law was designed as a strictly temporary measure due to lapse in six months after the end of the war. Thus, for the first time at the national level, Government intervened in the housing market as a result of pressure from below. More important than the 1915 Act *per se* and the second main consequence of the wartime conditions, was the increasingly obvious fact that the inadequacies of the private housing market could be overcome only by Government intervention which would ease shortage by increasing the supply of working class housing.[11]

Indeed, by 1919 housing had become a national political issue. Lloyd George's promise of 'homes fit for heroes' and the Coalition's Manifesto pledge that 'one of the first tasks of the Government will be to deal on broad and comprehensive lines with the housing of the people',[12] reflected a dramatic change in emphasis from the pre-war period. Even the Conservatives accepted the need for some state intervention — although they saw this as a temporary expedient necessary to overcome a crisis precipitated by war.[13] Lord Addison's 1919 Housing Act proposed, therefore, an extensive programme of municipal housing where the Treasury undertook to make good all losses incurred by local authorities in the provision of housing beyond the product of a penny rate and the rents they received. Two features of the scheme are worthy of special note:

(a) The Act made special provision for *working class housing.* Local authority housing became synonymous with working class housing, therefore.

(b) The Act was progressive in the sense that it was designed to help those most in need. However, who specifically was to be helped, together with the number of units built and the rents charged, was generally left to individual authorities. Therefore, the principle that local authorities should have discretion in access and allocation policies was established by the Act.

Addison's ambitious Act is generally agreed to have been a failure. A major problem was the nature of the subsidy. It was open-ended and in the face of rapidly rising interest rates in the 1919/21 period committed the Treasury to ever larger subsidies.[14] In addition, building

labour was short, and it was only a matter of time before the
Government, under Treasury pressure, acted to limit the programme.[15]
This was done in 1921 under the Housing and Town Planning Act
which limited production under the Addison Act to 170,000 – a figure
already reached in completed and contracted houses.

Writing in 1943, Marian Bowley accurately characterised the 20
years from 1921 as a period when housing policy 'was to swing
erratically in the winds of party politics and Treasury economy
campaigns. Each time the wind shifted the interpretation of policy
changed or a new experiment started'.[16] With the election of the
Conservatives in 1922 and until the advent of a Labour Government
in 1924, the party political wind shifted perceptibly against the public
provision of houses. The Ministry of Health, hitherto the hub of
post-war reconstruction, receded in importance as its main programme
collapsed under the 1921 Act. In fact, in 1923 the whole rationale of
housing subsidies changed, for in that year a law was enacted (the
Chamberlain Act) which reduced dramatically the role of local
authorities in housing. In essence, from 1923 'Local authorities could
build houses themselves [only] if they succeeded in convincing the
Minister of Health that it would be better if they did so, than if they
left it to private enterprise.'[17] An annual subsidy for up to £6 a house
was available under the Act, and any person, group or local authority
was eligible. Given the stricture favouring private enterprise, however,
few local authorities actually received the subsidy. While the public
sector role was reduced, state intervention in the housing market
clearly was not. A law providing private enterprise with a direct
subsidy is interventionist even by modern standards. The law was
regressive, however, as it clearly favoured those who could afford new
housing. Moreover, the 1923 Rent and Mortgage Interest Restrictions
Act went some way towards de-controlling those rents which had been
restricted by an Act of 1920, a fact which demonstrates that the
·Conservatives' interventionist policy was very much a flirtation with
state aid; a temporary intervention because of the continuing and
indeed intensifying housing shortage.[18]

Just one year later, however, the first Labour Government
re-established the central position of the local authorities in housing
policy. Under the 1924 Wheatley Act, unit subsidies remained, but
were increased to £9 a house for up to 40 years, and eligibility was
restricted to local authorities and public utility societies' rental
property. The system whereby local authorities could predict the size
of any subsidy and therefore calculate how much they would have to

contribute out of rents and rates was financially sound and persisted until 1967. In comparison with the Addison Act, this legislation was startlingly successful. As can be seen from Table 4.1 most public housing built between the wars was completed under this Act. While the Wheatley legislation was the most successful of Labour's short first ministry,[19] it was hardly revolutionary. Provision for the working class was the major objective, but as was the case with the Addison legislation the eventual beneficiaries were the 'deserving' or 'respectable' working class; very few of the unskilled or economically marginal population could afford the rents charged on the new housing.[20] But it was not a major aim of the Government to help the most disadvantaged, but instead to provide working-class houses. In doing this Labour also (perhaps mainly) hoped to stimulate employment in what was a depressed building industry (the building unions had lobbied the new Government long and hard) and to rescue small-scale private capital, traditionally the provider of finance for working class housing, from oblivion.[21] Labour also failed to control rents in the private sector. The 1924 Prevention of Eviction Act touched on the question of private sector rents, but this was a very minor piece of legislation. While the question of high rents (especially in Scotland, where housing shortage and high costs were more acute than elsewhere) remained an important issue for much of the 1920s, the salience of housing as a political issue generally declined. Public housing was proceeding quite rapidly, and although, when returned to power, the Conservatives reduced the per unit subsidy under the Wheatley Act to £6, falling costs provided an increase in production through to 1928 (Table 4.1).

Housing was not to return to the centre of the political stage until after the Second World War, partly because by 1926 the post-1918 reconstruction era had ended and public attention was diverted towards problems of unemployment and industrial relations; and partly because with the exception of Labour's short 1929-31 interregnum, governments' housing policies became increasingly conservative in character under the impact of the National Government's tenure of office.

Labour's ill-fated second term of office did produce new legislation, the 1930 Housing Act, which was designed to continue the Wheatley Act and to introduce a system of comprehensive slum clearance. Until 1930 few slums were cleared; the 1919 and 1923 Housing Acts did provide local authorities with small subsidies for slum clearance, but quite apart from the administrative difficulties involved in slum clearance,[22] the whole mood of the early and mid-1920s was favourable

Table 4.1: Numbers of Houses Built in England and Wales 1919-39 (thousands)

	1919 Addison Act	1923 Chamberlain Act	1924 Wheatley Act	1930, '36, '38 slum clearance	1935, '36, '38 decrowding	Private enterprise subsidised	Private enterprise unsubsidised
1920	0.6	—	—	—	—	0.1)	
1921	15.6	—	—	—	—	13.0)	53.8
1922	80.0	—	—	—	—	20.3)	
1923	57.5	—	—	—	—	10.3)	
1924	10.5	3.8	—	—	—	4.3	67.5
1925	2.9	15.3	2.5	—	—	47.0	69.2
1926	1.1	16.2	26.9	—	—	62.6	66.4
1927	0.9	14.1	59.1	—	—	79.6	63.9
1928	0.2	13.8	90.1	—	—	74.6	60.3
1929	—	5.1	50.6	—	—	49.1	64.7
1930	—	5.6	54.6	—	—	50.2	90.1
1931	—	—	52.5	—	—	2.6	125.4
1932	—	—	65.2	2.4	—	2.3	126.4
1933	—	1.4	47.1	6.0	—	2.5	142.0
1934	—	—	44.6	9.0	—	2.6	207.9
1935	—	—	11.1	23.4	—	1.1	286.4
1936	—	—	—	39.1	—	0.2	271.7
1937	—	—	—	54.7	2.0	0.6	274.4
1938	—	—	—	56.8	7.3	2.6	257.1
1939	—	—	—	74.1	14.3	4.2	226.4
Total	170.1	75.3	504.5	265.5	23.6	430.4[a]	2,455.6

Total: Local authority housing: 1,111.7; Private enterprise: 2,886.0.

a. Approximately 85 per cent of the subsidised private enterprise housing was built under the 1923 Chamberlain Act which was specifically designed to subsidise the private sector.

Source: Adapted from Marian Bowley, *Housing and the State* (1945), as reproduced in Peter Dickens, 'Social Change, Housing and State'.

to relieving housing shortage rather than to the wholesale removal of slums.

That the law changed in 1930 can only partly be attributed to the new Government, for in the late 1920s problems of overcrowding and poverty were increasingly seen both as linked to slum conditions and incapable of resolution through council building for artisans and the 'respectable' working class.[23] The poorest among the population were not benefiting from 'filtering up' caused by new building and, many argued, continuing rent control was inhibiting private landlords from increasing the supply of rental accommodation. These twin themes dominated government thinking after 1931. Slum clearance was greatly encouraged by Labour's 1930 legislation — especially as central government subsidies to local authorities were generous. In addition, every urban authority was obliged under the Act to submit a 5-year plan to the Minister of Health, stating housing conditions and plans for slum clearance. From 1931 Conservative-dominated National Governments continued slum clearance with new legislation in 1933, 1936 and 1938, and by 1939 some 273,000 units had been demolished.[24] They also made important moves to decontrol rent (although some properties remained controlled right up to 1959) and, from 1933, put a complete stop to the public housing system introduced under the Wheatley Act. The motives for doing so were as much economic as ideological. Strict fiscal conservatism was the prevailing orthodoxy, and housing subsidies were a natural victim in widespread and severe cuts in government expenditure. Public housing construction did continue, however (especially after 1936), but only as slum clearance rehousing. Because it was cheaper, this housing was of much lower quality than that built under the Wheatley Act, and the stigma of living in 'a council flat' — usually situated in a high density inner city apartment block — originates with the clearance projects of the 1930s.[25]

Conservatives have long congratulated themselves on their housing performance of the 1930s. They claim not only to have cleared slums at a rapid rate, but also claim responsibility for the very high level of private house building during the decade (Table 4.1).[26] However, private enterprise owner-occupied construction benefited enormously from the economic climate of the 1930s. Low interest rates, falling building costs, high levels of saving and abundant labour occurred simultaneously in an unprecedented fashion. As a result, the 1930s became a period when it appeared to many Conservatives that private enterprise owner-occupied housing could make the major

contribution towards easing housing problems — a fact which was to
have an important bearing on post-war Conservative housing policy.

Summarising the main developments in housing policy in the inter-
war period, the following features stand out:

(a) The politics of housing policy increasingly took the form of
arguments over whether the private or public sector could best relieve
overcrowding and provide an adequate supply of housing. While no
political party totally rejected a role for one or other of the sectors,
all along, and particularly from 1933, the Conservatives became the
party of the private sector and Labour of the public sector.

(b) The private sector shifted perceptibly during the period in favour
of owner-occupied housing and against private rental housing. Between
1914 and 1938, 2.9 million owner occupied units were added to the
housing stock while private rental housing declined by half a million.[27]
In percentage terms, private rental housing dropped from 80 per cent
to 46 per cent of the total, while owner-occupied housing rose from
10 per cent to 31 per cent. This was a result of economic factors
favouring owner-occupied development and penalising housing to rent.
Conservative policy probably did not intend this — although
Conservative Governments did support the growth of building societies
during the 1930s[28] — but the resulting availability of owner-occupied
housing for the lower-middle and middle class masses, meant that future
Conservative housing policies were likely to favour further extension of
this sector.

(c) At the same time, the inter-war period established public housing
as synonymous with council housing. A unit subsidy to local authorities
enabling them to build publicly owned and managed housing for the
working class became the model, and to many Labour MPs and Labour
supporters, the ideal form of housing tenure. But local authority access
and allocation policies went unchecked by central governments, and the
new bureaucracies of the local housing departments adopted rules and
procedures which clearly favoured the 'respectable' working class or
artisan class. This is true even of the low quality clearance estates of
the 1930s.[29] Moreover, rents charged in council housing were unrelated
to tenants' personal incomes, so even before the war, a universalistic
element in public housing provision had been established. Labour also
strengthened its antagonism toward privately rented housing which it
considered exploitative, and retained its conviction that owner-occupied

housing was inherently too expensive to cater for the mass of the population. Other forms of housing tenure —co-operative housing, shared ownership, and other forms of housing subsidy — interest subsidies for developers, trade unions and other organisations — were not developed.

(d) Housing policy decisions were taken in a little understood economic context. The highly favourable conditions for the development of owner-occupied housing in the 1930s were *dependent* on a very low level of activity in the economy, and in the more affluent post-war era such conditions were never to return. Generally, politicians and civil servants did not understand that the size and quality of housing production in both public and private sectors were intimately related to the availability of labour, building and land costs and interest rates, all of which were interrelated and partly dependent on macro-economic factors.

(e) While government policies in the immediate post-First World War period were influenced by a public aroused by housing shortage and overcrowding, the political salience of housing declined in the late 1920s and 1930s.

Housing and the Labour Government 1945-51

The Second World War transformed the objective housing conditions of the British. More than 200,000 houses were completely destroyed and a further half a million rendered uninhabitable as a result of enemy action.[30] At the same time, birth rates began to rise and new house building virtually ceased. This combination assured shortage, overcrowding and crisis, and by 1945 housing had become a key issue for the electorate.[31] Accordingly, both parties assigned a high priority to housing in the 1945 election. Moreover, compared with the pre-war period, the differences between the parties were relatively small. It was agreed that rent control, introduced universally in 1939, had to stay until shortage was alleviated, and both parties accepted that public housing had an important role to play. In a climate of shortage and economic controls so extensive that the market price mechanism had been suspended, the apparently highly interventionist stance of the Conservatives in housing policy was not surprising. However, they considered both rent control and public sector building as temporary expedients, whereas the new Labour Government promised that public housing would become the dominant form of housing tenure. Hence in

the House of Commons debates over the 1946 Housing Act the
Parliamentary Secretary to the Ministry of Health stressed that new
measures to extend public housing 'will provide an added impetus to
the building programmes of those local governing authorities whose
activities will furnish by far the larger part of the accommodation that
is necessary to satisfy our great housing needs'.[32] The new law provided
a Wheatley-type subsidy of £22 a house, one third of which had to
come from the rates. In Scotland, because of the need to provide
houses larger than the prevailing very small units, the subsidy was
variable, with larger amounts available for larger units. Conservative
spokesmen supported the subsidy, but were insistent that as time
progressed the private sector should increasingly be given a chance to
contribute to housing needs.[33]

Control of private sector housing construction was already in force
through a system of building licences introduced during the War and
it was Labour's intention to continue this system. Suggestions by Tories
that private interests should be given subsidies to enable them to add
to the housing stock were quickly dismissed by Aneurin Bevan the
Minister of Health in a typical parliamentary onslaught: 'The only
remedy that they [the Tories] have for every social problem is to
enable private enterprise to suck at the teats of the State.'[34] Via the
licensing system, a ratio of one private unit to five public was to be
established.[35] In addition, public housing standards were to be raised
to a minimum of 900 square feet per unit and local authority
borrowing for housing was to be arranged through the Public
Works Loan Board at protected rates of interest.

Apart from a short flirtation with a prefabricated housing
programme inherited from the Coalition Government, and the
introduction of New Towns in 1946 (which is dealt with elsewhere,
see Chapter 2), these measures were the essence of Labour's post-war
housing policy. As such, they contained little that was new. Unlike
income maintenance, health, planning, land use and nationalisation,
Labour had no grand strategy over housing. Housing was not covered
by a war-time report such as Barlow on the distribution of employment
or Beveridge on social security, and party thinking on the subject relied
in large part on the pre-war experience. To be fair, the combination of
land nationalisation (one of Labour's 1945 campaign pledges),
comprehensive planning with dispersal to the New Towns, licensing
and a large public sector borrowing from a public body at protected rates
of interest, would, if all implemented, have removed many of the
pre-war housing policy problems from public debate. Perhaps this was

intended; certainly Bevan planned for a high degree of social mix in public housing. Recalling in 1949 his intentions in 1945, he noted:

> I said that in my view. . .it was entirely undesirable that on modern housing estates only one type of citizen should live. I referred to them then as 'twilight towns', and said it was a reproach to our modern social planning that from one sort of township should come one income group. I said that if we are to enable citizens to lead a full life, if they are each to be aware of the problems of their neighbours, then they should be all drawn from the different sections of the community and we should try to introduce in our modern villages what was always the lovely feature of English and Welsh villages, where the doctor, the grocer, the butcher and farm labourer all lived in the same street. . .I believe it is a necessary biological background for modern life, and I believe it leads to the enrichment of every member of the community to live in communities of that sort. We believe it is essential that local authorities should also provide accommodation for single persons, for persons who are following professional life, and that they should provide for old people.[36]

As will later be shown, in the light of the subsequent development of public housing, these pledges were little short of revolutionary — as, sadly, they remain today.

Conservative housing policy was even less coherent than Labour's. The experience of the War had given Conservative politicians a close acquaintanceship with state controls and regulations which they continued to accept as necessary in the immediate post-war period. But apart from promises that the private market should eventually play a major part, Conservative policy was lacking. The precise ratio between public and private sectors went undefined, as did the ideal relationship between private rental and owner-occupied housing. It would be fair to say that Conservative policy in this period consisted of a grudging acceptance of controls and public sector involvement together with some rather hazy notions of returning to the market conditions of the late 1930s which were seen as ideal for the encouragement of mass production by the private sector.

As is well known, the 1945-51 period was beset with economic problems, many of which thwarted Labour's best laid plans for the reform of British society, and housing was to become a victim of successive central government cuts and compromises. Interestingly, housing was particularly susceptible to such cuts, for public housing construction involves a complex interaction of diverse factors from building and land costs and availability, to the nature of demand and the availability of public funds. From the outset, Labour's housing programme faltered as a result of severe material and labour shortages.[37] Gradually during the next few years, housing targets had to be reduced, so that the original plan to build 240,000 houses a year was never reached. As can be seen from Table 4.2, 1948 was Labour's best year when public sector production reached 175,000 and private sector 31,000. National economic policy was as important in reducing totals as were market forces such as the availability of materials. Fuel and balance of payments crises forced cutbacks in 1947, and in 1949 the Treasury imposed a 200,000 construction limit for the whole country.[38]

Regardless of these economic constraints, Labour was eager to press on with reform, and the 1949 Act officially removed the pre-war definition of public housing as housing for the working class and redesignated it as 'general needs' housing for all social classes. Bevan's idealism again comes out in the parliamentary debates on the Bill in which he emphasises how the new legislation would encourage local authorities to build a variety of housing types and architectural styles. There were however, no specific instructions in the Bill on how local authority access and allocation policies should be modified to achieve these objectives. How, for example, should local authorities distinguish between the poor and professionals when allocating housing? In the context of severe shortage, such questions should have been asked, for in 1949 a truly comprehensive and universal public housing programme was little more than a hope. At the same time, the pre-war universalistic element of rents being unrelated to tenants' personal incomes remained. Labour also maintained its coolness towards the private market throughout the 1945-51 period. In parliamentary debates Labour Members repeatedly showed antipathy towards building societies who were characterised as 'money lenders' charging interest rates above those which government agencies could charge. In fact, the Public Works Loan Board rates of interest charged to local authorities were kept low, varying between 2½ per cent in June 1946 and 3¾ per cent in November 1951.[39]

What of Labour's policy towards the private rental sector? Clearly, with public housing construction at a relatively low level, considerable stress in this, the main form of housing tenure, was likely. Moreover, with incomes low, rent control continuing, and materials and labour in short supply, the maintenance and improvement of what was a

Table 4.2: Houses Built in England and Wales, 1945-51[a]

	Local authorities[b]		Private builders		Total
1945-46	21,878	(42%)	30,657	(58%)	52,535
1947	87,915	(69%)	39,626	(31%)	127,651
1948	175,213	(85%)	31,346	(15%)	206,559
1949	147,092	(86%)	24,688	(14%)	171,780
1950	145,784	(85%)	26,576	(15%)	172,360
1951	150,497	(88%)	21,406	(12%)	171,903

a. Includes houses built by New Town Development Corporations, housing
   associations and government departments, and excludes temporary houses
   built by local authorities.
b. In Scotland the number of houses built by private developers has traditionally
   been low, and in the post-war period sank to very low levels. For example,
   in 1950 only 782 private houses were built out of a total of 25,811. Central
   Statistical Office, *Annual Abstract of Statistics* (HMSO, 1966), Table 56.
Source: J.B. Cullingworth, *Housing and Local Government* (London, George
   Allen and Unwin, 1966). Adapted from Table 4, p.52.

rapidly ageing housing stock (almost no new private rental housing had
been built since before the First World War) virtually ceased.[40] Apart
from the introduction of local authority improvement grants for older
houses under the 1949 Housing Act, however, Labour largely ignored
the private rental sector. Historically, Labour had viewed the private
landlord as the major source of exploitation in working class housing,
and his gradual elimination was stated policy. However, judging by its
legislative programmes, Labour intended to do this not by a planned
process of phasing out private rental housing and matching the demand
needs of private tenants with publicly available units — a process which
would have required a sophisticated understanding of the characteristics
of private rental housing — but instead by increasing the public stock
and, quite independently (and perhaps not entirely by intention)
encouraging the private rental stock to deteriorate.

  Summing up the housing policies of the 1945-51 period, we can see
that many of the pre-war problems remained. Labour's housing policy
relied almost entirely on a massive increase in local authority and New
Town housing, and broader perspectives on how such provision might
affect the dynamics of a complex housing market were largely absent.
Party thinking was strangely unformed on the housing question. There
was general agreement that property should be socialised, and that
those in greatest need should benefit most from public ownership. But

how these objectives could be reconciled with the economic reality of limited public funds, and the prospect, with decontrol, of an expanded role for the market price mechanism, was absent. In fact these constraints made nonsense out of housing policies which relied entirely on a rapid and massive increase in the size of the public sector. Aneurin Bevan understood this, and his insistence on the need to expand public housing construction partly contributed to his increasingly isolated position in the Labour Government — an isolation which culminated in his 1951 resignation over the imposition of health charges and increased defence spending.[41] It is testament to the poverty of thinking on housing elsewhere in the Labour Party that no suggestions were forthcoming on how policy might develop in the context of a mixed economy.

By essentially extending pre-war policies, Labour also left the local authorities with considerable discretion over their housing programmes. They were, of course, constrained by centrally imposed financial considerations, but in siting and tenant allocations they were left pretty much alone. Once the public housing programme was expanded, this local discretion was firmly entrenched in the local bureaucracies. It was also convenient for the central department (the Ministry of Health) to accept — and possibly reinforce — this bureaucratic demarcation. Constrained as it was by the Treasury and a continuing climate of crisis and shortage, it is not surprising that local discretion over areas *largely independent of economic factors* went unquestioned — especially given the lack of political direction from above on this question.

What evidence there is, suggests that private market interest groups were not an important influence during this period. Market forces were, after all, seriously constrained by a variety of controls which kept private housebuilding down to a minimum. In fact, identifying and assessing the role of interest groups is much more problematical in housing than in some other areas of urban policy. Housing is highly complex involving as it does a large number of interests and professional groups. But it is also highly political. Interested parties rarely have the sort of relatively simple focus which, for example, the TCPA and the RTPI have had in relation to the land-use planning policy system. As we will see, interested groups have been important in certain contexts, but housing policy has been far too much a party political issue for them to have dominated decision-making.

Housing was indeed a vital issue in the 1951 General Election, and the Tories made great capital out of Labour's failure to fulfil their own housing promises. Along with full employment, housing was second only to the cost of living as a domestic campaign issue.[42] Certainly, the Conservatives thought housing electorally important as is shown by their 1951 Manifesto pledge: 'A Conservative and Unionist Government will give housing a priority second only to defence. . .our target remains 300,000 houses a year.'[43]

The Conservatives and the Bifurcation of the Housing Market, 1951-64

On coming to power, the Conservatives set about fulfilling this pledge with some vigour. Their plan was to stimulate both the public and private sectors through increased subsidies and the relaxation of controls. Hence the 1952 Housing Act increased council house subsidies (including a one-third contribution from the rates) to £35 12s in England and Wales and £56 10s (maximum) in Scotland. At the same time housing standards were reduced, so as to squeeze more houses out of available funds. Bevan's 900 square foot minimum for a three bedroom council house had already been reduced by his Labour successor Hugh Dalton, 'provided that the sizes of the individual rooms and total amount of living space do not fall',[44] and the Conservatives' continuation of this policy reduced the average floor space of council houses from 1050 square feet in 1951 to 923 in 1955 and 897 in 1959.[45] These figures are significant, for they reflect the extent to which in the immediate post-war years Conservatives and (as will be discussed below) most Labour politicians viewed council housing as housing specifically for the working class. In Bevan's view, maintaining minimum standards in council housing was necessary to preserve the dignity of the individual tenant and attract a socially varied tenant population. The stigma of the 'council estate' would thus be avoided. Such considerations were irrelevant to most Conservatives, who wanted working class houses built fast to alleviate shortage. As can be seen from Table 4.3, the Conservative Government of 1951-5 was remarkably successful in doing this, achieving a public sector completion rate of over 200,000 in 1953-4 and 1955, a figure greatly in excess of that achieved by Labour during its last few years of office. Increased subsidies, reduced standards and eased controls, were largely responsible for the improved figures. Note, however, that throughout the Conservative period of office the ratio of public to private building shifted dramatically in favour of the latter. Indeed, the Government introduced a series of measures between 1952 and 1963 which specifically helped the owner/occupied sector and gradually reduced (at least until 1962) the role of public housing.

Housing and Slum Clearance   123

Table 4.3: Permanent Houses[a] Completed, United Kingdom, 1952-64

	Public sector[b]		Private sector		Total
1952	211,649	(85%)	36,670	(15%)	248,319
1953	261,937	(80%)	64,867	(15%)	326,804
1954	261,706	(74%)	92,423	(26%)	354,129
1955	208,330	(64%)	116,093	(36%)	324,423
1956	181,243	(59%)	126,431	(41%)	307,674
1957	178,806	(58%)	128,784	(42%)	307,590
1958	148,413	(53%)	130,220	(47%)	278,633
1959	128,402	(46%)	153,166	(54%)	281,568
1960	132,850	(44%)	171,405	(56%)	304,255
1961	122,434	(40%)	180,727	(60%)	303,161
1962	135,432	(43%)	178,211	(57%)	313,643
1963	129,927	(42%)	177,787	(58%)	307,714
1964	161,928	(42%)	221,264	(58%)	383,192

a. Includes flats.
b. Includes local authority, New Town Development Corporation, housing association, government department, Scottish Special Housing Association and Northern Ireland Housing Trust housing. However, in no year did *non*-local authority and New Town housing exceed 6 per cent of the total.

Source: Central Statistical Office, *Annual Abstract of Statistics*, no.103 (1966) (HMSO, 1966), adapted from Table 56, p.60.

Building for owner occupation was encouraged by the relaxation of controls in 1952 and the abolition of the licensing system in 1954. Also in 1954 the Tories abolished development charges on development land and thus seriously undermined Labour's 1947 land values policies (see Chapter 3, pp.80-1). In 1959 local authorities were given the power to grant 100 per cent mortgages for house purchase and building societies received £100 million Exchequer aid to lend on older houses. These measures together with economic conditions generally favourable to the building industry helped re-establish owner-occupied housing as the primary form of tenure in new properties.

At the same time, the aims and purposes of public housing were changed drastically by central government policy. It has already been noted how the Conservatives had never accepted the mass production of council housing as anything but a short-term post-war expedient to stem shortage, and from the early 1950s they went about the business of changing public housing from housing for 'general needs' to housing for more narrowly defined working class sections of the population. This transformation was by no means sudden, however, nor particularly well planned or thought out. The first change in policy concerned the emotive but uncontentious subject of slum clearance. Virtually no clearance of slums or improvements to properties had occurred since 1939, so an enormous backlog had built up. Harold Macmillan, the Minister in charge of the new Department of Housing and Local Government had long been an advocate of urban renewal,[46] and this together with public and interest group pressure for a revival of slum clearance,[47] meant that this became a central part of the Government's housing policy. But it soon became apparent that rehousing people from cleared areas was to become a major part of the public housing programme and would be achieved at the expense of general needs housing. So the 1954 Housing Repairs and Rents Act which revived the pre-war system of slum clearance and redefined the criteria for unfitness, together with a series of circulars requiring local authorities to put forward slum clearance proposals, immediately redirected local authorities towards the problems of rehousing people from cleared areas and away from providing general needs housing. In 1956 the Government actually withdrew the general needs subsidy; from then on, therefore, local authorities had 'to subsidise only those tenants who require subsidising, and only to the extent of their need'.[48] How this was to be done at the local level was, however, left to individual authorities, and there was no attempt to charge differential rents based on the differing income levels of tenants.

Judging by these measures the Government clearly intended to redefine the role of public housing, but it probably did not intend to reduce the role to the extent implied in Table 4.3. Indeed, there is evidence that external economic factors intervened so as to exaggerate the Government's antipathy to general needs public housing or, as some would have it, to public housing *per se*. In particular, the Government's decision in 1955 to withdraw local authorities' favourable access to the Public Works Loan Board and instead to make it the lender of the last resort after the open market, seriously affected their borrowing power in a period of rapidly rising interest rates.[49] Of course the Conservatives did not plan for higher interest rates, but once they had arrived it was up to local authorities to struggle along as best they could. In fact, high interest rates along with cuts in subsidies introduced in 1956 and the reduction in housing standards introduced earlier, threw many local authority housing departments into confusion. During the late 1940s their brief had been clear: they were to construct good quality family homes for most sections of the community. With the aid of central government subsidies, low interest rates, and, because of strict controls on land development, little competition with private enterprise over scarce land, this seemed a feasible objective. By the mid-1950s all had changed, however, and many housing departments found themselves obliged to build lower quality estates specifically for working-class families uprooted by slum clearance schemes. Given that many authorities (especially those Labour controlled) had already developed a bureaucratic culture where numbers were important, it was logical to build more lower quality homes rather than a few higher quality ones, and as the CDP Information and Intelligence Unit has noted, some of these houses were labelled slums even before they were completed.[50] Many local housing authorities also found themselves confined in spatial terms. For one thing they formed themselves in competition with a newly invigorated private sector over scarce land — a tendency aggravated by the extension of Green Belts to a variety of English cities during this period. These almost certainly encouraged higher density developments within city boundaries, rather than low density estates on peripheral suburban sites.

Conservative policy during the 1950s had three main objectives, all of which were linked to a basic philosophy that free market mechanisms could best solve Britain's housing problem. The first two — the relegation of council housing from general to specific needs and the encouragement of owner occupation have been noted. The third objective was to decontrol rents in the private sector and this proved the most controversial of all. Central to Conservative thinking on housing policy was that controls within this sector had greatly inhibited landlords' incentive to improve property and to increase its supply. In sum:

A relaxation of rent restrictions — the government claimed — would increase the supply of rented housing by encouraging conversions and new building, and discouraging sales and prolonged vacancies; it would increase the mobility of labour and reduce over-crowding and under-occupation; it would improve the condition of rented property by making it possible and profitable for landlords to do repairs, and the injustices arising from more than 40 years of rent restriction would gradually be eased.[51]

To achieve these apparently noble objectives, the 1957 Rent Act decontrolled what was estimated to be 750,000 better quality units in England and Wales and 60,000 in Scotland after an interim period

of 15 months. In addition, control was maintained on more than
4 million lower quality dwellings, but these were subject to graduated
increases in rent. Finally, any controlled house vacated by its tenant
was automatically decontrolled.

As represented by this law, Conservative policy was based on a series
of gigantic misconceptions as to the nature of the housing market.
These misconceptions have been adequately documented elsewhere,[52]
but they are worth reproducing in summary form. First, the
Government and the Ministry of Housing and Local Government
assumed that in 1957 the demand for housing roughly equalled supply.
In fact, as J.B. Cullingworth has pointed out in *Housing Needs and
Planning Policy*, the rate of household formation was increasing rapidly,
and in 1957 serious shortage was imminent[53] — especially among those
groups, the aged, young and single people, who tended to live in private
rented housing. Second the Government seriously over-estimated the
number of more expensive dwellings eligible for decontrol and seriously
underestimated the number of decontrolled units made available by
vacancies. Apart from a poor understanding of demographic changes,
therefore, the Government misunderstood the nature of a private rental
sector whose main characteristics were chronic underinvestment and
stagnation. As Malcolm Barnett has observed: 'Freedom not from
control but to make a fair return, was what landlords required,'[54] and
given the poor quality of the housing stock and the fact that the other
sectors of the housing market were heavily subsidised, no incentive
existed to invest in private rental housing, controlled or not. As it
turned out, the 1957 Act had little effect on the market in the North
and in Scotland, but in London where housing shortage was most acute
it almost certainly *reduced* the availability of private rental housing.
Many hitherto larger properties were subdivided and sold off. Security
of tenure vanished on decontrolled properties, rents increased rapidly,
and the much publicised if rare spectre of 'Rachmanism' — the
intimidation of sitting tenants to make them leave so that a property
could be sold or redeveloped — were all partly or wholly a result of the
Act. Worst of all, the housing stock most severely reduced was that
most used by disadvantaged sections of the population. Large poor
families, itinerant workers and the old suffered the most. Unable to
obtain council housing and in no position to buy, their housing position
gradually deteriorated and as it did so, so 'homelessness' increased.[55]

As can be seen from Table 4.4, there was an inexorable decline in the
private rental sector throughout the post-war period, the greatest drop
in absolute terms being between 1951 and 1966. This is significant, for

it was during this period that substantial cutbacks in council housing occurred. So the private sector tenant was squeezed by a reduction in private rental housing and in the rate of council house building. Moreover, council housing access and allocation policies continued to go unchecked by central governments, and the bias, long established in many authorities, in favour of certain social groups — especially the respectable working class family and increasingly the small family — continued.

By 1961 some shifts in Conservative policy were discernible. The Housing Act of that year reintroduced a general needs subsidy for council housing which specifically concentrated subsidies in those areas of greatest need, and production increased slightly (Table 4.3). In addition, £25 million was made available to housing associations to build rental housing, implying at least, that the Government was aware of the serious shortage in rental housing. As will be discussed later, however, housing associations and what might be called 'quasi'-public sector housing has never received much support from governments. Finally, in 1963 a committee was established to investigate the increasingly critical situation in the London housing market, and the Housing Act of 1964 created the Housing Corporation to provide advice and aid to housing associations.

When attempting to analyse Conservative motives in pursuing what effectively was a policy which further bifurcated the housing market into the owner occupied and public sectors and therefore produced a grossly inflexible housing situation for certain social groups, we must look to organisational and political factors. As Donnison has shown, both civil servants and politicians were extraordinarily ignorant of the

Table 4.4: Housing Tenure in England and Wales, 1951-76

Tenure	Dwellings (per cent)				
	1951	1961	1966	1971	1976
Owner occupied	31	44	49	52	55
Public sector[a]	17	25	27	29	30
Private rental sector	52	31	24	19	15

a. Local Authority, New Towns, Housing Associations, and government departments.

Source: *Housing Policy,* Cmnd.6851, 1977, adapted from Figure 2 and from *Council Housing: Purposes, Procedures and Priorities* (HMSO, 1969), Table 1.

nature of the housing market, and their access to and use of statistical data was sadly wanting.[56]   But as Barnett has pointed out, organisational failure usually has political roots:

> Ideas, policy proposals, plans, even research data, are as political as the clauses of a bill. They may direct action or force action along a particular line. This was clearly recognised by the civil servants in charge of the 1957 Rent Act, who carefully did little research and did it as secretly as possible. They worked out supporting evidence for decisions taken rather than evidence that might raise new and unwanted problems. Only in a transformed political climate would greater openness be possible.[57]

The political objective was to 'free the market' and thereby produce a more efficient allocation of resources. Conservative politicians intent on this end rode roughshod over information which may have led to a different conclusion. Even their own Party research department was ignored.[58] Moreover, the Parliamentary Labour Party, fierce as it was in opposition to the 1957 Act, argued in the same emotive and ideologically charged tones as did the Conservatives. Cool, rational appraisal of housing needs and how these related to rent control was absent on both sides.[59] Labour's long standing antagonism to private landlordism blinded the party to the need to seek rational solutions. The 'municipalisation' of the private sector was Labour's instantly conceived and totally impractical solution at the time.[60] As Barnett put it 'The campaign against the Bill, both in Parliament and in the country was completely unoriginal. The traditional phrases accompanied the traditional postures and led to traditional failures.'[61]

   It would not be over-harsh to apply this characterisation to Labour's thinking in housing generally during the 1951-64 period. While the Party was fraught with internal dissent and ideological conflict over the role of the state in the management of economic affairs, and over foreign policy, housing generated little intra-party controversy. Labour's housing policy essentially consisted of increasing the public sector in relation to the private and re-establishing rent control, and both left and right within the party accepted this.[62] Admittedly, by the early 1960s in the wake of the 1957 Act and the developing shortage in the private rental sector, some reappraisal occurred. Anthony Crosland, for example, argued in 1962 that 'quasi'-public sector or co-operative housing should play a much greater role in the housing market.[63] However, in the same piece, he pleaded:

The first essential is to relate the building programme more accurately to need, that is to shift the emphasis from middle-class housing (for at least *existing* middle class standards of accommodation are tolerable) to working class housing (where they are often intolerable). This will require additional government aid to sustain a larger municipal building effort [and] easier mortgage terms for owner occupiers.[64]

Little or no mention was made of local authority access and allocation policies, or of what to do about private rental housing, or how housing policy might be affected by macro-economic policy as determined by the Treasury. Even the complex but vital question of the relationship between land values, planning and housing policy received scant attention. Instead, policy was perceived in terms of working-class and middle-class housing — precisely the same frame of reference as used by the Conservatives.

Indeed, the whole period is fascinating not so much because of what was discussed and disputed in housing policy, but because of what was *not* discussed. All the issues debated — slum clearance, public *v.* private sectors, decontrol of rental housing — were precisely those which dominated housing policy in the 1930s. That the conditions of the 1950s and 1960s were vastly different hardly warrants mention.

As far as interest groups are concerned, the period witnessed two important developments. First, private sector institutions received a considerable boost from Conservative policies. Building societies grew very rapidly and became an important part of the policy system. However, while they did consult with government departments over issues of mutual concern, they remained, along with private builders, largely unregulated by central and local governments.[65] As noted in Chapters 2 and 3, from the 1950s on, the market reigned supreme as far as land values were concerned and builders and investors were constrained or encouraged as much by this as by Government housing policy. Of course, in an important sense this was what the Conservative Government wanted. It did not, however, want the rapid rise in land prices and hence housing costs which occurred between 1957 and 1964. With little control over the main actors in the land market, there was precious little the Conservatives could do about this, and this fundamental problem was to remain throughout the 1960s and 1970s. Second, the bifurcation of the housing market raised the spectre of 'homelessness' — a new label for an increasingly visible phenomenon which received publicity following the emergence of a lobby championing the cause of those most disadvantaged in housing.[66]

One final comment on the period concerns the political salience of housing as an electoral issue. Few dispute its importance in 1951, but there is evidence to suggest that by the election of 1959 its importance had declined. In that year just 9 per cent of the electorate considered housing the most important issue facing the country,[67] in spite of the prediction by many Labour politicians that the Tories' 1957 Rent Act would ensure their defeat at the next election.[68] However, by 1964 13 per cent of the electorate considered housing the most urgent national issue.[69] This no doubt partly reflects public perceptions of the failure of Conservative housing policy and in particular their encouragement of land and therefore house price inflation.

Labour and the Politics of Frustration, 1964-70

As in 1945, Labour came to power in 1964 amid a flurry of renewed intellectual activity within the Party and in a mood of great optimism. Much of the new thinking urged that Labour take on a new role as the party which would enable Britain to exploit the advanced technologies of the 1960s and, by applying them in a rational and socially constructive way, produce a wealthier and a more equal society.[70] In housing, however, with a few relatively minor exceptions, the policy agenda was not to change dramatically. Probably the main change in emphasis was the Labour Government's acceptance of owner occupation as socially and economically desirable. By 1964 the owner occupancy rate in England and Wales had reached 46 per cent[71] and the Labour Manifestos in both 1964 and 1966 made it clear that the extension of owner occupation would be Labour Government policy. There was, in fact, only a small decline in the proportion of private to publicly built dwellings in the 1964-70 period (Table 4.5), although the overall totals were very high by historical standards. On becoming Minister of Housing and Local Government, Richard Crossman commented on this apparently sudden shift in policy thus:

> It is a new thing for a Labour Government to admit that owner
> occupation is a normal and natural way for people to live and that
> living in council houses is an exception to that rule. Of course we
> wooed the owner occupier during the general election, but what the
> Party has never done before is to admit in public that if we give
> people favourable interest rates in logic we have to make sure the
> land is available on which their houses can be built. And if we are

going to take responsibility for providing the land, we must make
the local authority feel as concerned with owner occupation as with
providing rented accommodation. That is quite a shift in philosophy
and that is why it is strange that we spent only eight minutes
discussing the White Paper.[72]

The Housing Programme 1965-1970 was the White Paper in question
and indeed its contents did indicate an important departure from past
policy:

> Once this country has overcome its huge problem of slumdom and
> obsolescence and met the need of the great cities for homes to let at
> moderate rents, the programme of subsidized council housing should
> decrease. The expansion of the public programme now proposed is
> to meet exceptional needs. It is born partly of short-term necessity,
> partly of the conditions inherent in modern urban life. The
> expansion of the programme for owner occupation however is
> normal: it reflects a long term social advance which should gradually
> pervade every region.[73]

Richard Crossman should not have been so surprised at this change in
policy, for Labour's thinking on housing had received little fresh
stimulus for many years. In the late 1940s and early 1950s only Bevan
had a coherent view of the function of public housing, and as was noted
earlier, his concept of public housing as a universal form of housing
tenure had already been eroded by Hugh Dalton, his successor at the
Ministry of Health in 1951. Without any carefully worked out
philosophy, it was not surprising that the new Government should
advocate an expansion of owner occupation – especially given its
electoral popularity.

The concern with 'slumdom and obsolescence' noted in the White
Paper was the second major theme of the period. One of Labour's
first actions on coming to power was to carry out their election pledge
to put right what they saw as the evil consequences of the 1957 Rent
Act. So the 1965 Rent Act provided protection from eviction to
tenants in private unfurnished accommodation and introduced a form
of recontrol for many tenancies via a system of 'fair rents' where a
rent officer would assess rent in the event of a dispute.[74] But these new
measures were but a minor part of Labour's policy towards private
rental and older and deteriorating housing. What, above all, Richard
Crossman wanted was improved statistical data on the state of the

Table 4.5: Permanent Houses[a] Completed, United Kingdom, 1965-76

	Local authorities[b]		Other public sector[c]		Total public sector		Private sector		Total
1965	164,957	(42%)	9,115	(2%)	174,072	(44%)	217,162	(56%)	391,234
1966	176,871	(45%)	10,491	(2%)	187,362	(47%)	208,647	(53%)	396,009
1967	199,749	(48%)	11,498	(3%)	211,247	(51%)	204,208	(49%)	415,455
1968	187,984	(44%)	11,783	(3%)	199,767	(47%)	226,067	(53%)	425,834
1969	180,958	(48%)	11,450	(3%)	192,408	(51%)	185,917	(49%)	378,325
1970	176,926	(49%)	10,958	(3%)	187,884	(52%)	174,342	(48%)	362,226
1971	154,894	(42%)	13,268	(4%)	168,162	(46%)	196,313	(54%)	364,475
1972	120,431	(36%)	9,750	(3%)	130,181	(39%)	200,568	(61%)	330,749
1973	102,604	(34%)	10,953	(4%)	113,557	(38%)	190,571	(62%)	304,128
1974	121,017	(43%)	13,388	(5%)	134,405	(48%)	143,958	(52%)	278,363
1975	150,526	(47%)	16,891	(5%)	167,417	(52%)	154,696	(48%)	322,123
1976	151,655	(47%)	17,702	(5%)	169,357	(52%)	155,088	(48%)	324,445

a. Includes flats.

b. Includes local authority, New Town Corporation, Scottish Special Housing Association and Northern Ireland Housing Trust Housing.

c. Includes housing association and government department housing.

Source: Central Statistical Office, *Annual Abstract of Statistics*, 1975 (HMSO, 1975), adapted from Table 69, p.83, and from Table 16, *Housing and Construction Statistics*, no.23, DOE, 1977.

housing stock and by 1967 the publication of the Milner Holland report on housing in London, together with the report of the Denington Committee on older housing and the report on housing improvement possibilities in Deeplish Rochdale,[75] provided the Ministry of Housing and Local Government with much more comprehensive data on which to base any policy. It soon became clear that the number of unfit dwellings was greatly in excess of estimates made as recently as 1965. 1.8 million were so categorised in 1967 compared with 820,000 in 1965, and an additional 4.5 million were lacking an amenity or needed repair.[76] One reaction by the Government to shortage was to encourage systems building techniques. As early as 1959 a Research and Development Group consisting of architects, surveyors, sociologists and administrators, had been formed within the Ministry of Housing and Local Government to research new building methods. By 1966, Richard Crossman had accepted two systems methods recommended by the Group with enthusiasm, and a variety of local authorities (often working in co-operation with one another) adopted these techniques for high rise and other large scale public housing projects.[77]

In 1967, Labour enacted a major housing bill which touched on many of these problems. Its main provision, however, was a reorganisation of council housing finance. Increasingly during the 1950s and 1960s local authorities had experienced difficulties in keeping up their building programmes under the standard unit subsidy system. With rising interest rates and the improved standards of council housing which came with the implementation of the Parker Morris Report,[78] the Treasury subsidies were constituting a smaller and smaller proportion of total costs, and in the uncertain climate of a 'stop-go' economy, forward planning was rarely possible. To overcome these problems the 1967 Act introduced a new subsidy made up of the difference between the actual loan cost to a local authority and what it would have been at an interest rate of 4 per cent. The subsidy was limited, however, by the imposition of 'cost yardsticks' beyond which Treasury help would cease. At a stroke, therefore, the Government hoped both to improve efficiency and to facilitate increased production via forward planning. The 1967 Act also introduced the option mortgage scheme designed to provide low cost mortgages to those not paying income tax at the standard rate, and gave a generous subsidy to those authorities operating in 'priority areas'. These were originally designated under the Conservative Housing Act of 1964, but the 1967 Act greatly expanded aid to such areas which were those experiencing particular problems of overcrowding and slum housing.

Clearly the Government considered this new Bill a pathbreaking item of housing legislation. As Anthony Greenwood, housing minister at the time, commented:

> This is a proud moment for the Government and a great day in our social history. In two years we have restored security of tenure. We have provided machinery for fixing fair rents. A record number of houses have been built. We have helped the less prosperous ratepayers with their rates. Today we are commending to the House a Bill which symbolises our socialist housing philosophy. It helps councils to swell the stock of houses to rent and it brings home-ownership within the reach of large numbers of families to whom in the past it has been denied by low pay and the inertia of our predecessors.[79]

But the Act did not radically alter the relationship between the state and the housing market. A major flaw in the legislation was the assumption that the new subsidy system would remove public housing from the vagaries of national economic policy. In fact, and as will be shown later, this was not to be. At the time of passage Frank Allaun, Labour MP for Salford and an increasingly vocal critic of his Government's housing policies, realised this by pointing out that low interest rates and land prices were the key to a consistently high level of production.[80] Few Labour MPs agreed with Frank Allaun's prediction that Treasury restraint would soon transpire if interest rates remained high, and it took a Conservative to stress explicitly that if the Government's targets *were* met it would put great strain on the national budget.[81] It was also a Tory (Walter Clegg, North Fylde) who pointed out that there was a need to examine to whom local authorities were allocating housing.[82] In other words, simply increasing the stock of council housing need not necessarily solve housing shortages for those social groups who were at a disadvantage in relation to local government allocation and access systems.

Other problems remained. The option mortgage scheme relied on the incomes of lower and lower-middle income groups remaining at or below the standard rate of income tax. As it happened, fiscal drag over the next few years gradually reduced the original advantage of the scheme. Finally, the criteria for special slum clearance aid established by the Act were not based on totally reliable data – in spite of the publication of the already mentioned Deeplish study and the Denington Report which should have provided more rational data on which to decide which areas were most in need.

The poverty of Labour's housing policies during these years was to be revealed by a series of events in the 1967-70 period. First, after 1967, targets were met increasingly rarely. Frank Allaun's prediction of the key role which would be played by the Treasury was proved correct. In 1968 the Government cut the public housing programme by £82 million and the number of council housing starts fell from 213.9 thousand in 1968 to 154.1 thousand in 1971 (see also Table 4.5)[83] — although it should be acknowledged that at least some of these decreases resulted from the transfer of power to the Conservatives in many localities following local elections in 1968. Moreover, the quality of housing, in spite of Parker Morris standards, was changing — and often for the worse. More and more flats rather than houses were being built — many were high rise and from a social point of view, architecturally bizarre. As the CDP Information and Intelligence Unit has put it:

> Parker Morris standards, high rise flats, industrial systems building and the 1967 subsidies were using up enormous resources in slum clearance and replacement programmes. The cheap slum clearance houses of the 'thirties and 'fifties were being replaced by expensive and gimmicky designs which proved even more unpopular and unsatisfactory.[84]

As was pointed out in Chapter 2, the shift to high density development by local authorities in the 1950s was due at least in part to Conservative Governments' land-use and land-values policies. Labour did little to alter the forces making for high urban land costs.

In addition, the publication of the Cullingworth Report on *Council Housing Purposes, Procedures and Priorities* in 1969 revealed that the bifurcation of the housing market begun by the Tories in 1951 and continued by Labour in 1964 had led to a serious shortage of housing for single people, the old, racial minorities and large families. These groups could rarely afford good quality owner occupied housing and the many and varied allocation policies of local authorities were biased in favour of small, white families. In particular, the operation of residential qualifications, waiting lists, and the 'grading' of potential tenants according to such things as housekeeping standards tended to be discriminatory.[85] In sum, the provision of council housing was not related to social need; the most disadvantaged were not benefiting. Renewed and intensifying publicity on the problems of the homeless were added to what was rapidly becoming a debate on the long established organisation and traditions of local authority housing.

The Government had little opportunity — even if it wanted to — of entering this debate as it was defeated in June 1970 a few months after the publication of the Cullingworth Report. However, on the slum clearance and improvement front Government thinking was changing rapidly. The April 1968 White Paper, *Old Houses into New Homes*[86] represented for the first time an official challenge to the 50 year old assumption that Britain's poor quality housing stock could be transformed simply by clearance and rebuilding. Instead, the improvement of existing houses within specific locales was advocated. Improvement rather than demolition was to become the theme of the 1970s, but the 1969 Housing Act which followed the White Paper specifically promised to maintain existing levels of clearance, and at the same time established General Improvement Areas (GIAs) — specific locales within which local authorities could use improvement grants to raise housing standards. A concern with preservation rather than renewal was also reflected in new legislation to protect areas of historic interest. The Civic Amenities Act of 1967 broadened the concern for (although not the actual powers to preserve) individual historic buildings in an area context. Under the new law local planning authorities were permitted to designate certain areas as 'Conservation Areas' whose character was to be preserved and enhanced.

There can be little doubt that as far as *perceptions* of housing problems were concerned, 1964-70 was a period of change. Many of the assumptions of 1964 were under serious challenge by 1970. In particular, wholesale clearance, local authority allocation policies and the relationship between housing policy and interest rates and land values, were under close scrutiny. Indeed, the sheer weight of intellectual effort devoted to housing problems had increased enormously during these years. Starting with Richard Crossman's original efforts to collect and systematise data in the Ministry of Housing and Local Government, and culminating in the publication of a series of official and academic reports, almost a housing research 'industry' had emerged producing a wealth of independent views on the subject.

Much of the stimulus to this research derived from the failure of existing policies, and the research foundations laid in the 1960s were to prove extremely useful in the 1970s. As far as government programmes were concerned, however, little of this new thinking was actually translated into policy. By 1970 the major elements in housing policy remained the conviction that increased production of owner-occupied and council housing together with slum clearance would solve most of the country's housing problems. Even if one looks beyond actual policies to the policy agenda, some issues were not under close scrutiny. In particular, the possibility of creating a much expanded quasi-public or co-operative housing sector was little discussed. As can be seen from Table 4.5, housing association housing did not 'take off' during these years — possibly because local councillors and housing departments have viewed the associations as a threat to their own council housing domains.[87] At the national level, politicians did not lobby hard for the associations whose housing was seen as a relatively marginal supplement to existing programmes, rather than a major replacement.

Similarly, the whole relationship between housing and planning policy received scant attention. In 1968 the Government had announced the Urban Programme (see Chapter 7) which acknowledged the existence of inner city decay, but did nothing to relate decay to the wider issues of the location of industry and the policy pursued by all post-war governments of dispersing population — often via council housing — to new and expanded towns. Indeed, the spatial distribution of council housing was not on the policy agenda at all, either in terms of macro land use planning, or in terms of social segregation of council housing from owner occupied housing, and the segregation of different social groups *within* council housing. Generally, in fact, there was little sophisticated thinking on the extent to which inequality in housing provision, irrespective of tenure type, existed.

To be fair, it should be acknowledged that most of Labour's social programmes were seriously constrained by macro-economic policy during these years. In housing, Treasury imposed expenditure limits were no doubt important not only in cutting back production, but also in leading central and local housing bureaucracies to protect and hold on to existing positions, rather than to produce new and innovative programmes.

The political salience of housing remained relatively high throughout the period. In 1970, 10 per cent of the electorate considered housing the most urgent issue facing the country.[88] Moreover, a new housing lobby had developed whose main objectives were to promote the interests of the homeless and those most at disadvantage in private rental housing. With the addition of such groups as Shelter and the Child Poverty Action Group to the traditional interest groups involved in housing (local authority associations, building societies, builders, architects, surveyors, planners), the housing policy system was becoming increasingly complex.

1970-4: The Conservatives and the Politics of Ideology

While acknowledging that Party Manifestos have generally lengthened over the years, it is notable that the number of words devoted to housing in both Labour and Conservative Manifestos quadrupled between 1964 and 1970.[89] In part this reflects the increasing complexity of the housing issue, both in objective terms and in terms of party perceptions. During its period in Opposition, Conservative policy on housing had developed considerably. Indeed it could be argued that for the first time the Tories made an attempt to give some intellectual coherence to their housing policy, rather than, as had happened in the past, be content with modifying policies conceived by Labour Governments.

Their new philosophy was represented by the July 1971 White Paper *Fair Deal for Housing*,[90] the introduction to which made it very clear that the major reform planned by the Tories was to be in rental housing and in particular in council housing. The stated objections of reform were:

1. a decent home for every family at a price within their means;
2. a fairer choice between owning a home and renting one;
3. fairness between one citizen and another in giving and renewing help towards housing costs.[91]

Reform in the public sector was based on the largely correct conviction that subsidies were indiscriminate. In four ways, the White Paper claimed, injustice or 'unfairness' operated within the public sector. First, subsidies were unrelated to need. Ninety per cent of subsidy money was used to support rents irrespective of need. Second, the prevailing system did not give help to those authorities most in need. Many operating in the areas of great housing stress received less *per capita* aid than quite affluent areas. Third, the burden of subsidies was unfairly distributed. Many ratepayers and income tax payers were effectively subsidising council tenants whose housing conditions and incomes were higher than their own. Finally, huge discrepancies in the level of rents payable occurred between areas. In London, for example, average rents in 1970 varied between boroughs from £1.90 to £4.41 a week.[92]

The White Paper also pointed to the crisis within private rental housing where 50 years of rent control had destroyed any incentive to improve properties and expand the market, it pleaded the case for greater government help to improve properties, and it reiterated the

the Tory faith that owner occupied housing was beneficial to all.[93]

'Fair Rents' were to be the solution to most of these problems. All local authority rents were to be increased in stages to the 'natural' economic level — or that level representing the current value of the accommodation, given its age, character and location. The assumption of no scarcity in the housing market was made for the purposes of calculation — the same basis on which the Labour Act of 1965 had determined the rent of 300,000 private tenants. Those tenants who couldn't afford the increases would be given rebates. For the first time, therefore, a system of universal rent assessment was to be initiated in the public sector. Moreover tenants in the privately rented sector, 1.3 million of whom still enjoyed controlled rents, were to have their rents assessed on the same basis with those in most need receiving rebates.

By 1972 the White Paper had been translated into the Housing Finance Act. Needless to say its provisions were controversial, and Labour commentators were vociferous in opposition to it. It would be fair to claim that the political battles it inspired were the most intense on any housing issue since the war. Anthony Crosland, Shadow Minister for the Environment called it: 'the most reactionary and socially divisive measure that is likely to be introduced in the lifetime of this Parliament — and that is saying a good deal.'[94] Labour's main objection was that the Bill applied market criteria to what they considered were the non-market circumstances of council housing. In other words, the public sector was now theoretically to be expected to produce a fair return on investment. Such a concept was anathema to all those who considered housing a social service.

Other objections to the Bill were raised. The cost of granting rebates was likely to be high and their take up rate was likely to be low. Both of these predictions seemed realistic. As Peter Townsend noted in January 1973: 'There is plentiful evidence that all the means tests being operated in Britain are inefficient. Benefits do not reach substantial proportions of the families who are eligible for them. This seems to be particularly true of local authority rent rebates and the national rate rebate scheme.'[95] And under the new scheme some 40 per cent of tenants would be eligible for some sort of rebate, with the remainder assured of hefty rent increases over a four year period until the 'Fair Rent' level was reached.[96]

A further criticism was that with major changes in the pooling system whereby in a particular authority subsidised rents were equalised on properties of different age and quality, tenants paying 'fair rents' would effectively be subsidising those receiving rebates.

Other members of the community, in particular ratepayers and
taxpayers in owner occupied housing, would make no contribution.
Indeed, critics of the Bill latched most vehemently on to its failure to
change the advantaged position of owner occupiers. How, they argued,
could it be justified on grounds of social justice when the five million
public housing tenants would experience rent increases while the
nation's owner occupiers would continue to receive fairly massive
subsidies in the form of mortgage interest deducted from income tax?

Although it is difficult to measure in any precise way the motives of
the Conservative Government in deciding on this policy, certain facts
are clear. Firstly, increasing land and building costs together with high
interest rates had resulted in very expensive council housing. By 1970/1
subsidies had increased to £220 million, and had the existing system
prevailed there was every prospect of the subsidy bill increasing even
more rapidly.[97] Given the Conservatives' newly acquired devotion to
fiscal conservatism, cuts in these subsidies seemed rational. Moreover,
the Tories had long been advocates of selectivism in social policy, and
the non-means tested basis on which council tenants received subsidies
appeared a natural victim for radical reform. That the Conservatives
decided on fair rents in the 1970s rather than in the 1950s can be
explained partly by the different economic circumstances of the two
periods. In one there was a crisis in government expenditure and the
other not. Also, council housing finance was under fire from many sides
in the late 1960s. Labour was in the midst of preparing its own review
of housing finance when they were defeated — although Anthony
Crosland has made it clear that there was no possibility of Labour
introducing a 'fair rents' system.[98] But quite apart from the perceived
faults of the council housing system, the Conservatives had by 1970
acquired a new devotion to market principles in domestic policy. This
spirit of 'Selsdon Park' (after the 1970 meeting of the Shadow Cabinet
at Selsdon Park) was then also important in influencing the contents
of the Housing Finance Act.

Resistance to the Housing Finance Act came from many quarters,
including some Labour councils. In one of these, Clay Cross in
Derbyshire, resistance was total and not until successful legal action
against the recalcitrant councillors was completed, was it broken.[99]
As it turned out, the new Act did not result in a massive increase in
rents, largely because after 1973 the rate of inflation and earnings was
much higher than the step by step increases imposed by the Act!
(Table 4.6).

From February 1974 to January 1975 a rent freeze was imposed by the new Labour Government, and in 1975 the subsidy system was changed once again (see pp.144-5 below).

As Table 4.5 shows, council house building experienced its traditional dip during the final years of the Conservative Government, but this was a result as much of severe inflation as of deliberate government policy. Table 4.7 demonstrates how land prices and local authority building costs increased very rapidly indeed between 1970 and 1973. At the same time, the rate of interest local authorities have to pay for their housing requirements increased from 6.6 per cent in 1971/2 to 8.1 per cent in 1973/4.[100] This price explosion was to have profound effects on the total level of house construction, completions falling from 364,475 in 1971 to 278,363 in 1974 (Table 4.5), the lowest since 1952.

Fiery debate over the Housing Finance Act obscured the fact that other important housing issues were under review between 1970 and 1974. In particular, the whole rationale behind slum clearance policy was under attack. Slowly but surely, improvement grants for older property were increased and the rate of slum clearance decreased. Community groups, housing organisations such as Shelter, and informed academic opinion all became increasingly critical of clearance.[101] Two problems had emerged. First, families uprooted by slum clearance tended to be rehoused in large low quality inner city estates or in 'overspill' developments and it was not at all obvious that they were any better off in terms of the quality of community life, if not in access to basic housing amenities.[102] Second, the severe inflation in land and building costs had seriously reduced many local authorities' capacity to rebuild on cleared land. As a result, large tracts of land — especially in the high cost inner city areas — were lying waste waiting for redevelopment.[103] For the Government to advocate improvement rather than clearance was especially convenient, for it combined what seemed at the time to be a socially progressive policy with, relative to new building, relatively low government outlays.

So in their 1973 White Paper, *Widening the Choice: The Next Steps in Housing*,[104] the Government recommended a severe reduction in slum clearance and announced increased aid for the private rental sector by boosting the voluntary housing association movement. A second White Paper, *Better Homes, the Next Priorities*,[105] recommended a policy of gradual improvement for local authorities, with specific locales in severe stress receiving special help as Housing Action Areas. But before these measures could be translated into law, the Government was defeated in February 1974.

Table 4.6: Rents, Index Numbers of Rents, Average Earnings and
General Price Level, United Kingdom, 1959-76

	Rents (£ a week) (April)[a]	Rents (Index)	Earnings (men manual workers)	Index of retail prices)
1959	0.99	44	44	67
1964	1.32	58	68	76
1969	2.03	89	89	94
1970	2.27	100	100	100
1971	2.48	109	110	109
1972	2.75	121	122	117
1973[b]	3.44	152	142	128
1974[c]	3.75	165	163	149
1975	4.16	183	208	184
1976	4.77	210	243	215

a. Unrebated rents. Department of the Environment estimates 1969 and 1970
   for local authority housing.
b. Rent figure is for May.
c. Rent figure is for January.

Source: *Housing and Construction Statistics*, no.18, Table XXXV; *Housing
   Statistics*, no.23, Table VIII.

Parallel with renewed interest in improvement and rehabilitation came
increasing concern for Britain's threatened architectural and historic
heritage. Hence, the 1971 Town and Country Planning (Amendment)
and 1972 Town and Country Planning (Scotland) Acts gave local
authorities the power to purchase compulsorily any listed building not
being properly maintained by its owner. Later, under the 1974 Town
and Country Planning Act, the powers to make grants for the
improvement of buildings of architectural and historical interest, listed
or not, were extended.

The shift from clearance to improvement was the most important
development in housing policy during the 1970-74 period and, arguably,
since the Second World War. It was also a policy over which there was
little party disagreement. As far as political controversy was concerned,
the Housing Finance Act dominated the period. That this was so is not
surprising for it represented, very clearly, the apparently deep
ideological rift between the two main parties over the role of public
housing. As will be argued later, this rift did not derive from two
distinct and coherently thought out policy positions: prejudice played

Table 4.7: Index Numbers of Land and House Prices, United Kingdom, 1967-76 (1970 = 100)

	Second-hand houses[a]	New houses	Price index of local authority housing[b]	Building land for private owners[c] (price per plot)
1967	83	83	84	65
1968	90	86	89	73
1969	94	94	92	91
1970	100	100	100	100
1971	116	110	113	113
1972	155	139	136	185
1973	208	193	188	295
1974	218	223	217	290
1975	239	245	238	205
1976	259	263	253	203

a. UK figures for houses purchased with building society loans; from 1969 the figures are weighted averages of prices for individual types of houses, which exclude much of the effect of changes in the 'mix' of dwellings sold.
b. Tender prices for traditionally built one- and two-storey houses in England and Wales outside Greater London. Refers to tenders accepted in the years shown.
c. England and Wales.
Source: *Housing Policy, Technical Volume, Part 1*, Cmnd.6851 (1977), Table IV, 4, p.171.

as important a part as rational calculation, for the fact was that even in 1971/2, neither Government nor Opposition was fully aware either of the dynamics of the housing market or of the true nature of public housing.

What of the public during these years? Judging by opinion poll data, housing had declined in importance by some considerable margin. Only 1 per cent of the electorate considered it the most urgent problem facing the nation in January 1974, although 16 per cent considered it the second most urgent.[106] With large sections of the population now reasonably well housed, and the most acute problems remaining affecting the most disadvantaged, perhaps it is not surprising that the political salience of the issue had declined. But it was also during this period that most peoples' housing costs increased as never before. Rents, rates, house prices and mortgage interest rates all increased rapidly. Perhaps concern with these increases is reflected in the generally high concern over prices shown by many people in this period.[107] What is interesting is that as land and house prices soared, the Government simply stood back and watched. Perhaps, given the Conservatives' newly acquired devotion to the free market, this is not surprising. But even if they had wanted to intervene, the Conservatives might have found it difficult – after all, few mechanisms existed for the regulation of land prices, building costs or mortgage finance. Macro-economic policy and in particular interest rate levels did, of course, critically influence these factors – but they did so in a way quite unrelated to the objectives of housing policy. Building societies and other actors in the housing policy system were, therefore, not in a position 'to bring pressure' on central government. Instead, via the market mechanism they *reacted* to a general economic climate with consequences largely beyond the control of government. Almost the same could be said for the strengthening lobby representing the homeless and those in acute housing distress. If anything, the number of families involved here increased during these years as land and price increases further squeezed the private rental sector. Such groups as Shelter and the CPAG were certainly vocal in response, but, the shift from clearance to rehabilitation apart (which did not necessarily help the most disadvantaged), few government measures aided the lot of the homeless.

Reappraisal or Retrenchment?: Labour and Housing Policy, 1974-78

On coming to power in February 1974, the Labour Government's first housing measures were directed squarely at what were seen as the undesirable consequences of the 1972 Act. Council housing rents were frozen immediately, and the 1974 Rent Act gave full security of tenure to tenants in furnished accommodation. In 1975, the Housing Rents and Subsidies Act returned to local authorities the power to fix rents, and pending a major review of housing finance created a new subsidy scheme, which, although complex in detail, essentially re-established the principle that central government subsidies should have an element of predictability in an uncertain economic climate, and should consist in part of subsidising loan charges.[108]

While these changes do represent a return to the *status quo ante* of 1970, other measures taken by the Government during the period demonstrate that Labour's thinking on housing policy was becoming more sophisticated.

In particular, the 1974 Housing Act provided a new system of financial support for housing associations which, by 1976, had increased production in this sector to some 10 per cent of public housing starts (Table 4.5).[109] Quasi-public housing of this sort can provide much greater flexibility in management, and many of those groups – singles, the disabled, the elderly and one parent families – who find it difficult to qualify for council housing should, in theory, benefit. However, given that most housing associations rely on local authority nominations for tenants, it is not obvious that this sort of housing avoids the problems inherent in council housing management. The findings of the Cullingworth Committee on this subject were substantiated by the first comprehensive research on access and allocation policies which began to appear in the mid-1970s. Two broad patterns were discernible. First, a bewildering array of policies were being pursued by local authorities. Almost all discriminated unfairly against one group or other, and with few exceptions local councils proved reluctant to discuss or to publish the criteria employed in selecting and allocating tenants.[110] Second, research has gradually confirmed that when allocating tenants, most local authorities have divided them according to certain social or racial characteristics and thereby have created distinctive housing estates which can be characterised as 'problem' and 'respectable' estates.[111] These biases derive from the bureaucratic cultures of housing management departments and from the obvious fact that housing shortage has forced departments to discriminate between different social groups. The almost total absence of central government direction in this area is extraordinary given successive Labour Governments' avowed intentions to help the disadvantaged and to break down class barriers. In fact, in many instances council housing policies have increased spatial segregation between classes, both *within* council housing, and *between* council housing in general and those living in owner occupied housing.

While awareness of these problems exists and in the case of increased aid for housing associations awareness has been partly translated into policy – wide local discretion continues and, as will be discussed below, the Government has no plans to overhaul local authority access and allocation policies in any dramatic fashion.

Change was afoot in other areas of housing policy during these years. The 1974 Housing Act also embodied the 1973 Conservative plans to cut back even further on slum clearance and to concentrate instead on the improvement and rehabilitation of particular locales. To this end the Act established Housing Action Areas, within which local authorities were given broad powers to improve properties in areas of housing stress. A further important change in policy was an acceptance, for the first time, that government should play some role in regulating building society mortgage credit. As was noted earlier, the early 1970s were years of unprecedented inflation in house prices and land values. Building societies had been an unwitting contributor to this inflation by greatly expanding credit at a time when interest rates were high and the supply of houses limited. In order to stabilise the market, from 1974 a voluntary agreement between the Government and the societies was established which enabled the Government to provide short term loans which the societies could use when savings were low. Together with a self imposed policy of limiting credit when savings are high, this policy was designed to enable building societies to maintain a fairly stable flow of mortgage credit on to the market. It should be stressed, however, that the agreement was voluntary and *ad hoc* in nature, and even by 1978 statutory regulation of the societies was absent.

Between 1974 and 1977 the government was preparing a major review of housing policy, and in June 1977 a consultative green paper on housing policy was published covering every aspect of the subject from public housing to slum clearance and mortgage credit.[112] That the review appeared at all is testament to the many failures in housing policy which by the mid-1970s were apparent to all. Most experts agree, however, that the review represented more the consolidation of existing policies with some of the more obvious flaws ironed out, than a major reappraisal of housing programmes.[113]

Above all, the review failed to recommend any radical change in housing finance. To be sure, some changes in the details of public housing finance were advised, but the basic principle of local authorities receiving a subsidy to build public housing, the nature, management and location of which would largely be determined by them, remained.[114] Moreover, the tax subsidies received by owner occupiers, long the source of criticism for the left, and notwithstanding the limiting of relief to £25,000 on owners' principal homes introduced in 1975, were left untouched.[115] If, in fact, the green paper has a major theme, it is advocacy of the advantages of owner occupation and recommendation that it should become the dominant form of housing tenure. This view is not inconsistent with the policy which Labour first advocated in 1964, but by the mid-1970s, the desirability of owner occupation had become enshrined in Labour Government thinking. Hence in a 1976 speech on the forthcoming review, Peter Shore, Secretary of State for the Environment declared:

Owner occupation not only makes economic sense for the individual and the community, it also satisfies deep seated aspirations in our people. . .while we seek to give greater rights to people in all forms of tenure, there is a strong belief that to own the title deeds is to have an added assurance of independence and freedom. The spread of owner-occupation is of course wholly consistent with the principles and practice of my party.[116]

Accordingly, the green paper recommended a variety of schemes to extend owner-occupation, including 'low start' mortgages, special assistance for first time buyers, and higher percentage loans. In addition, 'intermediate' forms of housing tenure — and especially equity sharing between purchasers and local authorities or housing associations, were advocated.[117]

Most of the remaining recommendations of the review consisted of 'tidying up' existing policies or extending schemes already started. Therefore, further measures to stabilise the flow of mortgage finance, extentions to improvement grants and plans to increase the mobility of council housing tenants were all mentioned. On the general subject of council housing management, the green paper made all the right noises, but specifically rejected central control of access and allocation policies. So, recommendations that residential qualifications should be dropped, that more flexible allocation practices to help disadvantaged groups should be adopted, and that allocation policies should be published, were all central points, but the green paper resolutely stated that:

the Government wish to maintain their policy of giving the maximum freedom to authorities to interpret and implement national policies in the light of local circumstances. They therefore believe that proposals to control local authorities' allocation policies centrally — for example by laying down a statutory framework for allocation schemes — should be rejected.[118]

With regard to the private rental sector a similar picture emerges. No fundamental change in government help for the sector was forthcoming. Housing association and co-operative housing should, the green paper stated, be encouraged,[119] but no measures to arrest the contraction of private rental housing were announced. To be fair, the review did recommend that local authorities should take a strategic view of housing needs and resources in their areas and adjust policies not only in relation to the demand and supply of housing but also in relation to transport, employment, health and social service policies.[120] But without central guidelines on how this is to be achieved and with the continuing bifurcation of the market, it is difficult to envisage already hard-pressed housing departments so radically altering their policies to ease shortage and eliminate injustices, simply on this recommendation. After all, adjusting local housing demand with supply should have been standard municipal practice at least since the 1949 Housing Act introduced general needs housing.

In many respects then, the green paper is a profoundly conservative document. The ideological commitment to socialised housing, so strong in the 1945-50 period had been drastically modified by 1977. Now, it seems, Labour policy consists of broadly accepting the housing *status quo* and advocating small modifications in existing practices. On the other hand the Conservatives, with their continuing devotion to the free market, have become the party of radical change. A drastic reduction in the public housing stock mainly via increased council housing sales to sitting tenants remains Conservative policy, as does reform of council housing finance.

Party Politics and Housing Policy Since 1945: Some Conclusions

It would be a considerable over-simplification to characterise all post-war housing policies as failures. By most objective indices there has been a dramatic improvement in housing conditions and housing choice for most social groups.[121] However, if progress is measured in terms of *opportunity costs*, or of what could have been achieved given existing social and economic constraints, then a different picture emerges. Moreover, many of these lost opportunities must be attributed to party political influences and the often deeply rooted ideological differences between the parties. Such a view is not fashionable; among left wing critics of housing policy, structural economic factors are assigned the main role in determining the shape of policy.[122] Of course, the level of activity in the economy and macro-economic policies have had profound effects on the housing market. The general level of construction is intimately linked to such variables. In particular, changes in interest rates and government spending have been critical in producing the sometimes wild fluctuations in housing starts characteristic of the post-war period. However, many aspects of policy need not or could not be influenced by economic factors. Whether to spend money on clearance or improvement; whether to build public housing or to provide subsidies for private developers or owners; the extent of control of local authority access and allocation policies; the relationship between housing and planning policies; whether to give security of tenure to various tenancy types, are more political and social than economic questions.

It can therefore be argued that some of the more obvious failures in housing policy owe more to the political rather than the economic. Inflexibility is a characteristic of housing in many countries, and there are no capitalist or mixed economies where housing choice and residential mobility are consistently and uniformly high. However, in Britain, government policies have seriously reduced both choice and mobility for some social groups to a level far below that prevailing in some other countries. It is, for example, a shocking indictment of British housing policy that individuals or families moving to new locales effectively cannot rent properties — even temporarily — except those which can only be described as grossly overpriced and/or slums. Instead, the newcomer has to apply for local authority housing which almost always means a long wait, or he is obliged to purchase. For many, especially the poor, large families, the old and singles, these alternatives are usually unavailable.

The policies of party politics are largely to blame for this situation. Table 4.8 attempts to demonstrate how throughout the post-war period the housing policy agenda has been shaped by party politics. By party political salience is meant the extent to which a particular aspect of housing policy is considered important by the parliamentary parties, Governments and Oppositions. The high, medium, low scales are very general in nature being based on somewhat impressionistic analysis of parliamentary debates, political speeches, Government white papers and legislation. In the absence of comprehensive survey data it is not possible to measure public perceptions of different policies — even though the public have been more concerned with housing as a political issue than with other areas of urban policy in recent years. What Table 4.8 does show is the extent to which debate — and subsequently policy — has concentrated on relatively few issues. In particular, the public *v.* private debate, and the extent to which market forces should be given free play in rental housing have dominated party thinking throughout the period. In contrast, local authority access and allocation policies, the size and nature of quasi-public sector housing, and the relationship between housing policies and other urban policies have been given generally low priority and have rarely been major items on the policy agenda. Admittedly, the 1974 Housing Act and the recent housing policy review did make some gestures in the direction of these areas, but the 'traditional' issues continue to dominate housing policy. Such

Table 4.8: Housing Issues: Political Salience and Party Differences, 1945-78

Issue	Party political salience		Extent of party difference	
	1945	1978	1945	1978
Size of public sector	High	High	High	High
Council housing finance	High	High	High	High
Size of owner occupied sector	High	High	High	Medium
Security of tenure	Low	High	Low	Medium
Slum clearance	High	Medium	Low	Low
Private sector rent control	Low	Medium	Low	Medium
Tax policies: owner occupied sector	Low	Medium	Low	Medium
Improvement and inner-city housing policies	Low	High	Low	Low
Local authority access and allocation policies	Low	Low	Low	Low
Size of quasi-public sector	Low	Low	Low	Low
The relationship between housing and other urban policies	Low	Low	Low	Low

fundamental questions as the extent of inequality in housing provision, residential mobility, and spatial social segregation have virtually been ignored by the political parties. Yet, according to their avowed philosophies these issues should be of vital concern to one or other of the major parties. Inequality and segregation should be anathema to Labour politicians, but their policies have in many respects encouraged both. Similarly, residential mobility and the free movement of workers is surely a *sine qua non* of the free market. Yet Conservative policies resulting in the bifurcation of the market have *reduced* residential mobility.[123] In fact it may be possible to reverse the usual reasoning (that Britain's housing performance has been hampered by economic factors) and claim that housing policies have adversely affected Britain's economic performance by reducing the mobility of labour!

It is instructive that other societies, some of which have strong collectivist traditions, have avoided defining their housing problems in terms of a choice between the extremes of total private and total public ownership. As Table 4.9 shows, most comparable European countries have very substantial quasi public sectors, most of which cater for varied sections of the population. There is, of course, nothing inherently desirable about quasi-public housing, but it does seem likely that the decentralised and private management of such housing is less likely to result in the class segregation and bureaucratic inflexibility typical of British public housing.

Table 4.8 does oversimplify somewhat. In particular it does not reveal that while differences between the parties continued to be concentrated in certain policy areas throughout the period, the policy agenda within each of these areas did change — sometimes dramatically. So, the public/private sector debate in 1978 is a very different debate from that of 1945. Both parties now accept a major role for owner-occupied housing and as far as the Conservatives are concerned, public housing provision should be confined to those who through disability or 'inadequacy' are unable otherwise to rent or buy property. In 1945, on the other hand, they considered public housing an essential part of post-war reconstruction. Similarly, council housing finance continues to divide the parties, but the position of the Conservatives has changed substantially. In 1945 their dispute with Labour centred on their belief that subsidies were too high; now they challenge the very basis of the subsidy and want to inject free market principles into the system. It is, of course, not possible to say in any precise way whether the parties are more divided now than they were in 1945. In the sense that both now accept a major role for owner occupied housing, perhaps they are less divided now. Yet Labour's attitude towards owner occupation was changing as early as the late 1940s. If, indeed, a comparison is made between 1978 and the early 1950s when the rather exceptional post-war conditions had passed, then it could be argued that as far as the public sector is concerned, the parties are now more divided. The Conservatives are now firmly committed to a highly selectivist policy, while Labour continues to hold on to the belief that public housing should play a role in providing for working class citizens.

It is interesting, therefore, that while party ideologies have changed considerably during the period, important differences remain. Also, differences *within* the parties do not seem to have had a significant impact on policy. Admittedly, the Labour left led first by Bevan and latterly by Frank Allaun have always advocated a more prominent role for the public sector than has the Labour right, but this has not led to the sort of intense and often bitter intra-party division characteristic of such policy areas as defence or industrial relations. Public spending, of which housing is a major part, has been a source of party dispute, but debate has centred on general levels of public spending. Only rarely has the nature and quality of spending on housing been a source of intra-party rancour.

Within the Conservative Party differences over housing have been

Table 4.9: Housing Starts as Percentage of Total Housing Stock, by
Type of Builder, Selected Countries, 1971

Builder	Sweden	Netherlands	France	West Germany	UK	US
	%	%	%	%	%	%
National, county, and local governments	3.7	8.9	0.6	2.4	46.4	2.0
Quasi-public bodies	56.7	39.6	64.7	30.6		
Private builders	39.0	51.0	34.7	67.0	53.6	98.0

a. British housing association housing is included within the government category,
   although strictly speaking it should be categorised as quasi-public. Similarly,
   depending on the year, a small percentage of US housing starts are subsidised
   by federal low income (but not public) housing programmes.

Source: United Nations, Economic Commission for Europe, Annual Bulletin of
   Housing and Building Statistics for Europe, 1972 (New York, 1973), pp.40-42.
   Reproduced in Arnold Heidenheimer, Hugh Heclo, and Carolyn Tech Adams,
   Comparative Public Policy (New York, Macmillan, 1975) , p.72.

slight. Again, shifts in the policy agenda have occurred, but these
reflect changes affecting the whole Parliamentary Party, rather than
divisions within the Party.

To ascribe great importance to party politics and ideology in housing
policy does not mean that other factors have not also been important.
As noted, macro-economic policy and the specific role of the Treasury
have been a regular constraint on policy, and in particular on overall
housing production. As important, entrenched local authority housing
bureaucracies have shown considerable independence in certain areas.
Housing is, in fact, one of the most jealously guarded of all local
responsibilities, combining as it does great discretion with great
spending power. Officials of the Ministry of Housing and Local
Government and latterly the DOE have trodden very carefully when
advising governments on the ways in which local practices and
procedures can (or more frequently cannot) be changed. Admittedly,
implementation of the Housing Finance Act was successfully carried
out in the teeth of opposition from many Labour controlled authorities.
But housing finance along with overall levels of spending are areas where
local governments *expect* some control. In the crucial areas of
management, access and allocation, central governments either have
not wanted to or have lacked the political will to impose major changes
in local practices.

Interest groups have also had an important influence on policy. As noted, however, many of the housing interests — estate agents, builders, surveyors, architects, building societies — are largely free from *direct* central government regulation and control — even if they have been profoundly influenced by macro-economic factors. Also, unlike planning, no clear professional role can be discerned in housing. In planning, the views and research reports of professional planners and their organisations have been a significant influence in shaping the policy agenda. There is no equivalent of this in housing — although in specific instances such as building technology in the early 1960s, professional opinion has been important.

Since the mid-1960s groups representing those most disadvantaged in housing have grown in size and strength, and undoubtedly have been important in focusing public attention on the plight of the homeless. It would be difficult, however, to record any notable success for such groups. Governments may now be more aware of the problem, but at least at the central level, they have not produced the rather fundamental changes that would be necessary to transform the housing opportunities of the most disadvantaged.

In sum, in spite of the complexity of housing policy, there seems little doubt that many of the failings in housing since the war must be laid at the feet of party politicians. Dependence on fixed party positions deriving from certain ideological precepts has prevented debate on housing from focusing on such fundamental questions as access to housing, the extent of inequality in housing, and the effects of policy on occupational and residential mobility. Unlike planning and land values, housing has, of course, been of great electoral significance throughout the post-war period, and electoral considerations have been important in influencing policy on several occasions. But as will be argued in Chapter 8, in many respects party ideology has also prevented the formulation of policies according to rationally calculated electoral strategies.

Notes

1. *Housing Policy: A Consultative Document*, Cmnd.6851, 1977, Table 2, p.142.

2. Ibid., Table 1, p.141.

3. Comparison of the quality of housing between countries is problematical. British government figures (ibid., Table 1) imply that Britain's housing stock at least as measured by the 'plumbing' and overcrowding criteria is as good as, if not better than, comparable countries. But such figures hide the fact that much

of the poor housing in countries such as France, Italy, Norway and Japan is rural. If comparisons were based on urban housing, a quite different picture might emerge. For international comparisons of standards see Valerie A. Karn, *Housing Standards and Costs: A Comparison of British Standards and Costs with those in the USA, Canada and Europe*, Centre for Urban and Regional Studies, University of Birmingham, Occasional Paper, no.25, 1973.

4. Alan Murie, Pat Niner and Christopher Watson, *Housing Policy and the Housing System* (London, George Allen and Unwin, 1976). There are some exceptions to this general rule, the most important of which is Malcolm Joel Barnett's *The Politics of Legislation* (London, Weidenfeld and Nicolson, 1969). But see also, CDP, *Whatever Happened to Council Housing*? CDP, Information and Intelligence Unit, 1976; D.V. Donnison, *The Government of Housing* (Harmondsworth, Middx., Penguin, 1967).

5. Derek Barton, *A Hope for Housing*? (London, Mayflower, 1963). For short histories of government involvement in housing prior to 1914, see also Cmnd.6851, Technical Volume, Part 1, pp.3-7; J.B. Cullingworth, *Housing and Local Government* (London, George Allen and Unwin, 1966), ch.1.

6. Cmnd.6851, ibid., p.5.

7. Ibid., pp.4-6.

8. Ibid.; Barton, *A Hope for Housing*?, pp.13-14.

9. F.W.S. Craig (ed.), *British Election Manifestos 1900-1974* (London: Macmillan, 1975), pp.14-25.

10. For a good discussion of the 1915 Act and its social and economic context, see Peter Dickens, 'Social Change, Housing and the State: Some Aspects of Class Fragmentation and Incorporation: 1915-1946', paper before the Urban Change and Conflict Conference, University of York, 4-7 January 1977, pp.3-8.

11. Ibid., p.8; see also, Marian Bowley, *Housing and the State, 1919-1944* (London, George Allen and Unwin, 1945), ch.1.

12. Craig, *Election Manifestos*, p.29.

13. Bowley, *Housing and the State*, p.15.

14. Ibid., pp.22-3; Dickens, *Housing and the State*, p.13.

15. Dickens, ibid., see also Ruth Insacharoff, 'The Building Boom of the Interwar Years: Whose Profits and at Whose Cost?', paper before the Urban Change and Conflict Conference, York University, 4-7 January 1977, p.15; Bentley B. Gilbert, *British Social Policy, 1914-1939* (London, Batsford, 1970), p.158.

16. Bowley, *Housing and the State*, p.17.

17. Housing Act, 1923, 13 and 14, Geo. V. ch.24, section 1, quoted in ibid., p.37.

18. Bowley points out that the net shortage in 1923 was greater than in 1918, ibid., p.24.

19. See Carl F. Brand, *The British Labour Party: A Short History* (London, Oxford University Press, 1965), pp.98-100.

20. Bowley, *Housing and the State*, pp.113-31, Dickens, *Housing and the State*, p.16.

21. Brand, *Labour Party*, Dickens, *Housing and the State*.

22. For a good account of slum clearance in the inter-war period see, John English, Ruth Madigan and Peter Norman, *Slum Clearance: The Social and Administrative Context in England and Wales* (London, Croom Helm, 1976), pp.16-23.

23. Ibid., pp.19-20.

24. Ibid., p.23.

25. Dickens, *Housing and the State*, p.21.

26. This is a constant theme in post-war speeches and Parliamentary Debates

see for example, the speech by Willink (Croydon North), H.C. Deb.420 (1945-46), col.354-55.

27. *Housing Policy: Technical Volume*, Part 1, Table 1.24, p.39. Although of the 2.9 million added owner-occupied units some 1.1 million were transferred from private landlords.

28. Dickens, *Housing and the State*, pp.18-24.

29. See Bowley, *Housing and the State*, ch.8.

30. David Donnison, *The Government of Housing* (Harmondsworth, Middx., Penguin, 1967), p.163.

31. See David Howell, *British Social Democracy* (London, Croom Helm, 1976), p.130.

32. H.C. Deb.420, 1945-46, col.341.

33. The 1945 Conservative Manifesto pledged that 'Local authorities and private enterprise must both be given the fullest encouragement to get on with the job', F.W.S. Craig, *Election Manifestos*, p.115.

34. H.C. Deb.420, 1945-46, col.454.

35. Ibid.

36. H.C. Deb. 462, 1949, col.2126.

37. See David Donnison, *Housing Policy since the War* (London, Codicote Press, Occasional Papers on Social Administration, no.1, 1960), pp.15-16.

38. Barton, *A Hope for Housing*, p.38.

39. CDP, Information and Intelligence Unit, *Whatever Happened to Council Housing?* (London, CDP, 1976), p.19.

40. Cullingworth, *Housing and Local Government*, p.33.

41. See Michael Foot, *Aneurin Bevan*, vol.1, 1897-1945 (London, MacGibbon, 1962), ch.8.

42. David E. Butler, *The British General Election of 1951* (London, Macmillan, 1952), p.105.

43. Conservative Election Manifesto, 1951, in Craig, *Election Manifestos.*

44. Ministry of Housing and Local Government, Circular 38/51, 20 April 1951.

45. Quoted in Barton, *A Hope for Housing?*, p.36.

46. As early as 1925 Macmillan had established himself as something of a reformer in housing matters with his comment that 'Housing is not a question of Conservatism or Socialism. It is a question of humanity.' Harold Macmillan, *Winds of Change* (London, Macmillan, 1966), p.209.

47. See English, Madigan and Norman, *Slum Clearance*, p.24.

48. Quoted in D.V. Donnison, *The Government of Housing*, p.170.

49. Ibid., pp.168-9; CDP, op.cit., pp.18-19; by 1957 the PWLB rate was almost 7 per cent and it remained at around 6.7 per cent until 1964. J.H. Westergaard, 'Land Use Planning Since 1951', *Town Planning Review*, vol.35, October 1964, p.231.

50. CDP, *Council Housing*, p.19.

51. D.V. Donnison, 'Aftermath of the Rent Act', in Donnison *et al.*, *Essays on Housing*, Occasional Papers on Social Administration, no.9, Bell, London, p.7, quoted in M.J. Barnett, *The Politics of Legislation: The Rent Act of 1957* (London, Weidenfeld and Nicolson, 1969), p.44.

52. See in particular, D.V. Donnison, ibid.; D.V. Donnison *et al.*, *Housing Since the Rent Act*, Occasional papers in Social Administration, no.3, Codicote Press, 1961; *Rent Act 1957, Report of Inquiry*, Cmnd1246, 1960; Barnett, ibid. Much of the account below relies on Barnett, ch.13.

53. J.B. Cullingworth, *Housing Needs and Planning Policy* (London, Routledge and Kegan Paul, 1960), ch.12.

54. Barnett, *Politics of Legislation*, pp.252-3.

55. See J. Greve, *London's Homeless*, OPSA no.10, Bell, London, 1964; *Report of the Committee on Housing in Greater London*, Cmnd.2605, 1965 (Milner Holland Report). 'Rachmanism' derives from the activities of Peter Rachman, an unscrupulous landlord who operated in London in the late 1950s.

56. D.V. Donnison, *The Government of Housing*, pp.173-5.

57. Barnett, *Politics of Legislation*, p.5.

58. Ibid., pp.207-8.

59. Ibid., ch.11.

60. See *Homes for the Future*, Labour Party, Agenda for 54th Annual Conference of the Labour Party, London, 1956.

61. Barnett, *Politics of Legislation*, p.227.

62. It is instructive that the work which generated and reflected much of the new thinking, Anthony Crosland's, *The Future of Socialism* (London, Cape, 1956), hardly mentions housing at all!

63. A.R. Crosland, *The Conservative Enemy* (London, Cape, 1962), pp.189-90.

64. Ibid., p.189.

65. See Murie *et al.*, *Housing Policy*, pp.236-7.

66. See J. Greve, 'London's Homeless', and the Milner Holland Report.

67. *Gallup Political Index*, Report no.5 (London, 1959).

68. Of the 14 Labour members speaking in the Commons on the Rent Bill nine emphasised the importance of the electoral consequences of the Bill, D.V. Donnison, *et al.*, *Housing Since the Rent Act*, p.83. Barnett claims that the Act had no electoral impact whatsoever, ch.12.

69. *Gallup Political Index*, Report no.48 (London, 1964).

70. See Howell, *Social Democracy*, ch.9, also the Labour Manifestos of 1964 and 1966 in Craig, *Election Manifestos*.

71. D.V. Donnison, *The Government of Housing*, Table 10, p.186.

72. Richard Crossman, *The Diaries of a Cabinet Minister, Vol. One. Minister of Housing, 1964-1966* (London, Hamish Hamilton and Cape, 1976), p.383.

73. Cmnd.2838 (HMSO, 1965).

74. For a fuller discussion of this system see Murie *et al.*, *Housing Policy*, pp.183-5.

75. Milner Holland Report; Central Housing Advisory Committee, *Our Older Homes: A Call for Action*, Report of the Sub-Committee on Standards of Housing Fitness (HMSO, 1966); Ministry of Housing and Local Government, *The Deeplish Study: Improvement Possibilities in the District of Rochdale* (HMSO, 1966).

76. Quoted in John English *et al.*, *Slum Clearance*, p.33.

77. See 'The Work of the Research and Development Groups: 5, The MOHLG Housing Group', *Official Architecture and Planning*, March 1963.

78. Ministry of Housing and Local Government, *Homes for Today and Tomorrow* (HMSO, 1961).

79. H.C. Deb.738 (1967), col.676.

80. H.C. Deb.738 (1967), col.687-8.

81. H.C. Deb.738 (1967), col.693-8.

82. Ibid.

83. Central Statistical Office, *Annual Abstracts of Statistics* (HMSO, 1975), table

84. CDP Information and Intelligence Unit, *Whatever Happened to Council Housing*? (CDP, London, 1976), p.25.

85. *Council Housing: Purposes, Procedures and Priorities* (Ministry of Housing and Local Government, HMSO, 1969).

86. *Old Houses into New Homes*, Cmnd.3602, 1968.

87. Murie *et al.*, *Housing Policy*, pp.207-8.

88. *Gallup Political Index*, no.120 (January 1970).

89. F.W.S. Craig, *Election Manifestos.*

90. *Fair Deal for Housing*, Cmnd.4728 (HMSO, 1971).

91. Ibid., p.1.

92. Ibid., pp.1-2.

93. Ibid., pp.2-6.

94. H.C. Deb.826 (1971/2) col.48.

95. Peter Townsend, 'Everyone His Own Home: Inequality in Housing' in Townsend (ed.), *Sociology and Social Policy* (Harmondsworth, Middx., Penguin, 1976), p.102, and sources cited.

96. See 'Housing Act, 1972: A Guide', *New Society*, 28 December 1972, pp.734-7. Also, *One Nation? Housing and Conservative Policy*, Stewart Lansley and Guy Fiegehen, Fabian Tract 432, 1974; Anthony Crosland, *Towards a Labour Housing Policy*, Fabian Tract 410, September 1971.

97. *Fair Deal for Housing*, p.2.

98. H.C. Deb.82 (1971/2) col.49.

99. See D. Skinner and T. Langdon, *The Story of Clay Cross* (Nottingham, Spokesman Books, 1974).

100. *Housing Policy, Technical Volume*, Part 1, Table IV.6, p.174.

101. For a discussion of this change of mood, see John English *et al.*, *Slum Clearance*, pp.34-8.

102. Ibid., chs. 4 and 5.

103. See Robert McKie, *Housing and the Whitehall Bulldozer*, Institute of Economic Affairs, Hobart Paper, no.52, 1971.

104. *Widening the Choice: The Next Steps in Housing*, Cmnd.5220 (HMSO, 1973).

105. *Better Homes: The Next Priorities*, Cmnd.5339 (HMSO, 1973).

106. *Gallup Political Index*, Report no.162 (January 1974).

107. Of the electorate 29 per cent named prices as the most urgent problem facing the country in 1974, ibid.

108. For details of the new subsidy system, see *Housing Policy: a Consultative Document*, pp.82-3.

109. Ibid., p.80.

110. See in particular, Pat Niner, *Local Authority Housing Policy and Practice*, University of Birmingham, Centre for Urban and Regional Studies, Occasional paper no.31 (1975).

111. See Alan Murie *et al.*, *Housing Policy*, ch.4, and sources cited, North Tyneside CDP, *Some Housing and Town Planning Issues in North Tyneside: An Overview*, mimeo, 1976; David Smith and Anne Whalley, *Racial Minorities and Public Housing* (London, PEP Broadsheet no.556, 1975); David H. McKay, *Housing and Race in Industrial Society* (London, Croom Helm, 1977), ch.6, and sources cited; John English *et al.*, *Slum Clearance*, chs. 4 and 5.

112. Cmnd.6851.

113. See for example, Colin Ward, 'Peter Shore's Damp Squib', *Town and Country Planning*, October 1977, pp.421-2; Alexander Grey *et al.*, *Housing Rents, Costs and Subsidies* (London, Chartered Institute of Public Finance and Accountancy, 1978).

114. For a discussion of this problem, see Grey *et al.*, ibid.

115. See for example, Peter Townsend, *Sociology and Social Policy*, ch.6.

116. *Housing Tenure: A Speech by Peter Shore* (Department of the Environment, Press Release, 7 September 1976), pp.3-4.

117. Cmnd.6851, ch.14.

118. Ibid., p.79.

119. Ibid., pp.103-5.

120. Ibid., pp.42-3.

121. Ibid., ch.3.

122. See Dickens, *Housing and the State*; CDP Information and Intelligence Unit, *Gilding The Ghetto*, 1976; M. Ball, 'British Housing Policy and the Housing Building Industry', paper before the CES Urban Charge and Conflict Conference, York University, 4-7 January 1971.

123. See James Johnson, John Salt and Peter A. Wood, *Housing and the Migration of Labour in England and Wales* (Westmead, Farnborough, and Lexington, Mass., Saxon House/Lexington Books, 1974).

5 URBAN TRANSPORT POLICIES

> To me. . .the Ministry of Transport has always been a planning
> Ministry — not just a highway department for deploring the
> railway deficit. It must create the administrative and financial
> framework in which transport can serve the nation's social and
> economic needs. It must be a powerhouse of research, both
> economic and technological. It must work closely with other
> departments concerned with the same fields. (Barbara Castle,
> House of Commons, 1968)

That transport development affects the structure and growth of cities
is obvious. Some would go as far as to say that transport patterns are
the single most important factor in determining urban change. Certainly
the rapid growth of late nineteenth and early twentieth century
European and North American cities was facilitated by the electric
tramway and suburban railway.[1] More recently, the motor car and new
urban roads have in some instances allowed urban growth to proceed
at an even more rapid pace, and have also profoundly affected the
physical structure and social composition of cities.[2] Transport policy
has the potential, therefore, of greatly affecting land use, residential
location, occupational opportunity and mobility, and a host of other
phenomena affecting urban life. In one sense, *all* transport services,
including inter-urban roads and railways affect urban areas, for they
can influence residential and occupational mobility as well as industrial
location. Generally, however, the present chapter will be confined to a
discussion of *urban* transport policies, or those policies affecting public
and private transport patterns in urban areas.

Interestingly, British national governments did not develop a concern
for urban transport policy until after the Second World War — although
government involvement in transport generally goes back several
centuries. Unlike housing and land values, then, political parties have
not, until very recently, included urban transport problems in their
platforms. Perhaps this is understandable given the obvious and
immediate interest populations have in housing, and the central
ideological role of land in any left/right political dialogue. Urban
transport, by contrast, appears ancillary to these fundamental services.

This is especially true when it is remembered that the period of
most rapid (and disruptive) urbanisation in Britain was the nineteenth

century when state involvement in all aspects of urban society was low, and it was during this period that the basic pattern of road, tram and rail development was laid. With the partial exception of the London area, this pattern proved adequate until the rapid rise in car ownership in the 1950s. Unlike many other areas of urban and social policy, therefore, urban transport was not an important part of the national policy agenda in the period between 1900 and 1950.

Other policies, including some general transport policies, were important influences on urban transport in this period however, and before proceeding to the post-1945 period, it will be useful to mention these briefly.

The State and Transport, 1870-1945

One of the most important laws enacted in the urban transport field in the pre-war period was the 1870 Tramways Act. This law was designed to prevent the extension of local gas and water company monopolies to rapidly growing tramway networks. However, the quite severe restrictions imposed on the companies by the law resulted not in open competition but in some reduction in tramway construction and, more important, in the municipalisation of tram services.[3] When buses and trolleybuses began to replace and supplement the trams in the 1900s, it was natural that they too should be owned and operated by local authorities.

Most other pre-First World War legislation in the transport area affected urban areas only marginally. As far as roads were concerned the period was characterised by an increasing trend towards administrative centralisation, with local authorities losing most of their highway responsibilities to counties and to the nationally organised Road Board which was introduced in 1909.[4]

Between the wars, at least elements of a national transport policy emerged, although the primary concern of governments was with inter-urban rather than urban transport. Hence the creation of the Ministry of Transport in 1919 was precipitated in large part by a perceived need to rationalise inter-urban transport — and especially the railways.[5] London was a major exception to this general rule. London was experiencing particularly acute problems of traffic congestion, and in 1924 a London Traffic Act introduced a limited form of regulation of motor transport. More important, in 1933 the London Passenger Transport Act created a new transport authority (the London Passenger Transport Board) responsible for administering bus, tram and underground railway services throughout the metropolitan area.

Although passed by Ramsay McDonald's National Government this law was largely the initiative of Herbert Morrison, Minister of Transport in the 1929-31 Labour Government. Acting on the recommendation of the London Traffic Advisory Committee that proper co-ordination and the elimination of wasteful competition was necessary to improve communications in the conurbation, Morrison had pushed for the creation of a new authority and his efforts came to fruition in 1933.[6] The new Board was interesting because it operated independently of the London County Council (LCC) and the various boroughs, and because its jurisdiction extended well beyond the LCC's. It became, in fact, the only administrative body covering the true boundaries of the metropolitan area. More interesting for our purposes is the fact that the initiative to enactment came from a Labour Government. Labour had long been an advocate of the nationalisation and integration of transport services[7] and the London Passenger Transport Act was a first step towards that goal. The new law was acceptable to the National Government only because London's transport services (conventional railways apart) were already municipalised.

While some attempt was made to regulate the use and licensing of motor vehicles during this period, little interest was shown either by the political parties or by other interested groups in the basic relationship between vehicular traffic and cities – and this in spite of the fact that the number of vehicles increased from 388,860 in 1914 to over 3 million in 1938.[8]

Labour and Transport, 1945-51

The nationalisation of railway, road haulage, inland waterway and air services was a major part of Labour's 1945-51 programme and it was carried out in the post-1945 period. Where the new Government was less successful was in integrating transport services. Economic constraints, organisational problems and sheer lack of time were the main reasons for the limited success.[9] Apart from the suburban railway network (which was a major transport service south of the Thames) public transport in London was, of course, already integrated, and as originally conceived, the 1947 Transport Act was to be modelled on the London example. However, when finally enacted into law the legislation created a federal rather than unitary administration for transport, with separate executives for each of the transport modes operating with some independence under the central British Transport Commission.[10] Urban transport, as such, was not a concern of the legislation. Indeed, at this time there was little consciousness of urban transport as a separate policy area.

The only other major item of legislation in the transport field in this period, the 1946 Trunk Roads Act, was important for urban areas only in the sense that it established the principle of subsidising the construction of Class I or strategic roads with 75 per cent grants When large scale urban road development began in the 1960s the level of support was extended to all 'principal' roads — or routes which were considered important for regional communications, including many urban roads.

While the immediate post-war period saw few policy initiatives in the urban transport field, professional and bureaucratic thinking on the subject was by no means stagnant. In 1942 Alker Tripp had published *Town Planning and Traffic*[11] which distinguished between arterial, sub-arterial and local roads. Tripp's recommendation was that arterial and sub-arterial roads should be as free from pedestrians, junctions and standing traffic as possible. In addition, the document assumed that the most suitable pattern of road development was radial, and thus followed the general thinking of the time that ring or radial roads were the natural 'defence' against road congestion — especially, as Patrick Abercrombie had argued, in a large conurbation such as London.[12]

Many of these ideas received official approval in the 1946 Ministry of War Transport Manual *Design and Layout of Roads in Built-up Areas*[13] and, although during the ensuing ten years very little was done by way of new road construction, the idea that roads should be built to accommodate traffic, was firmly established. There was little appreciation either that such an approach implied an open-ended cost commitment by the government, or that new roads themselves could generate new traffic and therefore would not ease congestion. As it turned out, economic constraints such as fuel rationing, together with a very low level of car ownership during the immediate post-war years (see Table 5.1), assured a low political salience for the urban transport issue.

Some debate did occur between 1945 and 1951 on the question of car ownership and fuel consumption, with the Tories favouring eased controls, but the issue was minor in relation to such questions as nationalisation, housing, monetary policy and rearmament. Car ownership was, of course, concentrated heavily among Conservative voters, and many Labour MPs had long harboured an antagonism to the private car. In contrast, some Conservatives viewed government restrictions on motor vehicles as a denial of individual freedom. In 1950

Winston Churchill attacked Labour policy on motor taxation and fuel rationing partly on these grounds:

> People are not necessarily 'lower than vermin', because by their skill and thrift they have earned and saved enough money to buy a car or motor cycle. . .We realise the deprivation and often hardship involved in the strict rationing of petrol which the Socialist Governments have explored, and we are determined to put an end to it at the earliest possible moment.[14]

Yet, as William Plowden has pointed out in his comprehensive review of the relationship between the car and politics, these predictably conflicting policy positions were not translated into conflicting policy or even into an important party debate on the subject. Governments, Labour and Conservative, have always viewed motor taxation as an economic rather than ideological weapon. Revenue has been the primary consideration, not the inherent rights or wrongs of car ownership. Indeed, Conservative policy on motor taxation post-1951 is virtually indistinguishable from that of Labour.

The 1945-51 period was, then, remarkable for the absence of both policy and politics in the urban transport area. Significantly, it was *professional* opinion in the form of academic and official reports which made the only contribution to public thinking in the area. Perhaps this is not surprising. Urban transport problems were hardly an important element in party politics mainly because they were not perceived to exist. Moreover, urban transport and particularly traffic management appeared to be much more a technical than a political matter. The future development of large cities and how best to expedite the movement of people and goods in urban areas were subjects firmly in the realm of forward — possibly even utopian — planning. And while party differences in the general field of planning certainly did exist in the 1947-51 period (see chapter 2, p.38), during and immediately after the war an enormous enthusiasm existed in the political parties, in the civil service and among academics for planning *per se.* Moreover, concensus was strongest in those aspects of planning which did not appear to challenge existing power relations, or to impinge directly on the fundamental differences in policy which divided the parties in so many areas. Few perceived that the ethereal world of 'traffic management' and 'arterial and radial routes' was anything to do with party politics.

1951-62: The Politics of Neglect

In the transport area the 1950s were dominated by one overriding fact: the numbers of cars in use increased from 2.2 million in 1950 to over 8 in 1964 (Table 5.1), more than double the projected increase of 1945. In part because of this failure in predicting car ownership, local and central governments made little effort to adapt public policy to accommodate the car. Some relatively minor Road Traffic Acts were introduced in 1955 and 1958, sanctioning the use of traffic meters and other traffic management techniques. Significantly, these met with opposition not from any political party, but from the motoring organisations — the Automobile Association (AA) and the Royal Automobile Club (RAC). These organisations, together with the British Road Federation and its publicity offshoot, the Roads Campaign Council, formed what was to become known as the 'road lobby'.[15] Operating under an umbrella lobbying organisation, the Standing Joint Committee (SJC), the RAC and AA together with the Scottish RAC, had by the mid-1950s grown into a formidable political force. In 1954, the AA alone had more than 1.5 million members, and it espoused a philosophy towards transport policy which was at once coherent and attractive to car owners. In sum, the SJC wanted as little government interference with private motorists as possible, except that is, to accommodate the motorist and other road users via massively increased road construction. Their policy was, therefore, *laissez-faire* only in the sense that they advocated freeing road users from most forms of government controls. Government expenditure, on the other hand, had to rise rapidly if the motorists' highway needs were to be met. BRF and RCC policy, based on the perceived needs of thousands of commercial and industrial road users, was broadly similar. During the 1950s, the road lobby's priority was for a new network of inter-urban motorways, rather than for new urban roads. But the logic of their policy was that should the need be present, new urban roads should be built.

One of the most interesting features of this period was that with a Conservative Government in power preaching and practising de-regulation, the de-nationalisation of road haulage and steel and championing the cause of the private road industry and of the private citizen, a massive increase in road expenditure did not occur. Starting from a very low base, spending did increase — especially between 1957 and 1958 when expenditure on new roads increased from £30 million to £60 million. However, given the explosion in car ownership and in road haulage, the expenditure figure in 1961 of 98.9 million remained

Table 5.1: Motor Vehicles in Use, United Kingdom, 1946-74

	Year	Total vehicles	Cars	Year	Total vehicles	Cars
Sept.	1946	3,106,810	1,769,952	1961	9,965,300	5,978,500
	1947	3,515,444	1,943,602	1962	10,562,800	6,555,800
	1948	3,728,432	1,960,510	1963	11,446,200	7,375,000
	1949	4,107,652	2,130,793	1964	12,369,200	8,247,000
	1950	4,409,223	2,257,873	1965	12,939,800	8,916,000
	1951	4,677,888	2,380,343	1966	13,285,716	9,513,368
	1952	4,957,395	2,508,102	1967	14,096,000	10,302,900
	1953	5,340,222	2,761,654	1968	14,446,500	10,816,100
	1954	5,825,447	3,099,547	1969	13,751,900	11,227,900
	1955	6,465,433	3,525,858	1970	14,950,200	11,515,100
	1956	6,975,962	3,887,906	1971	15,434,400	12,580,600
	1957	7,483,489	4,186,631	1972	16,117,000	12,740,000
	1958	7,959,313	4,548,530	1973	17,014,000	13,521,000
	1959	8,661,980	4,965,774	1974	17,258,000	13,639,000
	1960	9,439,140	5,525,828			

Source: Reproduced from D.N.M. Starkie, *Transportation Planning, Policy and Analysis* (London, Pergamon, 1976), Appendix A, p.123.

small.[16]

According to the *Economist*, civil servants imbued with the elitist notion that car ownership ought to be confined to the middle classes were influential within the Treasury and Ministry of Transport at this time.[17] They may have held back expenditure on roads, therefore. Probably as important were the continuing economic difficulties of the Government which had a generally depressing effect on public spending. The Tory Administrations of 1951 and 1955 were not, in any case, enthusiastic about grand schemes in domestic politics. After the controls and interventions of the war and post-war period, they were keen to return, to if not *laissez-faire* politics, then certainly to the politics of minimal intervention. As we have seen in other areas of urban policy, this was translated both into more selectivist policies and into cuts in government expenditure.

William Plowden stresses that the last political conflict based on the assumption that the motor car was very much in the domain of the middle class concerned the efforts by the Conservatives to liberalise the use of cars during election campaigns. This parliamentary effort, culminating in a 1958 amendment to the 1948 Representation of the People Act, aroused fierce party controversy with Labour accusing the Conservatives of deliberately loading the political dice in favour of Tory voters.[18] From 1958 on, however, this particular issue was effectively removed from the political agenda by the rising tide of car ownership.

In other areas of urban transport the 1950s were a period of remarkable inactivity. Talk of integrating transport services, whether within urban areas or nationally, faded as the Conservatives dismantled the controls and regulations of the 1940s. Meanwhile, urban public transport services both in their administrative structures and operating procedures continued much as before.[19] Only with respect to the motor car did significant changes occur — and these largely independent of government policy.

1963-70: The Rise of Urban Transport Planning

By the late 1950s, academic and professional thinking on the relationship between towns and traffic was changing rapidly. British cities were becoming seriously congested. Meters and other traffic management schemes were slowly being introduced, but even as late as 1961 only 60 per cent of England's boroughs had thought about parking policy and only half of these were preparing plans.[20] With car ownership accelerating rapidly, commentators began to talk of traffic jams which would paralyse cities, possibly for days. As it happened, there was little evidence that this extreme situation could occur, but it added fuel to an intensifying debate on the subject.

Debate was concentrated, however, not in political circles, but within the world of professional planners and highway engineers and within the Ministry of Transport. As previously suggested, during the 1950s, MOT officials had little interest in mass-ownership motoring. Indeed, in the mid-1950s only 3 of the Ministry's 16 undersecretaries specialised in roads and road transport, and they were more interested in rural routes than urban roads.[21] After 1959, however, the emphasis within the Ministry changed. Civil Aviation, until then a part of the Ministry's responsibilities, was shed, and with the new Conservative administration, a new Minister of Transport, Ernest Marples (and a new Permanent Secretary, Sir James Dunnett) took over.[22] Administrative and personnel changes hardly revolutionised policy, however. Road Traffic Acts were passed in 1960 and 1962 giving the Ministry greater power over local authorities to introduce traffic management schemes, and increasing penalties for driving offences.

These measures were, however, small modifications of existing policy rather than radical departures from it.

If policy did not change drastically, professional thinking did — largely as a result of the publication of the Buchanan Report in the Summer of 1963.[23] Much has been written on this Report and its influence, and this is not the place for a comprehensive summary of its contents. Several aspects of the Report are worthy of particular note, however:

1. It was set up by the Ministry of Transport: 'to study the long term development of roads and traffic in urban areas and their influence on the urban environment'.[24] Its members included planners, architects and academics and it was supervised by a Steering Group consisting of architects, and local and New Town officials. Party politicians played some role in setting up the Committee. Ernest Marples was a highly active 'Executive type' minister who believed in the radical rethinking of existing practice[25] — but it is unlikely that politicians influenced the committee's findings.

2. There seems little doubt that the Report produced a permanent shift in the focus of debate. After publication both those (in any case a dwindling minority) who advocated restrictions on car ownership, and those who thought that urban congestion problems would 'work themselves out' without government intervention, lost influence and were rarely heard from again. Instead, Buchanan's observation that traffic in towns was unavoidable and bound to increase in volume, and that the central question of public policy was to balance accommodation of traffic with preservation of the urban environment, began to dominate thinking on the subject.

3. At least in theory, Buchanan's approach to traffic in towns was comprehensive. He was concerned not just with cars in urban areas (which had tended to be the case in earlier debate) but with all traffic including bus transport and the relationship between urban road and rail transport. And, for the first time since the famous wartime reports, the whole question of the relationship between urban transport policies and other urban policies was raised by Buchanan. Hence the Report refers to population and investment capital movements, and to how public policy — and especially transport policy — might be adapted to encourage planned growth without allowing the extremes of overcrowding and sprawl to develop.[26]

While Buchanan's approach to urban transport was in theory comprehensive, an examination of the Report's specific focus reveals a very considerable bias in favour of private cars and of the comprehensive redevelopment of cities. Most important of all, the Report made the *a priori* assumption that the motor car was beneficial and that its use should be maximised. This is clear both from the Report and from Professor Buchanan's later statements on the subject. For example, in an article published in 1964, he wrote:

> We. . .always returned to the view that the motor vehicle was an incredibly useful method of transport, offering advantages possessed by no other invention to date, nor, as far as we could see, by anything in the foreseeable future. This led to our 'fundamental standpoint' of accepting the motor vehicle as beneficial and then seeking to understand what needed to be done to cities in a creative and constructive way to enable it to be exploited within them. The case for restriction would have to emerge, we argued, from the demonstrated impossibility, or great difficulty, or great expense, of meeting the full demand for the use of motor vehicles. I remain absolutely convinced this was a sound approach, and that had we started in any other way our study would have carried no confidence with the public.
>
> I would expect any local authority studying the problems of its area to proceed broadly as we did, that is, to investigate how far it is possible to go with the motor vehicle and to allow the case for restriction to emerge in the negative 'feedback' manner described. There is nothing to prevent the local authority at any stage costing out alternative methods of discharging the movements, provided they can think of them. In practice, this is likely to boil down to one main issue — how much of the *journey-to-work* load can be discharged by private cars, and how much must be carried by public transport.[27]

In sum, the motor car should be accommodated within cities and the limits to this accommodation should be environmental and cost factors. Accessibility was defined in terms of the private car and: 'within any urban area as it stands the establishment of environmental standards automatically determines the accessibility, but the latter can be increased according to the amount of money that can be spent on physical alterations'.[28] Buchanan held strongly to the notion of the city as a compact, vibrant and cohesive unit with a thriving central area, and protected by green belts and planning laws from both overcrowding and sprawl. The objective of maintaining this essential character and at the same time accommodating the private car led to two important conclusions. First, the large scale redesigning or restructuring of central cities would be necessary if restrictions on the car were to be kept at a minimum. Separation of pedestrians from traffic both horizontally and vertically, involving vast engineering work, would therefore be necessary. Clearly, such plans are very different from traffic management schemes which accommodate cars within existing physical layouts and which had increased in popularity during the late 1950s and early 1960s. Second, in order to facilitate the free passage of through-traffic and to give adequate access for local traffic to the main arterial routes, a network of urban motorways would have to be built. Needless to say, both of these could only be facilitated by greatly increased central government expenditure.

These are the logical conclusions of the Report's findings rather than specific recommendations. Indeed, as far as larger cities are concerned, Buchanan had serious reservations as to the applicability of the 'total redesign' alternative.[29] The cost would be too high and the damage to the environment great. But the theoretical underpinnings of the analysis which put a premium on motor car accessibility applied as much to the large city as the small town. As Stephen Plowden has put it:

> In large towns, the weakness in Buchanan's concept of accessibility becomes fatal. There is a real danger that the environmental losses in restructuring the town in the way his design principles indicate would exceed the environmental gains, and the costs involved even in modest solutions along the lines that he suggested are likely to be exorbitant.[30]

Finally, the implied 'solutions' of traffic in towns effectively relegated public transport, and especially rail transport, to a residual role. With the rise of mass ownership of cars, only a minority of the population, so the Report implied, would need public transport. But this minority was virtually ignored in the analysis, and a further 'minority', pedestrians, found themselves being fitted in to new traffic schemes rather than have traffic adapted to their needs.

Few doubt the significance and influence of *Traffic in Towns*. It is true that the Report made no specific recommendations, and instead provided policy makers with a frame of reference within which to operate. But the basic philosophy of the study has been adopted by local authorities on a wide scale. Even in London, in many ways the city least amenable to Buchanan-style solutions, its influence has been great. As Douglas Hart has commented: *'Traffic in Towns* has had a profound impact on thinking about the way in which London could approach its traffic problem, and Buchanan and his consulting firm, Colin Buchanan and Partners, have subsequently developed and elaborated "Buchananism" with regard to the capital in their role as consultants to the Greater London Council.'[31] As Hart later demonstrates, London's particular traffic plans based on a complex network of urban motorways were not to come to fruition, but in dozens of other cities, large and small throughout Britain, city centres have been reconstructed and new urban roads (including urban motorways) built at least partly on the Buchanan Report's assumptions.

During the 1960s solutions to urban problems were increasingly seen in terms of high-cost grand designs, and this must explain at least in part the success of 'Buchananism'. A fascinating document reflecting the ethos of the times and the coming success of the Report was published by the British Road Federation in 1963. *People and Cities* was the report on a conference sponsored by the BRF and the Town Planning Institute — largely in response to the Buchanan Report. Almost every contribution congratulates the bold new approach of *Traffic in Towns* and heralds the coming motor age with excitement and enthusiasm.[32] The speakers included planners, architects, civil servants, surveyors, engineers, as well as Buchanan and Ernest Marples, the Minister of Transport. More significantly, the conference was attended by more than 1000 delegates drawn mainly from the planning and engineering departments of myriad local authorities, but also including foreign and academic representatives.[33]

Concurrent with this rising enthusiasm for accommodating the car, came calls for the commissioning of transportation studies. Pioneered in the United States, these consisted of a comprehensive study of transport needs, demands and patterns in particular cities or conurbations. By analysing present and future individual journeys within a locality or zone and between localities, transportation studies could be used to plan transport needs for years ahead. The sophisticated survey methods and data analysis techniques utilised by the studies have greatly increased our knowledge of urban areas both in the United States and, since the commissioning of transportation studies in the UK in the 1960s, in Britain. However, these early transportation studies, like most purportedly technical solutions to complex problems, had serious weaknesses. As Stephen Plowden notes, the interests of pedestrians and cyclists were ignored.[34] More importantly, the studies tended to project from existing conditions and trends, and therefore greatly favoured the role of the motor car in future transport needs.[35]

The early and mid-1960s were, then, a period of great change in the field of urban transport planning. But change owed very little, if anything, to party politics. The Buchanan Report was welcomed by both Conservative and Labour spokesmen, and the Parliamentary debate on the Report shows both parties broadly in support of car ownership and of adapting cities to cars rather than car use to cities.[36] The only deviant view came from a few members of the Labour left. Referring to 'the most hideous lobby of all — the motorists' lobby', Anthony Wedgwood Benn called for restrictive motor taxation to control the use of cars in cities.[37]

In their reaction to changes in professional thinking, the parties were generally united, and at least until 1967, national urban transport policy did not diverge along party lines. This point is particularly interesting because between 1962 and 1967 urban transport policy became a political issue for the first time, and, almost 'beneath the surface' of national politics, important changes in policy were underway.

It is relatively easy to explain the increased political salience of this issue. Car ownership had soared, cities were congested and the Buchanan Report had been given great publicity. It is not surprising, therefore, that in their 1964 Manifestos (and to a much lesser extent in the 1966 Manifestos) both parties gave space to urban transport problems. The Tories promised 'to apply the principles of the Buchanan Report to comprehensive campaigns in town replanning. As an immediate step, expenditure on urban roads will be trebled'.[38] Part of Labour's platform was different in emphasis. 'Labour believes that public transport, road and rail, must play the dominant part in the journey to work. Every effort will be made to improve and modernise these services.'[39] But in effective contradiction to this, the Manifesto continued: 'Urgent attention will be given to the proposals of the Buchanan Report and to the development of new roads capable of diverting through traffic from town centres.'[40]

Expenditure on new roads did increase rapidly during this period from £190 million in 1964/5 to £504 million in 1970/1,[41] although most of the increase went towards inter-urban rather than urban roads. But with little direct intervention from Whitehall, local authorities all over the country were preparing and in some cases actually executing plans to reconstruct central areas and to build new roads. The Ministry of Transport aided this trend by making funds available for urban roads, and in 1965, setting up an Urban Unit within the Ministry to advise on urban traffic and road building schemes.

Hence, there existed a climate in which new urban road building schemes were encouraged — even though no specific legislation prescribed them. As far as urban transport is concerned this policy continued with little modification until the change of government in 1970. Yet the period of 1965 to 1970 was one of intense political debate both in the transport area generally and with respect to urban transport in particular. Party differences over the general principles of transport policy had, of course, existed for some years, with the nationalisation issue dominating debate. By 1964, however, Labour was proposing not nationalisation but the *integration* of transport services to eliminate wasteful competition. Claiming that Conservative policy, by encouraging competition between different transport modes, had produced waste and inefficiency, Labour was intent on rationalising and co-ordinating all transport services.[42]

To this end, a White Paper, *Transport Policy*, was published in 1966 proposing an integrated transport system.[43] Urban transport was considered a crucial part of this system and the White Paper made two important proposals in this area. The first was essentially an official recognition of 'Buchananism':

> As Professor Buchanan has pointed out, to meet modern traffic needs, to protect the environment and to relieve congestion, our large cities and towns will need over the next generation a modern network of high capacity traffic routes. These networks will call for massive investment in road construction. We now have an expanded urban road programme, growing and gathering momentum. Even so, its present scale cannot be regarded as more than a beginning of the inevitably long and expensive job of providing enough road space in our towns. A bigger programme will be needed in the 1970s, its extent and timing properly related to the resources available for the road programme as a whole. The Government's aim is to see that primary networks needed for the main traffic flows and for the establishment of environmental areas will be built as soon as resources allow.[44]

Given that reconstruction was a long-term undertaking the White Paper proposed increased investment in smaller scale traffic management with the Ministry of Transport taking the lead in encouraging local authorities to adopt such schemes.[45]

Public transport was the second major focus of the White Paper's plans for urban transport, and in this area, a major reorganisation was proposed. London apart, urban public transport had undergone virtually no major organisational change for decades. Noting this, and the fragmented and often inefficient administrative structure prevailing in many cities, the White Paper announced a major rationalisation and integration of transport on a conurbation-wide basis. This involved both administrative rationalisation and the integration of transport planning with planning of land use. The logic of transportation studies — that transport needs could only be measured by analysing changes in employment and population - was, therefore, being adopted as official policy. Recognising that such changes would have to wait upon the reports of the Royal Commissions on the reform of Local Government, the White Paper proposed the setting up of interim transport authorities based on the 'urban region' or conurbation.[46] Finally, the White Paper announced the Government's intention to increase the subsidies available to local authorities for public transport to a level comparable to those offered for road construction.[47]

A further White Paper, *Public Transport and Traffic*, giving greater detail to these proposals was published in December 1967.[48] The new metropolitan-wide transport administrators were to be named Passenger Transport Authorities (PTAs) and Greater Manchester, the West Midlands and Tyneside were immediately designated as PTA recipients. In addition, grants of 75 per cent were to be introduced for investment in public transport capital projects (the same as for urban roads) and smaller subsidies were proposed for the purchase of buses.[49]

The reorganisation measures applied only to urban areas outside London. Separate legislation, transferring transport responsibilities from the London Transport Executive to the Greater London Council was being prepared for that city.[50]

Recognition of a major (and possibly enhanced) role for public transport might appear to be a radical departure from the policy pursued down to 1964, but on closer examination this apparently important innovation produced few fundamental changes. The ensuing 1968 Transport Act *was* a major item of legislation — possibly the single most important legislative Act of the Labour Government's tenure — and it included radical changes in such areas as country and inter-urban bus transport. However, in urban transport, the major administrative reform represented by the PTAs applied to only four conurbations, although others were added following the reorganisation of local government in 1972, and from 1974 the new county councils were given the responsibility of co-ordinating transport services. More importantly, at least until the early 1970s, the major feature of urban transport policy was not the enhancement of public services, but the pursuit of Buchanan-type solutions. Road expenditure continued unabated and the reconstruction of city centres to accommodate the car reached a climax during these years. Many local variations existed with some cities (such as Glasgow) deciding on more extensive reconstruction than others (such as many of the cities with centres of historical interest), but it would be quite misleading to characterise this period as one when public transport received a new lease of life. It was, rather, an era when technical solutions were seen as sufficient to overcome urban transport problems, and when, in the face of rapidly increasing car ownership, Labour could not be seen to be giving massive support to public transport.

Perhaps the strangest feature of these years was the sudden eruption of party rancour over urban transport issues. In retrospect, the 1960s were years of continuity rather than contrast in urban transport policy; the main objective difference between the parties being the level of expenditure each was prepared to commit to transport (with Labour favouring greater expenditure on public transport). But Labour's commitment to the integration of urban transport and to conurbation-wide planning was to be adopted by the Conservatives in the post-1970 period, so this was hardly a point of great controversy. Yet between 1966 and 1970, the Labour Government, and in particular, the Minister of Transport, Barbara Castle, came to be identified in some quarters as anti-motor car and pro-public transport. The reasons for this are not difficult to identify. *Public Transport and Traffic*, the White Paper published in December 1967, and the subsequent 1968 Transport Act, made it clear that the Labour Government believed in some role (if not a dominant role) for public transport, and it was predictable that the road lobby should see this as a threat to the hitherto unbridled rise of the motor car. Moreover, Mrs Castle was on the left of the Labour Party political spectrum and it was all too easy to brand her policies as socialist, or even extremist.[51] Hence, the BRF, the motorists' organisations and the Opposition in Parliament all condemned Mrs Castle's attitude to transport, as well as criticising certain aspects of the Transport Bill. Mrs Castle's own inability to drive and her successful efforts to impose a 70 mph speed limit and introduce a breathalyser test to detect drunken drivers were seen as confirmation of her anti-car stance.[52]

There was, however, an important distinction between the

opposition of the road lobby and that of the Conservative Party. Front
Bench Opposition spokesmen based their attack as much on fiscal as
on ideological grounds. Peter Walker, the Conservative spokesman on
transport put the Opposition's position on the 1968 Bill thus:

> I do not condemn the Right Honourable Lady for this. She has
> always been a left wing, extreme Socialist. Those who I do blame
> are the Prime Minister and the new Chancellor of the Exchequer
> for allowing this piece of legislation to come forward at this
> particular time. . .There is nothing in the Bill which will improve
> confidence in Britain.[53]

In other words, at a time when Britain was experiencing particularly
acute economic problems, the Government was preparing to increase
public transport subsidies. Walker made no mention of the
Conservatives' continuing devotion to massively increased road
subsidies, nor did he respond to Barbara Castle's boast that Labour had
increased road building by over 100 per cent in money terms between
1964 and 1968.[54] Indeed, the new Labour policy was hardly socialist
in design. Rather than the 1968 Act being a major device for the
redistribution of transport resources from private to public control
(which was what the road lobby claimed) it proposed the *rationalisation*
of transport services. It was, then, technocratic in nature; witness
Barbara Castle's presentation of the second reading of the Bill:

> To me. . .the Ministry of Transport has always been a planning
> Ministry — not just a highways department for deploring the railway
> deficit. It must create the administrative and financial framework in
> which transport can serve the nation's social and economic needs.
> It must be a powerhouse of research, both economic and
> technological. It must work closely with other departments
> concerned with the same fields.[55]

In any case, the Conservatives could hardly deny the logic of providing
help to public transport, given the indisputable fact that a substantial
minority of the public would always have to rely on buses and trains.

Labour's apparent devotion to public transport needs, then, to be
kept in perspective. Within the Party, the left were undoubtedly more
antagonistic to the private car than were the right,[56] but as translated
into legislation, policy was based on the assumption that the
continuing rise in car ownership was inevitable, and Governments had

a responsibility to see to the transport needs of the 'residue' of non-car owners. On the question of journeys to work and the use of cars in central city areas, policy was much more ambiguous. Vague talk about 'road pricing' and limiting car ownership which was prevalent in the early 1960s, remained vague. Few important differences between the parties existed, although a kind of 'phoney war' waged in Parliament and in the press gave the impression that significant political party conflict did exist.[57]

Britain's townscape was very different in 1970 compared with 1963. With the aid of speculative capital, government subsidies, and fuelled by the expansionist civic ethos of the period, Buchanan-like 'solutions' had transformed many central city areas. At the same time, although government spending on public transport began to increase after 1968, decline was the main characteristic of public transport during the 1960s. This accepted, in marked contrast to the 1950s, planning for both the car and public transport was attempted — even if in most cases this meant accommodation of the rising tide of car owners.

1970-8: The Politics of Retrenchment

On coming to power in 1970, the Conservatives made no significant change in policy towards urban transport. Neither party Manifesto gave as much prominence to the area in 1970 as they had given in 1964 or 1966. Perhaps this was because policy *had* developed considerably during Labour's terms of office. Roads were being built, city centres adapted to meet the needs of private motorists (and to a lesser extent to limit the freedom of the motorist), and some (but much smaller) changes were under way in public transport. Possibly as important was the fading of enthusiasm for the grand schemes and hopes of a 'New Britain' which the two Labour Governments of the 1960s had promised. Economic constraints were partly responsible for this, but as important was the increasing realisation that the bold new urban initiatives in housing, slum clearance, redevelopment and transport bore significant social and environmental costs. In transport, vast new urban road schemes came under mounting criticism during the late 1960s and early 1970s, and, following the substantial cutbacks in public expenditure which began in 1973, the spectre of planning blight — derelict land and buildings awaiting the construction of new roads — became increasingly common in some cities.

As was emphasised in the last section, the Labour Party's devotion to public transport during the 1960s was more apparent than real. The rise of the motor car continued inexorably during their tenure in office. Between 1966 and 1970 private car traffic in urban areas increased by 22 per cent, bus and coach traffic declined by 13 per cent[58] and greatly increased spending on roads together with a commitment to Buchanan-type solutions, revealed the true position in the urban transport area. It is not at all surprising that the Conservatives continued this policy in 1970. They were, after all, the Party most closely associated with the interests of the road lobby even if the greatest increase in road spending ever had occurred under Labour between 1966 and 1970. Moreover, for *any* Party to have reversed the trend towards private car transport, would have required such profoundly radical policies – extensive road pricing, limitations on car ownership – as to be electorally inexpedient. However, as can be seen from Table 5.2, the Conservatives also continued the programme of subsidies to local public transport initiated by Labour in 1968. (The most relevant figures here are surface transport infrastructure grants which increased from £25 million to £50 million between 1971/2 and 1973/4.) But note also the high level of and continuing rise in road expenditure during these years.

Other changes were afoot in the 1970s which were to produce significant changes in urban transport policy. Generally, however, these were not a product of party politics. One important administrative innovation was the creation of the Department of the Environment (DOE) in 1970. This 'super ministry' combined the Ministries of Housing and Local Government, Transport and Public Buildings and Works, and the underlying rationale for the reorganisation was that the related interests of these departments would benefit greatly from administration integration. But there is little evidence that the creation of the DOE had much impact on transport policy. Generally speaking, transport administration within the DOE carried on much as before, largely independent of influence from the rest of the new agency.[59]

A much more important development was the mounting opposition to major road construction in urban areas. During the late 1960s and early 1970s a variety of environmental and 'defensive' groups worked hard to stop the construction of new urban roads. Some of these, such as Transport 2000, had the specific aim of promoting public transport. Others such as the Council for the Protection of Rural England and Friends of the Earth were primarily concerned with environmental protection. In addition, dozens of *ad hoc* local groups were formed to fight against particular schemes. In London for example, the London Motorway Action Group and the London Amenity and Transport Association were formed specifically to prevent the construction of the

Table 5.2: Public Expenditure in Roads and Surface Transport —
Urban Transport, Great Britain, 1971-4 (£ million)

	1971/2	1972/3	1973/4
Roads, new construction and improvement:			
principal roads	145.0	160.0	175.0
other roads	25.0	30.0	30.0
other expenditure (including lighting)	25.0	25.0	30.0
Roads — Maintenance:			
principal roads	40.0	40.0	45.0
other roads	30.0	30.0	30.0
other expenditure (including lighting)	20.0	20.0	20.0
	285.0	305.0	330.0
Surface transport			
support to nationalised industries	30.0	30.0	30.0
bus fuel grants	15.0	15.0	15.0
infrastructure	25.0	45.0	50.0
other passenger transport	35.0	30.0	30.0
	105.0	120.0	125.0

This table does not include figures for administration, nationalised industries
capital expenditure, research. etc.

Source: *Urban Transport Planning*, 2nd Report from the Expenditure Committee,
vol.1, Report and Appendix (London, HMSO, 1972), appendix 1, Table 3,
p.ciii.

London orbital motorways. By protesting at the official inquiries which
had to be held before all major road proposals were approved, lobbying
MPs, organising letter writing campaigns, and by some direct action,
such groups were important in focusing public attention on road
plans.[60] In December 1972 the anti-road lobby received its first official
boost with the publication of the House of Commons Expenditure
Committee Environment and Home Office Sub-Committee Report on
Urban Transport Planning. Chaired by a Conservative, this all-party
report came down strongly against increased spending on roads. Having
culled evidence from a wide variety of sources, the Report's
recommendations were fascinating for their projection of a spirit of
'urban siege'. For environmental, social and cost reasons, the continued
accommodation of the motor car was, the sub-committee argued,

untenable. An immediate halt to all new urban road schemes was
proposed, as well as the introduction of more restrictive traffic
management techniques and the promotion of public transport.[61]

So rather than proposing grand schemes the sub-committee pleaded
that policy be changed before British cities as traditionally known were
effectively destroyed. Hence it claimed that:

> Paradoxically an increase in road expenditure causing more urban
> road building tends to exacerbate the other urban problems of
> housing, health, education, etc. The United Kingdom has a particular
> structure of urban fabric which makes its adaptation difficult, and
> the repercussions of the urban roads programme on the stock and
> quality of housing is causing particular concern.[62]

In some respects, the Report was the most intelligent document on
urban transport to have appeared. For example, it did not argue for an
immediate switch to the currently popular 'rapid transit' or rail-based
metropolitan wide transport schemes. Recognising that, apart from
being expensive, the success of rapid transit schemes is difficult to
predict, the Report recommended that feasibility studies into rapid
transit development should be undertaken.[63] The Committee was, in
other words, sensitive both to environmental factors and to economic
and political reality.

The Report also launched into a considerable critique of the
administration of transport services at the central and local levels.
Under the 1968 Act a complex (and, according to the sub-committee,
in some respects indecipherable) system of grants for local transport
had been introduced. The Report therefore recommended that a new
system of block grants should replace the array of categorical
programmes, with the DOE overseeing carefully worked out plans for
urban transport.[64] The administration of transport planning within the
DOE was also criticised — mainly because it was perceived to be too
fragmented — and the Report accordingly recommended increased
bureaucratic co-ordination in the transport area. Most importantly,
it called for one minister within the DOE to be responsible for transport
and land use in urban areas. As these responsibilities had hitherto been
strictly divided between the Minister for Local Government and
Development and the Transport Minister, these were radical proposals
indeed.

Press response to the Report was generally favourable;[65] by early
1973 sentiment against the unlimited use of cars in towns had risen

perceptibly. Predictably, however, the road lobby were fierce in their opposition to the MPs' recommendations, with Anthony de Boer, Chairman of the British Road Federation, declaring that 'if road schemes are halted now, this will distort completely the whole programming of urban development'.[66]

Official reaction to the Report came with the publication of a White Paper on urban transport planning in the summer of 1973.[67] This document demonstrated just how far thinking on transport had changed since the mid-1960s. Notwithstanding the introduction of PTAs, which were extended to several more conurbations following local government reorganisation in 1972, and the sometimes quite ambitious schemes integrating rail and road transport (such as the Newcastle Metro system) initiated by some authorities, there was no *substantive* change in policy between 1968 and 1973. This accepted, the *emphasis* and *style* of policy changed considerably. Hence, the White Paper made sympathetic noises about public transport subsidies and, while it did not accept in total the Committee's call for a halt to the urban road programme, it did ask authorities to reconsider their road plans.

As in 1970, the change of government in 1974 produced few immediate urban transport policy initiatives although, on coming to power, Labour promised a major review of all aspects of transport policy. What transpired nearly three years later in December 1976, was a consultation document[68] which was extraordinary for its apparent abandonment of 'traditional' Labour policy. Remember that, at least in emphasis and rhetoric, Labour policy throughout the post-war period had emphasised the need to integrate all transport services. To a lesser extent, but especially from 1968 onwards, extensive subsidies for public transport were stated policy. Moreover, the incorporation of the MOT into the DOE in 1970, provided, at least in theory, the vehicle for comprehensive transport planning including relating transport policy to other aspects of urban policy such as housing and land-use planning. But in September 1976, Prime Minister James Callaghan decided to split transport away from the DOE, and although the two departments do retain some important administrative links, the decision formally to separate them hardly helped the cause of integrated policy. Moreover, even within transport policy the consultation document eschewed notions of integrated policy. Instead it proposed a 'managed market' approach to transport planning. As Peter Hall has put it:

The job of government, it [the consultation document] argues, is to set a framework which reflects social, environmental and resource considerations. But within this, people – either as private individuals, or transport operators – would be free to take their own decisions about what kind of transport to use. This means a heavy emphasis on fiscal measures – such as taxes on heavy lorries, which reflect the resource costs of building and maintaining the roads on which they run, and the environmental costs they may impose on roadside communities. It also means selective subsidies for particular groups of people – such as the carless poor, the young, the old and infirm. In particular, the report defiantly stresses, there should be no curb on the growth of car ownership, the use of cars should be restrained only in congested urban areas; and new roads will still be needed to cope with traffic growth.[69]

In other words, the Government proposed abandonment of the idea of comprehensive planning based on a public transport solution, and instead opted for an openly pragmatic solution based on existing trends and on the costs and benefits of particular transport modes. Even the heavily subsidised British Rail South East commuter services were not sacrosanct, for the consultation document specifically recommended that British Rail be required to adapt services to a reduced subsidy.

As a result of the publication of the document the Labour left found itself for the first time since the War seriously at odds with official Labour Government transport policy. Also, for the first time since 1945, the road lobby found itself in broad agreement with a Labour Government.[70] What explains this apparent reversal in policy? It seems probable that the personality of Anthony Crosland, until 1976 Secretary of State for the Environment, was highly influential as was the role of transport economists within the DOE.[71] It may even be that the Department of Transport was hived off in anticipation of the change in policy. Basically, Crosland's philosophy was based on notions of selectivism and fiscal responsibility rather than the universalism which hitherto had been influential on Labour thinking – even if it had not always dominated policy. It is, of course, impossible to say whether or not and to what extent Crosland was influenced by civil service advice, although it can be said with confidence that throughout the 1960s and into the 1970s the style of civil service operations in transport changed from very traditional to technical and analytical.[72] Armed with transportation studies and cost-benefit analyses it seems likely that civil servants were influential in steering the development of policy towards technical solutions and away from *dirigiste* solutions based on broad principles of social justice.

But it would be simplistic to portray the evolution of policy in this period as strictly internal to the civil service. Of great relevance was the economic climate and the growing fiscal crisis in the national economy. Policies based on perceived economic need with a residue of highly selective policies based on notions of social justice, became generally more popular in this era, with both political parties leading the way.

In fact, some of the more technocratic elements in the consultation document were dropped when the Government published a follow-up White Paper, *Transport Policy*, in June 1977.[73] In marked contrast to the consultation document, the White Paper put great emphasis on public participation in transport and it no longer recommended that public transport subsidies be reduced. Its main conclusions were:

> — expenditure in support of public transport and to moderate increases in fares will not be reduced, as had been planned, despite the declining share of public expenditure which can be devoted to transport. This will mean more support for buses, and less for road construction;
> — more responsibility for planning transport to meet local needs should be devolved to local government since the most practical and democratic approach to co-ordination is local;
> — greater emphasis should be placed on getting value for money, both in the financial regimes for the public sector industries and in the framework for decision-taking on particular schemes and services;
> — there should be a more systematic and open involvement of people, Parliament, transport operators and unions in the continuing debate on transport and the formulation of policy; and this should be promoted by the regular provision of information by Government and the industries.[74]

By no means, however, did the White Paper represent a return to the *status quo ante* of 1975, for it still recommended great emphasis on cost factors. For example, the proposal by the Greater London Council that they take over British Rail commuter services in the South-East was rejected as potentially too expensive. It is too early to explain why the Government withdrew some of the more 'hard headed' options contained in the consultation document, although it is possible that local authority and Labour Party opposition was important. What can be said with certainty, however, is that by 1977 hopes of comprehensive and integrated urban transport planning had been all but abandoned.

Instead, a much more pragmatic approach to urban transport problems based on the assumption of limited and even declining resources, had been adopted. This acknowledged, public transport expenditure did increase in relation to road expenditure both for urban areas and generally. As can be seen from Table 5.3, the White Paper proposed a fairly drastic cut in road expenditure, together with a much smaller drop in spending on public transport. Undoubtedly, fiscal considerations were as important here as notions of the relative merits of the two transport modes. It was, simply, politically easier to cut road expenditure in a climate of growing grass roots opposition to grand urban road schemes. In fact, by 1976 opposition to some of the more ambitious plans had reached near hysterical proportions. Led by John Tyme, a vehement opponent of new roads, several public inquiries were disrupted in the hope of halting the DOE's plans.[75] The protesters' claim that public participation in the form of inquiries was largely a sham had some credence, for in spite of all the official noises about the advantages of increased participation, the fact that public involvement only came at the *end* of the planning process put the public at a considerable disadvantage when faced with complex technical arguments justifying what in effect were decisions already taken.[76]

The 1970-77 period was, then, remarkable for the absence of party differences in the urban transport policy area. Unlike the late 1960s when, at least in terms of rhetoric, the parties differed, the 1970s could be characterised as a time when both political parties responded in similar fashion to a rapidly changing economic and political climate. The high expenditure programmes of the late 1960s and early 1970s became economically untenable in the mid-1970s. At the same time, opposition to urban roads at the grass roots level and within Parliament gradually gained momentum. Therefore, the undoubtedly significant move away from road expenditure and towards public transport in this period owed much to factors external to the central government transport policy-making machinery. Government and parties *reacted* to the wider policy environment, rather than were influential in shaping the policy agenda.

Table 5.3: Inland Surface Transport Public Expenditure,ᵃ Great Britain, 1971-8 (£ million at 1976 Survey Prices)

	1971/2	1973/4	1976/7	1977/8	End of decade (Cmnd. 6721)	Now proposed
Local transport capital:						
roads and car parks	525	565	370	265	(275)	260
public transport investment	75	135	175	165	(155)	155
Current:						
subsidies to buses, rail, etc.	10	40	210	180	(105)	185
concessionary fares	10	35	90	95	(100)	120
roads maintenance	480	485	440	420	(420)	400
administration, etc.	125	135	160	150	(135)	135
Central government support:						
British Rail						
passenger	135	250	325	310	(315)	295
freight	—	—	40	15	(—)	—
National Freight Corporation	15	2	30	25	(—)	—
Grants towards new buses, railway siding, ferries, etc.	10	20	25	30	(30)	30
Motorways and trunk roads:						
construction	485	495	460	370	(425)	380
maintenance	65	100	80	70	(80)	80
Other surface transport programmes: ports, BR pensions, research and central administration, VAT, etc.	105	95	215	205	(160)	160
Total	2,040	2,360	2,620	2,300	(2,200)	2,200
National surface transport industries investment	265	320	325	330	(360)	360
Less investment financed by capital grants included above	15	15	115	125	(120)	120

a. These figures are not comparable with those of Table 5.2 which referred to specifically urban transport expenditure. In the above table, Local Transport expenditure figures include administrative and research costs, as well as non-urban local expenditure which are not included in Table 5.2.

Source: Transport Policy, Cmnd 6836 (HMSO, 1977) p.61

Conclusions

In contrast to housing and land use, the two main political parties in Britain have only quite recently acquired an interest in urban transport policy. Certainly, the parties have long been divided on the question of state intervention in transport generally, and some of the most acrimonious disputes in post-war policy have occurred over transport nationalisation and subsidies. Generally, however, these have been confined to inter-urban rather than urban transport. Only during the Labour Governments of 1964 and 1966 did party dispute over urban transport appear to reach significant proportions — and as has been demonstrated this dispute was more rhetorical than substantive. It is true that the tentative moves towards public transport represented by the 1968 Act were initiated by a Labour Government, although on coming to power in 1970, the Conservatives continued this general policy trend.

Party politics may not have been instrumental in changing policy, but there can be no doubt that policy changed dramatically during the post-war era. The size of government subsidies for urban transport — and especially road transport — increased rapidly from the early 1960s to the early 1970s. Armed with these subsidies, and in partnership with private capital, local authorities have effectively rebuilt significant central areas of a number of British towns and cities. Since 1974 substantial cutbacks in subsidies have occurred and the shift to public transport has become more real than apparent. But, again, it is hard to attribute this change to party politics. Clearly, we will have to look elsewhere for explanations of urban transport policy in the post-war period.

Perhaps implicit in the foregoing analysis is an important role for interest groups. The road lobby along with the motor manufacturers have often been given the credit for the essentially road-based policies dominant in the 1960s,[77] and, on the other side of the political coin, environmental and *ad hoc* action groups have been credited with having successfully pressured government into abandoning road schemes in the 1970s.[78] It is, of course, notoriously difficult to assess the precise role of interest groups in the policy-making process[79] — especially given the complex variety of factors which operate in the formulation of policy. As William Plowden has noted:

It is clear that the influence of the motor interests is at least variable and uncertain. Even apart from this, to explain official policy as a

whole as a product of successful lobbying would be profoundly to
misunderstand the character of British government and the ways in
which decisions on policy ar   — and have been — made.[80]

Plowden then pinpoints the crucial role of civil servants whose
interaction with politicians often occurs independently of external
influence such as that exerted by interest groups.[81] That this is
frequently true of British government is indisputable but at the same
time, civil servants, politicians and interest groups operate in particular
ideological environments which must help shape the extent to which
particular interests are favoured or penalised at any one time. As far as
urban transport is concerned, in the period between 1960 and 1970
ideas were moving rapidly in favour of accommodating the motor car.
Massively increased car ownership with its electoral implications must
have been influential in precipitating this change, as was the ascendent
ethos of civic expansion and redevelopment which were directly aided
by Tory land policies discussed in earlier chapters. In such a climate,
the influence of the road lobby was likely to be considerably greater
than at other times.

   In the same way, professional influence in the shape of information
and advice provided by the Buchanan Report and by planners, surveyors
and highway engineers within local and central government, was
important during a period when governments were highly receptive to
apparent 'solutions' to urban traffic congestion which did not penalise
too strongly the rising ride of car owners. Interestingly, economic
constraints did not prevent the rapid and steady rise in road
expenditure during the 1960s, and even in the early 1970s when the
economic climate became increasingly hostile, road expenditure
continued at almost the same rate of increase as before. No doubt one
reason for this was the perception among civil servants and politicians
of the strategic economic importance of new roads and of the motor
industry. Unlike urban public transport, new roads, both inter-urban
and urban, were viewed as essential to the free movement of goods,
and therefore to the health of the economy.[82] Again, it would be
misleading to attribute this policy to the lobbying efforts of the British
Road Federation and other interested groups. It would be more
accurate to say that the economic and political climate was right for
greatly increased road expenditure.

   Similarly, during the 1970s the apparent success of the anti-urban
road lobby has to be placed in historical context. Economic arguments
in favour of massive road programmes faded as the environmental costs

of such enterprises became increasingly apparent.[83] At the same time, from 1974 in a climate of intensifying national fiscal crisis, it was logical to cut expenditure in an area where political opposition was mounting. It should also be remembered that by 1974/5 the basic inter-urban road network had been completed, and although many urban road schemes were only half complete (in the case of London, hardly begun) the economic arguments for urban roads had never been as strong as for inter-urban highways. The climate was right, therefore, for a cutback in urban road construction.

It would not be inaccurate to claim that urban transport policy since the war has resulted in large part from the interaction of certain ideas about the nature of urban form and urban society, with a complex of economic needs and constraints. In some instances, the central actors have been transport and planning professionals and civil servants in the transport ministries and the Treasury. If the policy agenda has been set by these actors, others — in particular local authorities, politicians, interest groups and the public — have reacted to and often reinforced existing trends. This is not to deny that in some cases party politics have been important — in particular, the trend towards public transport subsidies which was initiated by Labour under the 1968 Transport Act — although meaningful change in this area did not occur until the mid-1970s.

Like so many areas of policy, efforts to integrate urban transport with other aspects of urban policy have been few and far between. During the late 1960s an appreciation of the close linkage between land use and transport policy slowly emerged, and the 1972 Committee recommended strongly a close administrative co-ordination in this area. However, this came to nothing, and references to the integration and co-ordination of transport policy with other urban policies had by 1976 all but passed from the political and bureaucratic vocabulary. It is true that at the local level, the adoption of sophisticated planning techniques have led local authorities to see transport policy in the context of a larger framework involving housing and land use. Public transport policy is now much more advanced in this respect than twenty years ago. However, *national* policy on the interrelationship between transport, housing, land use, and other aspects of urban policy remains remarkably undeveloped. Indeed, the 1970s were notable for the retreat by Labour Governments from the integration of transport modes and of transport services with other urban policies. This is unfortunate, for when problems are seen as interrelated, fundamental questions on the distribution of public goods are inevitably raised. For example, carefully relating the construction of an urban motorway to public transport policies *and* to housing, land-use and economic policies, raises questions of social justice as well as perceived economic need. Asking 'who gets what?' or 'who benefits and who suffers as a result of construction?' is the essence of social planning and is an essential element in any coherent urban policy. Perhaps a major reason why political parties have shied away from such questions is that by emphasising them, their political salience is raised. Interested groups and populations become more aware of their positions and their rights and political battle lines are drawn. This is likely seriously to hamper or to delay the proposed construction as well as to challenge the assumptions on which existing transport policy is based.

Notes

1. See C. McKim Norton, 'Metropolitan Transportation', in G. Breeze and D.E. Whiteman (eds), *An Approach to Urban Planning* (Princeton, Princeton University Press, 1953).

2. Arnold J. Heidenheimer, Hugh Heclo and Carolyn Tech Adams, *Comparative Public Policy: The Politics of Social Choice in Europe and America* (New York, St Martin's, 1975), ch.6.

3. K.M. Gwilliam, *Transport and Public Policy* (London, George Allen and Unwin, 1964), p.87.

4. Ibid., p.86.

5. See Philip S. Bagwell, *The Transport Revolution from 1770* (New York, Barnes and Noble, 1974), ch.9.

6. Ibid., pp.269-70.

7. See the Labour Manifestos of 1918, 1924 and 1931, in F.W.S. Craig, *British General Election Manifestos, 1918-1966* (Chichester, Political Reference Publications, 1970).

8. Bagwell, *Transport Revolution*, p.270.

9. See Gwilliam, *Transport and Public Policy*, chs. 6-11.

10. See Bagwell, *Transport Revolution*, p.304.

11. Alker Tripp, *Town Planning and Road Traffic* (London, Arnold, 1942). References to Tripp's work are based largely on the summary provided by Stephen Plowden, *Towns Against Traffic* (London, Deutsch, 1972), pp.13-22.

12. For a good discussion of Abercrombie's work, see Douglas A. Hart, *Strategic Planning in London: The Rise and Fall of the Primary Road Network* (Oxford, Pergamon Press, 1976), pp.71-87.

13. As reported in Stephen Plowden, *Towns Against Traffic*, p.11.

14. Quoted in William Plowden, *The Motor Car and Politics, 1896-1970* (London, Bodley Head, 1971), p.329.

15. William Plowden's discussion of the influence of the road lobby is excellent, and the following section is partly based on his analysis, ibid., pp.338-95.

16. Ibid.

17. Ibid., p.346.

18. Ibid., pp.346-7.

19. One exception was the demise of the tram and trolley car. Both were seen as inflexible and incompatible with higher road traffic denisities. Their disappearance (significantly, they lasted longest in Scotland where car ownership was low) was hardly a centrally planned policy, however. Municipalities replaced them with buses on a piece-meal basis and according to local conditions.

20. According to a BRF survey, quoted in Plowden, *Motor Car and Politics*, p.370.

21. Ibid., p.349.

22. Ibid., p.350.

23. *Traffic in Towns: A Study of the Long Term Problems of Traffic in Urban Areas*, Reports of the Steering Group and Working Group appointed by the Minister of Transport (London, HMSO, 1963).

24. Ibid., Introduction, p.7.

25. Following Bruce Heady's classification in *British Cabinet Ministers* (London, George Allen and Unwin, 1974); See also Colin Buchanan, 'Traffic in Towns'. in *People and Cities*, Report of the 1963 London Conference organised by the British Road Federation and the TPI (BRS, London, 1963), p.15.

26. *Traffic in Towns*, paras.54-7.

27. *Traffic Engineering and Control*, vol.6 , no.1 (May 1964), p.39, quoted in Stephen Plowden, *Towns against Traffic*, pp.36-7.

28. *Traffic in Towns*, para.116.

29. This is clear from *Traffic in Towns'* treatment of London, ibid., paras.290-371.

30. Stephen Plowden, *Towns against Traffic*, p.41.

31. Hart, *Strategic Planning*, p.88.

32. *People and Cities*.

33. Ibid., 'List of Delegates', pp.281-300.

34. Stephen Plowden, *Towns against Traffic*, p.35.

35. Ibid.

36. William Plowden, *Motor Car and Politics*, p.354.

37. Ibid., p.355.

38. F.W.S. Craig, 'Conservative Election Manifesto, 1964', *British General Election Manifestos*, p.220.

39. 'Labour Election Manifesto, 1964', in Craig, ibid., p.235.

40. Ibid., p.236.

41. William Plowden, *Motor Car and Politics*, p.355.

42. Craig, *Election Manifestos*, pp.235 and 275.

43. *Transport Policy*, Cmnd.3057 (HMSO, July 1966).

44. Ibid., p.12.

45. Ibid., pp.12-13.

46. Ibid., pp.13-14.

47. Ibid., pp.14-15.

48. *Public Transport and Traffic*, Cmnd.3481 (HMSO, December 1967).

49. Ibid., Summary, pp.31-3.

50. *Transport in London*, Cmnd3686 (HMSO, July 1968).

51. William Plowden, *Motor Car and Politics*, pp.355-6, 385-6.

52. Ibid., p.385.

53. H.C. Deb.756 (1968), col.1320.

54. H.C. Deb.756 (1968), col.1282.

55. Ibid., col.1282.

56. The 1967 Fabian pamphlet, *Urban Transport: Public or Private* (Fabian Research Series, No.261) advocated the use of loans to aid public transport and preferred few restrictions on private cars, while the Labour left favoured straight

subsidies and cutbacks in road building.

57. Both the *Economist* and *The Times* attacked the Bill for its emphasis on public transport subsidies.

58. Quoted in *Urban Transport Planning*, 2nd Report from the Expenditure Committee, vol.1, Report and Appendix (London, HMSO, 1972), para.19.

59. Ibid., paras.166-70.

60. See Hart, *Strategic Planning*, ch.5.

61. *Urban Transport Planning.*

62. Ibid., para.104.

63. Ibid., para.45.

64. Ibid., paras. 127-48.

65. 'Better Public Transport Now', *Guardian*, 19 January 1973, p.3.

66. Reported in the *Guardian*, 19 January 1973, p.3.

67. Cmnd.5366 (HMSO, 1973).

68. *Transport Policy: A Consultation Document*, vols. 1 and 2 (HMSO, 1976).

69. Peter Hall, 'Rail, Roads and Pavlov', *New Society*, 16 December 1976, p.561.

70. Ibid., pp.561-2.

71. Ibid., p.561.

72. This is reflected in the language and style of the consultative document's technical sections, *Transport Policy*, vol.2, Technical Papers. For a review of how policy has become more technical and analytical, see D.N.M. Starkie, *Transportation Planning, Policy and Analysis* (Oxford, Pergamon Press, 1976).

73. *Transport Policy*, Cmnd.6836 (HMSO, June 1977).

74. Ibid., para.293.

75. See 'M-Way Rebel Strikes Again', *The Sunday Times*, 12 September 1976, p.2, and *The Times*, 16 September 1976, p.2.

76. See 'Road Objectors: Why the Ministry Arouses Anger', *Sunday Times*, 10 October 1976, p.5.

77. See, for example, the comments by Anthony Wedgwood Benn on p.171.

78. See John Grant, *The Politics of Urban Transport Planning* (Earth Resources Research, 1977); Dilys Hill, *Participating in Local Affairs* (Harmondsworth, Middx., Penguin, 1970), ch.4.

79. Paul E. Peterson, 'British Interest Group Theory Re-examined', *Comparative Politics*, vol.III (1971), pp.381-402. See also, Graham K. Wilson, *Special Interests and Politics* (London, Wiley, 1978).

80. William Plowden, *Motor Car and Politics*, p.39.

81. Ibid.

82. See Martin Buxton, 'Transport', in Rudolf Klein (ed.), *Inflation and Priorities* (London, Centre for Studies in Social Policy, 1975), pp.153-69. Colin Buchanan and Partners, *The Conurbations* (London, British Road Federation, 1969).

83. The 1977 White Paper strongly emphasised the environmental dimension, and stressed that future road schemes should be confined to those where either a clear economic advantage existed, or environmental gains would be reaped (such as with the building of by-passes). *Transport Policy*, para.308.

6 REGIONAL ECONOMIC AND INDUSTF LOCATION POLICIES

There are few things more forlorn than the industrial parks
dedicated by George VI in the late 1930s in the North
Country. The planners seem to have thought that new
industries would set up rather like shopkeepers, all in tiny
spaces along neat village paths. In truth. . .the design of these
centres *declared* that industry was past in that part of Britain.
What governments design, as against what they say, is what
they really mean. (Daniel P. Moynihan, *The Public Interest*,
1978.)

Important differences exist between regional economic and industrial
location policies and the other areas so far covered in this book. For
most of the post-war period politicians and bureaucrats at the national
level have treated industrial location as a discrete issue. Rarely has it
been seen as related to the 'mainstream' urban policies such as housing
and land use. Reflecting this separate status, the Department of the
Environment and its predecessors have not been responsible for
industrial location and regional revival.

However, as was stressed in Chapter 1, regional revival via controls
over industrial location was a major element in post-war reconstruction.
Moreover, in contrast to France and Italy, Britain's regional decline has
mainly affected urban rather than rural settlements, so attempts at
revival must be seen as part of urban policy – even if this has not
always been recognised by politicians. In fact, recent reappraisals of
policy towards the inner city have linked regional policy to other
urban policy issues for the first time and an appreciation of how and
why this change has occurred is important. Finally, irrespective of the
regional dimension, industrial location has a profound effect on urban
structure and form. While the causal links between industrial location
and housing, population and transport patterns are complex, the
relationship between them is indisputably intimate. It is not necessary
to accept every element of Castell's urban theory – which posits the
view that advanced capitalism based on 'collective consumption'
determines spatial forms – to recognise the central importance of
investment patterns for urban society.[1] In this context the present
chapter has three main objectives. First, to summarise the main

industrial location policies pursued by successive governments since 1945; second, to explain why governments have pursued some strategies rather than others; and third, broadly to discuss the relationship between location policies and urban problems — especially those of the inner city.

The Discovery of a Regional Problem and the Failure of Planning: 1930-45

In the 1920s unemployment averaged around one million annually and the depression of the early 1930s sent the figures for the unemployed in the UK above three million. Unfortunate as this was for British society it soon became apparent that the incidence of unemployment was unequally felt across the regions of Britain. Thus, though London and the South-East were experiencing unemployment rates of 15 per cent, the level in the North, North-East and Central Scotland was anywhere between 25 and 35 per cent of those eligible to work.[2]

It is now clear that the government of the day saw this problem of industrial decline in the traditional sectors of the economy as only a temporary phenomenon. There was little appreciation of the fact that the problem of unemployment was not first and foremost a problem of temporary depression but rather a problem of decline in traditional industries caused by inefficiency and lack of competitiveness.[3] The depression of the 1930s appeared in the guise of regional unemployment because traditional industry had been regionally concentrated in the industrial North of England and Scotland. Now, as economic depression hit the Western economies, it was the least efficient and least profitable sectors of the economy which suffered first and closed their doors to employees. Similarly, when the upturn in the economy occurred it was the profitable, competitive modern industries of petro-chemicals, electrical engineering and motor manufacturing that led the way. The traditional industries of shipbuilding, coal mining, textiles and iron and steel production would never again regain their dominant role in the economy.[4] As these new industries were less tied by the need to locate near to sources of raw materials it was inevitable that they would locate near their markets which were increasingly in the South-East and Midlands. Thus, to what appeared as a relatively temporary downturn in demand causing unemployment was added a structural change in the economy.[5]

This was not clear to decision-makers in Government in the 1930s. On the contrary, the idea that the Government should assume assume a major role by intervening to correct imbalances in the economy was likely to be anathema to politicians in the inter-war National Governments.[6] The policies pursued at this time were the complete antithesis of the state intervention and control which would have been necessary to plan the future development of the regions of the economy. Thus policies aimed at balancing the budget and defending the pound dominated. This approach was seen in the infamous cuts in welfare and unemployment benefits and the imposition of means tested welfare benefits.[7]

Some government intervention did occur during the 1930s — mainly to deflect social and political unrest — but the measures adopted were either ill conceived or hopelessly underfunded. Hence the Special Areas (Development and Improvement) Act of 1934 designated industrial South Wales and Scotland, West Cumberland and North-East England as Special Areas in which public works would be initiated. However, stringent expenditure controls and the limitation of the schemes to sewage work and the encouragement of a return to the land doomed the Act to failure. Further *ad hoc* measures were introduced in the 1936 Special Areas Reconstruction (Agreement) Act, which provided loan capital for small businesses through a government agency, and the 1937 Special Areas (Amendment) Act.[8] This latter measure was the first attempt positively to encourage firms to locate in the Special Areas. Treasury loans, public trading estates built for the private sector at favourable rents and rate and income tax benefits for up to five years after location were all provided. The Government also endeavoured to place its own rearmament factories in these areas.

These measures were, however, likely to be of only limited utility since only a sum of £2 million was provided in the way of total loan capital for the Special Areas Loan Committee of the Treasury. The upturn in world trade, rearmament and a boom in consumer goods rather than government measures were the major factors lowering unemployment to the 1¼ million level in 1939. If these measures were limited in their impact on unemployment levels, they were also singularly ineffective in changing the basic economic structures of the regions. It has been estimated that few light engineering firms — the growth industries of the 1930s — developed in the Special Areas at this time. Indeed, the prosperous London area was estimated to have attracted 44 per cent of all new factory development in Britain between 1932 and 1938.[9]

Though the Government of the day was not particularly concerned with intervening to solve the problems of unemployment and regional imbalance, a number of interests and groups were. Local authorities were increasingly concerned with the problems facing their inhabitants and with the ways in which public expenditure cuts reduced their ability to help. At the same time, the trade union movement, though still quiescent after the defeat of the 1926 General Strike, was agitating with the Labour and Liberal Parties for a solution to the unemployment problems.[10] Even younger members of the Conservative Party were looking at ways in which the state might intervene to aid the economy without distorting the role of the private sector.[11] These amorphous pressures for change were largely unorganised and failed to go to the heart of the structural problem of decline. However, they were influential in forcing the Government to act.

It has been argued that many of the experts involved with administering the limited government relief at this time were aware of the interconnected relationship between unemployment, economic decline and regional imbalance.[12] Individuals, like Sir Malcom Stewart (first Special Commissioner for England and Wales) began to argue that the policy of industrial relocation could only work effectively if there was also a control on the prosperous regions. It was realised that it was not enough simply to provide encouragement; industry had to be restrained from locating where it would best prefer if the policy was to work at all. In this, the Special Commissioner and others tapped the nascent vein of positive planning which was exemplified in the Fabian Society and the embryonic planning pressure groups – the TCPA and the TPI.[13] The belief that society could and should be planned to eradicate cankers of deprivation and decline was beginning to gather political support at this time and this, along with the more formal political pressures outlined above, was sufficient to force the Government to appoint a Royal Commission in 1937 to look into the problems of the distribution of the industrial population.

The subsequent *Barlow Report*, published in 1940, did not make the mistake of limiting its analysis of unemployment to the problems of the economy, even though these were crucial.[14] On the contrary, the Report argued that economic and physical developments were fundamentally interrelated and should be planned for together. Thus population, housing, land use and economic forces were all shaped by and interactive upon one another. Barlow argued that the Depressed Areas could not be enhanced without controls on the more prosperous regions and this required an integrated and positive approach to planning which linked together the economic and physical aspects of society. This was indeed the apotheosis of positive planning in Britain so far this century. The Report called for action on three fronts. The less prosperous regions were to be redeveloped, population and industry was to be decentralised from the prosperous areas, and a 'reasonable' balance of industrial development was to be achieved within each individual region.[15]

Unfortunately the promise of the Report was never to be fulfilled after 1945, and the return to an emphasis on unemployment relief in the context of limited dispersal and industrial development control has been the basis of policies ever since. To understand how this came about, and how the integrated planning approach advocated by the Barlow Report was overturned, one must appreciate the role of political forces in shaping policy decisions.

The broad aims of the Report were accepted but there was fundamental disagreement over the methods to be adopted in implementing it. The majority on the Commission sought to follow the 'line of least resistance' politically by allowing the existing President of the Board of Trade to appoint an Advisory and Research Board which would assist him in locating industry and also regulate the location and development of industry in London and the Home Counties. This was a far cry from the intentions written into the Report's analysis and was testament to the lack of real support for these planning goals by a significant section of the Commission. At the same time it also revealed that the majority, at least, were aware of the likely administrative pressures any more radical institutional approach might receive from existing government departments.[16]

The role of the Treasury and the Board of Trade did not, however, deflect three members of the Commission from arguing for a more radical approach:[17] an autonomous Board to be responsible for providing inducements to firms locating in every region of the country along the lines of the former Special Areas Commissioners. This Board would also be responsible for regional boards instituted to administer the responsibilities of the national Board. Even this approach, though attempting to loosen existing institutional bonds, was not as radical as might have been envisaged if the Report's goals were to be fulfilled, because it failed to bring together locational control and regional inducements under one planning body. Nor did it attempt to relate these functions to physical development.

The most radical approach to be suggested and the institutional solution to the goal of integrating economic and physical planning, was outlined by three further Commissioners in a further Minority Report.[18] The Report argued that the town planning functions of the Ministries of Health and Transport, the housing functions of the

Ministry of Health, the inducement powers of the existing Board of Trade, plus the newly envisaged powers of locational control and land-use planning should be amalgamated under a Cabinet Minister in a new Department of State. Although this statement did not really outline a policy for the control of national economic and financial policy in this embryonic Planning Ministry, it seems obvious that this would have been necessary. The fact that Lord Reith (the Minister given responsibility for working out these divergent proposals in the Reconstruction Secretariat during the War) was sacked by Churchill for presuming to intimate that such a development (as well as land nationalisation) might be necessary, is testament to the centrality of organisational infighting and political ideas in shaping policy.[19]

It is fairly clear that the Treasury, Board of Trade and Ministries of Health and Transport were well aware of the potential threat to their own organisational base and functions by the mooted Planning Ministry. Any Ministry responsible for physical planning and locational controls in the micro sectors of the economy would be in a strategic position in the government machine and therefore able to dictate to other departments.[20] This fear, plus the fact that Churchill and many senior Ministers were not themselves as enamoured of state planning as some of their contemporaries, was itself enough to spell the early demise of a central Planning Ministry. Added to this was the fact that under war-time conditions normal party political and interest group activities would be at a minimum allowing the civil service far greater autonomy in determining policy than in normal times.

Whatever the major reason, it was clear by 1944 that though there would be land-use (physical) planning, industrial location control, dispersal policies and regional incentives, these policies would not be co-ordinated together under one administrative arm. As the post-war legislation reveals, the existing departments maintained their responsibilities even as these powers were extended. This meant that due to institutional inertia and political opposition the goal of national and regional planning to solve the problems of economic imbalance, growth and unemployment could not be achieved. A return to *ad hoc* policy and electoral expediency was indicated by the fact that the two parties could only really agree to achieve what no one in 1944 could have rejected: full employment. Thus, though the 1944 Coalition White Paper, *Employment Policy*, has been seen as a major innovation it was in fact a defeat for an integrated economic and physical planning approach to Britain's social and economic problems.[21] While the document alluded to the use of regional economic policies, amongst other things, to solve unemployment problems, the real importance of the White Paper was to concentrate regional policies on solving employment problems whenever rises in unemployment threatened government popularity. To be effective in the context of what Barlow had intended, regional policies for the economy would have been only part of an integrated approach to national-regional-local economic and physical planning. So the unemployment role of post-war regional policies had been created and largely as a result of the political and institutional myopia at the heart of central government decision-making between 1940 and 1945.

By 1945, therefore, industrial location policy had taken on certain distinctive features:

(a) Although some experts recognised the need for a close relationship between physical planning and industrial location, policy during the war years had gradually moved away from this idea at the national level and towards a strict separation of physical from economic planning.

(b) As a policy area industrial location had become virtually synonymous in the minds of politicians and civil servants with the problems of regional imbalance. Inter-regional inequalities and their correction were the main items on the policy agenda. Few thought in terms of intra-regional or intra-conurbation patterns of investment. The failure to combine regional policy with physical planning was likely to compound this bias, for the co-ordination of all planning functions was more likely to reveal complex patterns of industrial change within regions and metropolitan areas.

(c) In the wake of the structural unemployment of the 1920s and 1930s, regional policy had developed into a strategy for the relief of unemployment. As we shall see, this concern rather than a strategy to encourage economic growth, was to have a profound effect on post-war regional policy.

Planning Without Institutional Co-ordination: 1945-7

When Labour returned to office in 1945 it was not really in a position to alter the broad framework already mapped out by the civil service and Coalition Government. Indeed, the first major piece of legislation, the 1945 Distribution of Industry Act, had been largely formulated prior to the July election.[22] This Act did go some way to create the sort of positive state role of assistance for the Depressed Areas which Barlow had intended. The old Special Areas were abolished to be

replaced with larger Development Areas covering Central and North
Eastern Scotland, the North-East, South Wales, Cumbria and parts of
Merseyside and South Lancashire (see Map 6.1).

Map 6.1: The Development Areas: 1945-60

Development Area

The pre-war powers of the old Special Areas for grant aid and loans were maintained in the Board of Trade, which was additionally given powers to build advance factories, reclaim land and improve local infrastructure to encourage new industrial development. Though a new Planning Ministry had not been created and the Treasury and the Board of Trade had maintained their roles in macro and micro-economic policy-making respectively, the 1945 Act did give the state some of the positive interventionist powers that had been intended in the Barlow Report. Clearly, however, the broad aim was one of ameliorating the conditions of unemployment in these areas rather than consciously planning on a national basis.

As a result of raw materials shortages in 1945 the Government also created a licensing system to control the use of materials and to ensure that they were used effectively in the period of reconstruction. In the 1947 Town and Country Planning Act locational controls over all new industrial development over 10,000 sq.ft. (or 10 per cent of the existing industrial site) were instituted. Under this Act the Board of Trade was given responsibility for administering this system of industrial development certificates (IDCs) without which no local authority would grant planning permission for new industrial development. By 1947, therefore, it was clear that a form of regulatory locational control for the whole of the country had been created, supplemented by limited positive powers for the Development Areas. In this way, Barlow's advocacy of controls over employment opportunities in the prosperous areas was supported by aid for firms locating in the less advantaged regions of the country. But by failing to create a Planning Ministry, neither national economic or financial policy nor physical policies (which were with the separate Ministries of Town and Country Planning, Health and Transport) were to be co-ordinated with these largely micro-economic powers. Without such co-ordination, it was unclear how the Board of Trade could ever effectively fulfil its obligation to solve regional imbalance and thereby create a balanced distribution of industry within each region.[23]

The Labour Government on entering office in July 1945 was committed to a programme of policies aimed at nationalising certain crucial sectors of the economy. Though many Labour and trade union activists saw this as the first step on the road to a socialist society, this programme of increased state intervention was in fact the limit to which Labour thinking had developed on the role of the state in the economy.[26] For many leaders it was clear that once this policy had been implemented then they had very little idea of what was to follow.

Given this intellectual redundancy at the heart of the Labour movement it was inevitable that, in the period when the initial enthusiasm for office and policy innovation had wained, established actors and relationships would reassert themselves in the policy process.

Thus, though the Labour Party was more committed than any of the other parties to a planned economy, their concentration on nationalising the heavy industrial sector rather than reconstructing the economy allowed the Treasury and other established departments to maintain their existing boundaries of responsibility. Therefore, the Labour and Barlow goal of a planned economy would now be increasingly difficult to achieve.[27] Since much of the initial post-war support for the Labour Party had stemmed from the perceived failure of the Conservative Government to solve the problems of unemployment and depression in the 1930s, and because most of Labour's support was resident in the Development Areas, it is not surprising that the Labour Government used the building licence system extensively to ensure that a large proportion of new development was located in the Development Areas to assist employment rather than planning goals. The Government also encouraged the Board of Trade to use its IDC controls vigorously in the pursuit of this aim, as well as converting munitions factories in the regions for the use of new industry on favourable terms.[28]

The lack of a coherent direction in Labour policies and the increasing reliance on existing institutional practices and perceptions was plainly seen by 1947. The balance of payments crisis of that year led to a return to established Treasury orthodoxies relating to sound financial policy. In other words, in order to protect sterling, a policy of public expenditure cuts, plus a voluntary incomes policy, was introduced. The idea of solving the problems of the economy by a policy of national planning for growth and economic reconstruction had been defeated in the face of an attachment to sound money policies at the centre of the policy process.[29] The consequences for regional policy were quickly apparent. All advance factory construction was curtailed in 1947 and Board of Trade expenditure on factories fell by a half. Only 17 per cent of new industrial development in Britain was located in the Development Areas between 1948 and 1950 compared with over 50 per cent between 1945 and 1947.[30] In a crisis therefore, entrenched and established departments at the centre of the policy-making process would be bound to dictate policy to a government which lacked a clear policy. As a consequence, Conservative and Labour Government positions between 1947 and 1960 bore a striking similarity to one another.

Regional Policies in an Era of Full Employment: 1947-60

As we saw, any attachment to the planning and growth rationale for regional policies was finally rescinded by the Labour Government in the 1947 balance of payments crisis. As a consequence of this, until the Conservative Government's reappraisal of 1963, regional policies were to be limited to reacting to the needs of electoral expediency in the context of rising or falling unemployment. Any last vestige of the integrated planning approach was to be destroyed by continuing prosperity and relatively full employment in the 1950s.

As a result of the 1947 crisis, exports became a more important objective for the Labour Government than locational problems, and this new emphasis was aided by the fact that unemployment levels continued to fall from almost 400,000 in 1946 to just over 200,000 in 1951. Given that unemployment rather than planning was to be the major objective of government action in the regions there was less need to assist positively the Development Areas. This new direction was to be seen in the period of 'bonfire of controls' by Harold Wilson at the Board of Trade after 1947. What this meant in effect was that building licence controls were gradually phased out and the IDC system was relaxed. The emphasis was now to be on encouraging any and all industries to develop where and how they felt fit if this assisted the push for export growth. Only in 1950 was there a return to more limited assistance for the less prosperous areas under the Distribution of Industry Act of that year. This Act, which empowered the Board of Trade (with Treasury consent) to provide further grant aid and loan capital to firms locating in the Development Areas and to assist financially with the housing and resettlement of key workers, exemplified the close connection between regional policies and unemployment which rose above 300,000 temporarily in 1950.

The return of Churchill's Conservative Government was hardly likely to result in a move to the planned restructuring of the British economy. The Conservative leadership was opposed to planning and the new government was committed to further cuts in public expenditure and state controls. As a result, the new Government further relaxed IDC controls and in 1954 abolished building licences altogether.[31]

So, though the new Government did not abolish the Development Areas and IDC system, it failed to use the controls available to it to alter the balance between the prosperous and less developed regions.

This was amply revealed by the fact that between 1956 and 1960 the Development Areas obtained only 11.5 per cent of new jobs compared to the South-East's 58.2 per cent.[32] The Conservative Government was therefore able, due to a combination of rising prosperity and industrial production and falling unemployment, to ignore the need to restructure the economy and end the dependence of the Development Areas on traditional industries. In a sense, they were not forced to confront this problem because a boom had taken place in these very industries (coal, steel and shipbuilding) in the 1950s.[33]

It was also true, however, that the Conservative Government was opposed to a larger state role at this time and unlikely, even in periods of rising unemployment, to conceive of the state's function in terms of restructuring the economy. Any assistance, when it was unavoidable, would be aimed at limited aid to existing firms and small inducements to new firms locating in areas of unemployment. Unemployment, not planning for higher growth and efficiency, would be the catalyst for action, and in this approach the Government was aided by the fact that the Labour Opposition and the trade union movement were also bankrupt in terms of innovative ideas on regional and national economic policy. The Labour Party spent the mid-1950s arguing over the rectitude of further nationalisation and controls. The trade unions, in a period of relatively sustained economic growth and low unemployment, were unlikely to question existing policies.[34] Unfortunately, even when unemployment rose at the end of the decade, neither of these actors would argue for anything more than specific aid for the areas of unemployment as opposed to the overall structural needs of the economy.

The response of the Conservative Government to the ending of the post-war boom in 1958 (when unemployment rose to half a million in 1959) was therefore predictable. IDC controls were tightened everywhere, but in the Development Areas a return was made in 1959 to the building of advance factories. In addition the 1958 Distribution of Industry (Industrial Finance) Act added 'Development Places' of especially high unemployment to the existing Development Areas,[35] which were eligible for special grant aid and loans after Treasury and Board of Trade approval. It is, of course, notoriously difficult to demonstrate convincingly the precise link between government policies and electoral circumstances. Certainly, an election was due before May 1960 and with unemployment rising in 1958, the Government's regional policy may well have been motivated by electoral expediency. Whatever the motivations, the employment focus of the new policies had very little to do with the Barlow Report's emphasis on integrated restructuring of the national and regional economy.

Conservative Reappraisal: 1960-4

On returning to power, the Conservatives at first continued the employment focus of existing policies. Indeed, their first piece of regional legislation, the 1960 Local Government Act, revealed the way in which the Barlow goal of an ideal pattern of industrial and physical distribution had been diluted until unemployment relief was the primary goal of policy. The Act swept away the former Development Areas of the 1945 Act and replaced them with Development Districts based on those local employment exchange areas with the 4½ per cent rate of unemployment (Map 6.2). Within these districts the old Board of Trade inducement powers to new industry were improved. Building grants based on 85 per cent of the difference between the cost of construction and a property's value on completion were to be given, and the old Development Area industrial estates companies were abolished and replaced by three Industrial Estate Management Corporations in England, Scotland and Wales.[36]

Any notion of regional balance or economic restructuring was now rejected by Reginald Maudling at the Board of Trade as the post-1960 policy assisted those areas, wherever they might be, which were suffering unemployment. The criterion from 1960 would be 'need' rather than 'potential' for growth and regional revival.[37] This Act marked, therefore, the first major break with post-Barlow legislation. The Conservative Government reverted to the aim of limited assistance on a purely selective basis with no overall co-ordination or integration. The other major difference with the 1960 approach was that it was more heavily funded and allowed the state a more positive, if limited, interventionist role.

Ironically this reorientation came at a time when the pendulum of policy was to swing very quickly in the opposite direction, for professional economists were beginning to discuss the idea of 'growth-point' (or pole) regional development.[38] One of the major factors shaping Conservative policy in 1960 was the realisation that cities like Edinburgh and Manchester were prosperous within the regions obtaining government assistance. On the other hand there were areas, like the South-West, which suffered high unemployment but were not eligible for aid under the 1945 Act. The 1960 Act sought to discriminate therefore on the basis of need across the country as a whole to deal *only* with unemployment. Economists, however, realised (or at least have argued the case)[39] that if unemployment and growth were to be harnessed together in regions then it was necessary to concentrate mainly on their prosperous centres in order that their continuing and enhanced prosperity would draw additional job opportunities to these regions as a whole. The corollary of this was of course that there were some declining areas which would have to be left to die naturally because there was no hope of their revival. This was the antithesis of the policy being adopted by the government in 1960 which sought mainly to help the areas which were in decline.

There were other 'straws in the wind' during this period which would assist a reappraisal of policy. The Macmillan Government, realising the relatively poor growth rates experienced by Britain since 1945, had, in 1961, unsuccessfully applied for membership of the EEC. This application had in itself generated a degree of national introspection which would have been unthinkable in the 1950s. One consequence of this was the study of French indicative planning leading to arguments that this approach would solve Britain's economic problems.[40] In a sense, the French approach was nothing more than a continental version of Barlow. The French Plans were however primarily economic rather than physical/economic in character.[41] This growing clamour by economists and some politicians for a more active governmental role in the regions was also assisted by the fact that in 1962 and 1963 unemployment rose from 300,000 to well over half a million.

Added to these broad economic trends, developments on the political front were increasingly propelling the Government towards a change in policy. Macmillan and Selwyn Lloyd, the Chancellor, had created the tripartite National Economic Development Council (NEDC) in 1961 in an attempt to get both sides of industry talking together and with the Government, about the needs of the economy. This body, which was the Conservative response to demands from the Federation of British Industry (FBI) for French style planning and trade union demands for an end to poor growth and high unemployment, was itself to come out in favour of a return to regional planning and growth areas.[42] The 1963 NEDC paper, *Conditions Favourable for Faster Growth*, pointed to the need for 'growth points' in larger Development Areas, within a National Indicative Plan, as one means of solving the national economic problem. The idea, as in Barlow, was to maximise employment opportunities in the depressed areas in order to use the under-employed workforce to increase national growth. It was estimated that a 50 per cent reduction in regional disparities would lead

Map 6.2: Development Districts: 1960

Development District

to a 1.3 per cent increase in national economic growth.[43] Thus, though the NEDC did not really call for the integration of physical and economic developments, a return to planning with a regional dimension was indicated.

There were, of course, other forces operating at this time and these, arguably, were of potentially more significance than NEDC or Macmillan's hopes of future planning.[44] Though the Conservatives had obtained an increased majority in 1959 they had fared badly in the North-East and Scotland, areas with endemic unemployment continuing deprivation. It was clear by 1963 that, with unemployment continuing to hit these areas disproportionately, the Conservatives' chances at the next election would be even worse.[45] This in part helps explain why a Scottish Development Department had been created in 1962 to co-ordinate all physical planning responsibilities under the Scottish Office.[46] The creation of this agency added a further institutional pressure for a regional/area dimension to be adopted. At the same time, economists like Cairncross and Tothill had completed work on the problems of growth and unemployment in Scotland, and Odber had done the same for the North-East.[47]

These varied political pressures in a period of economic dislocation and relatively high unemployment, with a general election approaching, probably forced the Government to act. Unfortunately the Government, due in part to the problem associated with back-bench Conservative hostility to state intervention in the economy, was unable or unwilling fully to accept the goal of indicative planning.[48] The Government's response was to 'fall between two stools'. In 1963 it acted on two fronts: it extended selective assistance for the areas of unemployment in the country as a whole, and accepted the 'growth areas' approach in Scotland and the North-East.

In line with the 1960 Act, the 1963 Local Employment Act sought to aid all districts with high unemployment throughout the country. The emphasis was to extend capital grants (10 per cent of the costs of machinery and plant, and 25 per cent of the costs of buildings) in the Development Districts when this would lead to extra employment. As a supplement to this the 1963 Budget also made provision for 'accelerated depreciation'. This was a further capital based measure allowing firms in Development Districts to reduce their tax liability in new investment in plant and machinery to zero until the full cost of the investment had been recovered.[49]

This selectivist, capital intensive approach was supplemented by an acceptance of special aid for the North-East and Central Scotland. In

January 1963 Lord Hailsham was appointed as 'Minister with special responsibility for the North-East' and at the same time the Scottish Development Office was given responsibility to draw up a regional plan in a new Scottish Development Group.[50] These Regional Plans, emphasising that the 'growth-point' approach be adopted, resulted in White Papers in the autumn of 1963 and the transfer of Edward Heath to hold the new office of Secretary of State for Industry Trade and Regional Development and President of the Board of Trade. One of his acts was to set up a Regional Development Division to prepare similar plans for the country as a whole.

In spite of these important innovations which came just before the General Election of March 1964, the old primacy of unemployment relief, with growth and restructuring coming a poor second was the main characteristic of this period. The main emphasis was on selective, limited assistance to areas of high unemployment, buttressed by 'growth-point' policies in the areas of highest unemployment which might generate electoral problems. This was not the coherent and integrated approach of either the positive (Barlow), or indicative (NEDC), planning variety. Though the Scottish and Hailsham Plans indicated that there was a mismatch between physical and economic planning, and that selectivity nationally was detrimental to a policy of aiding economic restructuring, the policies adopted in 1963 did not indicate that the Government was prepared to put growth and integrated planning above the short-term electoral and political benefits to be gained from being seen to be doing something about unemployment.

Labour and the Second Failure of Regional Planning: 1964-6

At least as judged by the employment criterion, it was clear by 1964 that regional policies had failed (see Table 6.1). Instilled with a new resolve to solve the regional problem, the Labour Government produced a variety of initiatives in the period between 1964 and 1966. For a variety of reasons, however, these efforts failed to transform the position of the regions. Indeed, as Table 6.1 shows, the relative position of the poorer regions was no better in 1966 than in 1962.

One of the boldest initiatives of the period was the creation of a Department of Economic Affairs (DEA) responsible for national planning and growth. Theoretically, at least, the DEA was to be responsible for long term economic strategy while the Treasury managed the short term financial needs of the economy. The problem for the DEA in this respect was that, given the emphasis on the short-

Table 6.1: Unemployment Rates in the Regions: 1960-70 (%)

	1960	1961	1962	1963	1964	1965	1966	1967	1968	1969	1970
South East	1.0	1.0	1.3	1.6	1.0	(0.9	1.0	1.7	1.6	1.6	1.6
East Anglia						(1.3	1.4	2.1	2.0	1.9	2.2
South West	1.7	1.4	1.7	2.1	1.5	1.6	1.8	2.5	2.5	2.7	2.9
East Midlands	1.0	1.1	1.6	2.0	1.0	0.9	1.1	1.8	1.9	2.0	2.3
West Midlands						0.9	1.3	2.5	2.2	2.0	2.3
Yorkshire and Humberside						1.1	1.2	2.1	2.6	2.6	2.9
North West	1.9	1.6	2.5	3.1	2.1	1.6	1.5	2.5	2.5	2.5	2.7
North	2.9	2.5	3.7	5.0	3.3	2.6	2.6	4.0	4.7	4.8	4.8
Wales	2.7	2.6	3.1	3.6	2.6	2.6	2.9	4.1	4.0	4.1	4.0
Scotland	3.6	3.1	3.8	4.8	3.6	3.0	2.9	3.9	3.8	3.7	4.3
Northern Ireland	6.7	7.5	7.5	7.9	6.6	6.1	6.1	7.7	7.2	7.3	7.0
United Kingdom	1.7	1.6	2.1	2.6	1.7	1.5	1.6	2.5	2.6	2.5	2.7

Source: Jacques Leruez, *Economic Planning and Politics in Britain* (London, Martin Robertson, 1975), adapted from data on p.155.

term in British government and administration, it was inevitable that longer term calculations would be continually prey to modification in the light of short-term financial expediency.[51] As is now clear, the embryonic National Plan itself was eventually overtaken by the need for public expenditure cuts to defend sterling in 1965 and 1966.[52]

If the National Plan was defeated by inter-departmental conflict then the goals of regional planning and an integrated economic and physical approach were also similarly overturned — though not by Treasury dictate. The DEA was given responsibility for regional planning (though not for IDCs) in 1964, taking over these functions from the Board of Trade. To make this system work it would have been necessary to ensure that a regional tier of administration and government was created, both to advise on and to implement national and regional plans. The problem with this was that such an approach would have immediately questioned existing local authority/central government relationships. This would have been less of a problem had these responsibilities been with the DEA: they were unfortunately in the Ministry of Housing and Local Government (MHLG). We have seen elsewhere (Chapter 3) how this Ministry and its Permanent Secretary

(Evelyn Sharp) were able to defend themselves against similar threats to their responsibilities from the new Ministry of Land. It was clear that the MHLG would not be willing to countenance such a new departure.[53]

In response to this opposition the DEA was only able to create *advisory* regional boards consisting of civil servants representing and co-ordinating the work of the Whitehall Departments which had responsibilities in the regions. In addition, Regional Councils consisting of representatives from local authorities, trade unions and industry, as well as expert planners and academics were created.[54] While these bodies did draw up regional development plans, the fact that they were administrative and advisory structures without powers to implement policy led to their being largely ignored. It is clear that civil servants on the Boards were more prone to think of problems in terms of their own department's needs rather than those of the region. In this way the regional strategy was largely undermined before it began. Nor was it assisted by the fact that the National Plan had finalised before the Boards and Councils had the opportunity to meet and discuss their future potential. Ironically, by the time these bodies began to report in 1965 and 1966 the National Plan had been destroyed by national financial crisis.[55]

The DEA was eventually wound up in 1969, with its responsibilities passing to the Treasury, Ministry of Technology and Ministry of Housing and Local Government.[56] In retrospect, the DEA's demise is not surprising given the failure to provide the institutional framework necessary to co-ordinate economic and physical aspects of development. Small wonder that there was a mismatch of effort as both the DEA and MHLG commissioned studies, plans and strategies. The DEA plans emphasised the economic future and the MHLG studies the physical environment.[57] MHLG control of physical development was further emphasised in the 1965 Control of Office and Industrial Development Act. The Act attempted to extend the Government's dispersal policy by creating an Office Development Permit (ODP) system for London and the South-East: any future office development in these areas would first require an ODP. This was an extension of the IDC system to office development in response to the boom in white collar and office employment in the 1950s and 1960s. Ironically, this one opportunity to bring physical and economic policies together was lost. Rather than the Board of Trade supplementing its IDC powers, responsibility for ODPs was given to the MHLG. The DEA, which had encouraged the original ban on any new office development in London in November 1964, was not given either of these powers even though they were, arguably, central to any regional planning approach.

By 1966, with the demise of the National Plan and the failure to co-ordinate economic and physical planning, Labour's attempt at indicative planning was also at an end. This unfortunately also meant that Labour's bold attempt to put regional economic growth and reconstruction at the centre stage of policy-making had failed. From 1966 onwards the Government would increasingly revert to the policy of considering the social and political aspects of unemployment first and growth and reconstruction second — if at all.

Labour and Indiscriminate Regional Aid: 1966-70

With the demise of the indicative planning approach in 1966 and the need to do something to aid the regions and deflect the criticism of the left-wing of the Party, Labour decided to resurrect its traditional approach to regional unemployment.[58] It therefore abolished the highly selective Development Districts and returned to the much broader concept of Development Areas. As before, these areas would include some prosperous and some poorer localities. Unlike the Conservative emphasis on selectivity and helping only the district suffering from unemployment 'need', Labour was prepared to give indiscriminate aid to large areas whether they had pockets of prosperity or not. In this way Labour also rejected the 1964 Conservative reappraisal favouring 'growth-point' assistance in Central Scotland and the North-East. There would be little emphasis on growth potential after 1966.

The explanation for this indiscriminate approach is fairly simple. Even if it does not make much economic sense to give aid to areas which are never likely to prosper (whatever the level of financial aid from the Government), Labour Governments are always likely to pursue these incongruous policies because of their political base and ideological commitment. The Party at an emotive or ideological level — goaded by the conscience of its left-wing — is committed to easing the lot of the working man. This means that it is difficult for the Party when in office to be seen to be pursuing policies which might be interpreted as an attack on traditional Labour supporters' livelihoods. So, while a policy of aiding those prosperous regions with the greatest growth potential might make economic sense, it does not make much political sense for Labour Governments. This also explains why it is that legislation after 1966 was indiscriminate. Labour dominated local authorities are disproportionately found in disadvantaged areas of the country. Indeed, it is probably true to argue that most of the areas which would be left to die under a 'growth-point' policy would be disproportionately Labour in political complexion. Any policy which would seem to discriminate against these areas would not only create tremendous conflict between local and central government but it would also, presumably, alienate the local electorate from the national and local party.

As a consequence, the 1966 Industrial Development Act returned to assisting less prosperous regions on a largely indiscriminate basis. The new Development Areas were larger than those under the 1945 Act and covered 40 per cent of the land area, and 20 per cent of the population of Britain (Map 6.3). The indiscriminate nature of the aid was revealed not only in the area covered but also in the fact that tax incentives were abolished and replaced by cash grants for investment. Labour was antipathetic to tax incentives and allowances because they were only available to profitable firms. The new system, which abolished 'free depreciation' and tax allowances, was based on a cash grant every time a firm made an investment. These grants were available in the country as a whole, but the rate in the Development Areas was 40 per cent whereas the maxium elsewhere was only 20 per cent. The Development Areas also had additional benefits of 25 per cent building grants and 85 per cent grants for land reclamation. Finally, the 1966 Act extended the use of IDCs to storage and scientific research buildings, and the level of permissible development in the South-East and Midlands before applying for an IDC was reduced from 5,000 to 1,000 sq.ft. These latter measures indicated that Labour was now more prepared to use IDC controls than the previous Conservative Government and also that the Government was at least aware of the fact that the scientific and tertiary sector of the economy had outgrown manufacturing throughout the 1950s and was also, therefore, in need of control. Interestingly, educational establishments were not controlled even though they were in a period of major growth.[59]

Having laid this framework for regional economic policies, as unemployment rose, Labour had little alternative but to assist those areas in most need. The thrust of the 1966 Act had been to encourage regional dispersal to aid unemployment, and in the context of continuing high unemployment in the regions after 1966 a further series of measures were introduced.

Cash grants were raised to 45 per cent in 1967, Selective Employment Tax (SET) was introduced in 1966 and was supplemented by the Regional Employment Premium (REP) in 1967. SET was introduced to encourage manufacturing by allowing employers in

Map 6.3: The Expanded Development Areas: 1966-71

Development Area
Intermediate Area
Special Development Area

manufacturing, across the country as a whole, to claim back the value of this tax plus a premium of 7s 6d for every male employee in work each week. After 1967 this premium was paid to employers only in the Development Areas following public expenditure cut backs after devaluation. In the same vein, REP further assisted the Development Areas by giving an extra 30s per week to employers for every employee in manufacturing work. By these means the Government hoped to encourage labour intensive industry as well as to induce manufacturing firms to locate in the depressed areas. While the Government understood the need to encourage manufacturing industry, it seriously underestimated the forces at work favouring the growth of some parts of the tertiary sector. Indeed, between 1965 and 1975 employment in manufacturing as a whole declined by 12.5 per cent.[60]

It was also becoming increasingly obvious that the Development Areas were far too arbitrary a category for aid. They contained some quite affluent cities (such as Aberdeen and Inverness) as well as badly depressed conurbations (such as Glasgow) and declining coal mining communities. In addition, a variety of communities *outside* the Development Areas were experiencing as high or higher levels of unemployment as communities within them. In response to these anomalies, the Government introduced Special Development Areas covering parts of West Cumbria, Lancashire, South Wales, North-East England and Central Scotland in 1967 providing special additional help for industry (see Map 6.3).

Partly in response to this new distinction between Development Areas and Special Development Areas, local authorities in Lancashire, South and East Yorkshire and the South-West began to lobby the Government arguing that in periods of rising unemployment they too were deserving of help. Indeed, their case was a good one. Cities like Hull were clearly experiencing more difficulties than some of the relatively affluent service centres such as Aberdeen and Edinburgh. A committee of inquiry was called (the Hunt Committee on the Intermediate Areas)[61] which when it reported in 1969 recommended that parts of South and East Yorkshire as well as most of the North-West should be designated Intermediate Areas. The Committee also advocated at least a partial return to the 'growth point' approach by suggesting that with the aid of incentives similar to those available in the Development Areas, the Intermediate Areas should become growth centres within their sub-regions. This involved 'downgrading' some of the existing Development Areas (such as Merseyside) to Intermediate status. Such a step would, of course, have been politically very difficult for Labour to take, and when the Intermediate Areas concept was adopted (under the 1970 Local Employment Act) no change was made in the status of existing Development Areas. Instead some incentive aid was provided for seven small areas in the North-East, Lancashire, North Humberside, South-East Wales, Plymouth, Leith, and the Yorkshire, Nottingham and Derbyshire coal fields (see Map 6.3).

The major innovations in regional policy from 1966 – the extension of the areas eligible for support, the introduction of SET and REP, and the appreciation that variations within declining areas existed – were all evidence of the Government's bias towards employment based solutions to regional revival. It is true that the creation of the Special Development Areas showed some appreciation of the varied pattern of industrial change within the regions, but as we will later demonstrate it was a crude device given the complexity of change not only within the regions but throughout the United Kingdom. As before, no attempt was made in this period to examine investment and employment trends *within* conurbations; and at the national level regional policy remained largely detached from policies in housing and land use.

The Conservative Regional Rationalisation and 'U' Turn, 1970-4

As we saw in earlier chapters, the 1970 Heath Government embarked on a variety of social and economic policies based on selectivism rather than universalism and incentive rather than blanket subsidy. Regional policy proved to be no exception. Rationalising the industrial base of regions became the key objective, with employment considerations taking second place. Hence in the White Paper of October 1970, *Investment Incentives*,[62] investment grants were replaced by tax allowances. In addition, REP was to be phased out, and SET replaced by Value Added Tax. The rationale of this approach was clearly to encourage further efficient firms while forcing the inefficient either to rationalise or to 'go to the wall'.[63] Regional aid was also to be provided by the maintenance of building grants which were raised from 25 to 35 per cent in the Development Areas, and from 35 to 45 per cent in the Special Development Areas. This policy further underlined the desire to concentrate on capital subsidy rather than the now rejected labour subsidy of SET and REP. To support this general move to rationalisation greater emphasis was placed on individual firms locating where *they* wanted – which was achieved by the relaxation of ODP and IDC controls. This was somewhat incongruous given that the Government had attempted to improve regional balance by ensuring that service industries in the Development Areas should receive only the national, as opposed to (higher) regional, tax allowances.

Apart from this, the major thrust of Conservative policy in 1970 was logical and fairly clear. The Government was not rejecting regional assistance, since it maintained the previous Development, Special Development and Interm_diate Area division. However, the approach from 1970 was confined largely to helping only those who could help themselves.

Clearly the new Government was able to overcome the difficult political choices which have always forced Labour to reject the most economically logical solution. The Heath Government was also, presumably, well aware of the need to solve the problem of the declining traditional industrial base of British industry. Unfortunately, because of contradictions in its own policies and a crisis, in part generated by external forces, this approach had to be summarily rejected in 1972.

In 1970 unemployment was relatively static at around the half million mark and the Government was able to introduce the bulk of its economic measures. From 1970 on, unemployment began to rise until, in 1973, it was over 800,000. This trend was to make the operation of the Conservative 'Selsdon' approach unworkable. The Government, though less tied to aiding areas of high unemployment poltically, could not in a period of high unemployment and rising inflation totally ignore the situation. Having no short-term measures to counter these trends, the Government was forced to resort to traditional methods of assisting the declining industries whether they were profitable or not. This meant a return in 1972 to the recently rejected Labour approach of investment grants and massive state aid.

It is probably true that, though external forces played a crucial role in the policy 'U-turn', the approach initially adopted by the new Government in part contributed to the need to rethink regional policies. The unprecedented rise in commodity prices, and later the rise in oil prices, all contributed to the costs of production for firms.[64] With the costs of production rising it was inevitable that the least efficient firms in the economy, which were disproportionately located in the declining regions, would be the first to face collapse and have to close. This process, fuelled by inflationary pressures and a declining rate of profit,[65] would also have the effect of raising the levels of unemployment. Of itself this would not have been a problem since it was broadly in line with what the Government had intended: inefficient and non-competitive firms were forced either to rationalise or to die.

Unfortunately for the Government it had not been expected that this process would generate the levels of unemployment that it did — nor that it would affect some of the largest industrial concerns in the country. The need to assist British Leyland, Rolls Royce and the Upper Clyde Shipbuilders had not been part of the Government's scenario: these were firms which were supposed to be able to compete and look after themselves.[66]

By 1971 it was clear that regional unemployment was growing to levels which would soon become politically intolerable. Since the Government was also involved at this time with politically contentious industrial relations legislation, it was only a matter of time before it would have to act.[67] Under the 1972 Industry Act, therefore, the Government reintroduced investment grants under the new title of Regional Development Grants which were payable to the Development Areas and Special Development Areas at the level of 20 and 22 per cent respectively for building, plant and machinery investment. The Intermediate Areas were to obtain 20 per cent grants in respect of buildings only. These grants were to be in addition to the existing tax allowances and free depreciation which were extended by an allowance for 100 per cent free depreciation in the first year on all investment in plant and machinery throughout the country. At the same time, IDC controls were raised to a level of 15,000 sq.ft. of permissible development before IDC application became necessary — except within the South-East Planning Region where the limit was raised from 5,000 to 10,000 sq.ft. IDCs were, furthermore, to be waived for all development in Development and Special Development Areas. Finally, Intermediate Area status was extended to the North-West, Yorkshire and Humberside Planning Regions (see Map 6.4).[67] The Act instituted some important administrative changes. A new Minister for Industry was created with responsibility for attracting industry to the Development areas. To aid this purpose an Industrial Development Executive was created which was to be responsible for administering the new regional development grants and specific selective aid written into the Act. At the same time, an Industrial Development Board was formed to advise on problems and priorities. Within each of the regions of Scotland, Wales, the North, North-West, South-West and Yorkshire and Humberside, a Regional Industrial Director was instituted who was directly responsible to the new Minister for Industrial Development within the DTI and who was to be assisted in the administration of regional aid and subsidies by a Regional Industrial Development Board. These Regional Boards were to fulfil the same advisory role as that

Map 6.4: The Assisted Areas: 1972-7

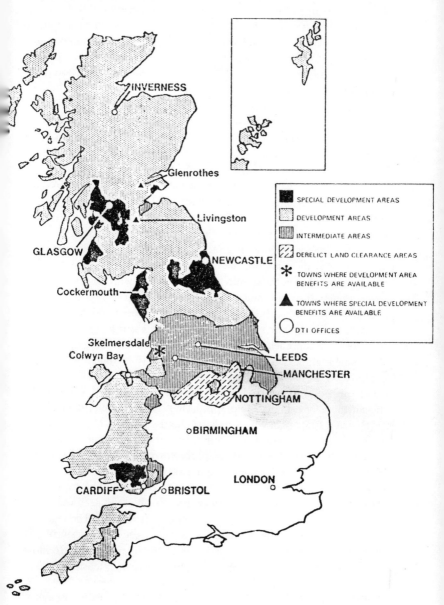

undertaken by the national Board. In particular, they were to assist the Regional Director make decisions concerning applications for the selective aid written into the Act. This regional structure was also given 'teeth' for the first time since each Director was to have autonomy in allocating up to £500,000 in state aid. It can be argued that the 1972 volte-face was one in which both the scope and method of government regional policies changes substantially. There would be a return to investment grants and a new regional structure would assist in regional growth across a broader spectrum of the nation's economy. It would not be true, however, to argue that the overall Conservative goal of 1970 had been rescinded.

The initial Conservative conception had been that the private sector should rationalise itself so that increased efficiency would be introduced into the varied regional economies. The aim of policy after 1972 was still ostensibly the same. The regional economies would be encouraged to rationalise and become more competitive, but now through government choosing 'growth centres' within the regions on a selective basis. This was the real rationale for the new regional DTI structure: the aim was to allow those individuals conversant with each region the means to help the Government choose 'winners' for its regional assistance. Once more, this aid would be given irrespective of whether or not this reduced unemployment. Indeed, it is worth emphasising that the 1972 approach was premised on the understanding that Government aid was *not* to be tied specifically to job creation. On the contrary, as the legislation reveals, all of the cash grants were to be for capital projects rather than labour intensive schemes. This was, arguably, the antithesis of earlier Labour approaches. Labour after 1966 had developed a strategy based on indiscriminate capital and labour aid across the Development Areas, with selectivity based on unemployment 'needs' criteria. The Conservative approach was subtly different. Within a broadly indiscriminate capital aid programme for all the Development Areas, the 1972 Act sought to give selectivity for growth through further *capital* grants; job creation for those in need was not to be the primary function of this increased financial aid. The real aim was to defend the industrial base from collapse in a crisis until those firms which would and could help themselves responded to more favourable conditions. The policy was, therefore, an extension of the rejected 1963 'growth-point' approach on a larger scale.

This point is important because it underlines the fact that though the Conservative Government was responding to various pressures — rising unemployment, TUC and Confederation of British Industry (CBI) demands for action, rising inflation and a declining industrial base — its policies still maintained their own peculiar stamp.[68] Rather than simply returning to the policies of its predecessor, once the initial policy package had failed the Government attempted to maintain its overall goal even though conditions had changed. This underlines the fact that there are real, if subtle, differences between the parties when they come into office. However, this cannot be taken too far because it may well be the case that the most striking factor in British policy making is the similarity which the parties show in what they *reject* as viable alternatives for policy. An integrated and positive economic and physical planning system is arguably one of the policy options which falls into this category of political 'non-starters'. The Conservative Government between 1972 and 1974 was, however, forced to retreat from its reconstruction ideal and to return to *ad hoc* unemployment relief due to the continuous rise in unemployment. This had been partially seen in the 1972 Industry Act's providing finance for extra job-training schemes by increasing grants to firms providing jobs in the Development and Special Development Areas. In February 1972 these measures were supplemented by a Department of Employment, Training Opportunities Scheme, which was to be financed for four years at a cost of £100 million to provide more training centres and allowances. These limited measures were further assisted by the 1973 Employment Agencies Act which established a licensing system for such agencies, and the 1973 Employment and Training Act which rationalised the administration of unemployment and job creation by creating the quasi-public agencies: the Manpower Services Commission, the Employment Services Agency and the Training Services Agency. By these various means it was intended that job placement and retraining would be less inefficient and more able to speed the process of finding a job.

The period 1970 to 1974 is, therefore, instructive because it reveals the degree to which Governments are able to maintain an independent direction in regional policies. Clearly, the Conservatives' initial approach was long-term and did not really have the opportunity to work because of external pressures. However, these were inconsistencies in the policy. The 1971 reduction of Corporation Tax to 40 per cent and the decision to extend free depreciation from 20 to 80 per cent across the country as a whole had the effect, it is argued, of undermining the differentials between the regions — thereby contributing to further regional decline and rising unemployment. Whatever the basic cause of the continuing decline of the regions in this period it is true that the Conservative

Government could pursue an independent policy direction as the 1972 Act's lack of consistency *vis-à-vis* earlier legislation reveals. However, the continuing rise in unemployment and decline of traditional industries, while not determining policy, acted as a negative constraint on what would be possible. Like it or not, and using whatever method they might choose, the Conservative Government was not able to pursue the policy it preferred because of the continuing commitment to 'full employment' in British politics.

Labour Policy in a Period of Continuing Crisis: 1974-8

In the period since 1974, industrial location policy has been dominated by one overwhelming fact: unemployment has risen steadily and since 1976 it has hovered around the 1¼ to 1½ million mark — the highest figures since 1940. Two consequences have resulted. First, the Government has continued with *ad hoc* tinkering in the form of unemployment relief. Second, as the recession has bitten deep into a wide range of British industries located in a variety of cities and regions, new light has been thrown on the complexity of regional decline and on the relationship between the problems of the regions and those of the inner cities.

As was noted in Chapter 2 (pp.59-60), the first Labour Government of 1974 came into office amid a flurry of renewed debate on the role of the state in the economy. The 1973 Party document, *The 1973 Labour Programme*,[69] had advocated the nationalisation of a whole range of industries and financial institutions and proposed the introduction of a powerful central planning machinery (although not, significantly, the close co-ordination of physical and economic planning as advocated by Barlow). Once in office, however, the Labour Governments of February and then October 1974 pursued much more gradualist policies than either *The 1973 Labour Programme* or the February 1974 Manifesto (which was largely based on the 1973 document) advocated.

In regional policy, the Tories' 1972 Act was continued — although the Government quickly revealed its commitment to unemployment relief by continuing and doubling REP, and by tightening the IDC system so as to help those areas experiencing the worst levels of unemployment. Also, the 1975 Industry Act, although it did introduce a National Enterprise Board (NEB) and some additional planning machinery, gave the new Board few financial resources and it avoided the more problematical nationalisation issues.[70]

By the summer of 1976 the positive economic planning approach desired by the left had been defeated. Though there is as yet little real evidence, it is probably true that the same institutional constraints on innovation in the Whitehall machine (which were felt in 1944/5 and 1964/5) were in operation once more. A fullblown NEB would have meant a significant challenge to both the Treasury and the Departments of Industry and Employment, not to mention the implied potential threat to the Department of the Environment's physical planning powers. Added to these pressures, it seems clear that there was significant opposition within the Government and Labour Party to any such innovative moves. It has been argued that Harold Wilson himself, then the Prime Minister, took over the final deliberations of the 1975 Industry Act to keep it out of the hands of the politically suspect Secretary of State for Industry, Anthony Wedgwood Benn.[71] It is also probably true that Wilson was not acting alone in this. Obviously, the 'City' and the major banks, not to mention the CBI and large multi-national corporations, viewed the prospect of nationalisation with some alarm and their views were well represented in government. Indeed, the threat seems to have stimulated the banks into direct action. They created Finance for Industry, a private equity bank providing capital for investment in manufacturing industry. This move was clearly an attempt to counter the charge by the left that insufficient investment capital was being channelled into manufacturing industry compared to property and overseas opportunities.

Having abandoned radical solutions in economic policy generally, the Government continued with short-term unemployment relief measures in the regions. As unemployment reached the million mark the Government announced a Temporary Employment Subsidy in August 1975.[72] This measure was aimed specifically at the deferral of planned redundancies affecting fifty or more workers in the Assisted Areas and was intended to last one year. At the same time, the Manpower Services Commission was given a grant of £30 million to help it provide jobs of social value for young people who were unemployed in areas of high unemployment. Similarly, any firm taking on school leavers from the unemployment register was to be subsidised at the rate of £5 per week. These measures were intended to run to the end of 1976.[73] In October 1975 the Job Creation Programme was announced to supplement these measures. An extra £30 million grant was to be given to create jobs mainly in the Assisted Areas. It was estimated that this scheme would provide 15,000 short-term jobs.[74] As unemployment continued to rise in 1976 it became apparent that the Government would have to extend the scope of these measures. The Temporary Employment Subsidy (TES) was modified to allow for redundancies affecting 25 workers to be included in the asistance programme and the Job Creation Programme (JCP) was given an additional £10 million in January 1976.[75] In February the TES was extended to cover loss of work affecting 10 workers and the JCP was given an extra £30 million to finance its extension beyond summer 1976 when it was due to close.[76] In May 1976 this piecemeal approach was continued by the granting of an additional £15 million to extend the earlier Conservative Training Opportunities Scheme (TOPS), the JCP and other retraining schemes operated through the Manpower Services Commission.[77]

This policy of temporary provision of finance, aimed largely at finding jobs for school leavers, or subsidising employment in the Assisted Areas, was given a novel aspect in September 1976 when the Job Release Scheme was introduced. As unemployment continued at the million to one and a half million level it was decided to encourage people to retire early so that their jobs might be available for the young unemployed. This scheme, which was confined to the Assisted Areas, allowed anyone to retire a year early on a £23 a week tax free allowance. The programme, costing an estimated £73 million, was expected to run until June 1977. At the same time it was announced that an additional £15 million was to be provided for the JCP.[78]

In December 1976 in the face of ever higher unemployment, the Government extended the scope of the TES and JCP. The TES, with an additional £60 million, and the JCP with £15 million more, was to run until April 1977.[79] The TES was further funded in March 1977 with an additional £172 million to keep it in operation until March 1978. The Budget in March 1977 also introduced another approach in the creation of the Small Firms Employment Subsidy. This scheme gave a £20 per week subsidy to encourage small firms in Special Development Areas to take on extra employees.[80]

In the 1974-8 period, the short term problems which have plagued all post-war governments — sudden increases in unemployment, external economic pressures — became particularly acute. As this occurred, it became apparent that the spatial pattern of industrial change (some would say industrial decline) had modified somewhat. As Table 6.2 shows, even by 1974, Scotland and the Northern region of England had improved their position relative to the rest of the country, while the position of Yorkshire and Humberside had declined. While no complete agreement exists on explanations for this trend, it is almost certainly related to continuing expansion in Scotland and the

North of some service industries (notably education, health and government), the revival of the coal mining industry and (to a small extent) the rise of the offshore oil and gas industry.[81] However, while the overall relative position of some regions improved between 1961 and 1975, the particular position of some inner areas such as Glasgow and Gateshead as well as certain vulnerable smaller towns such as Hartlepool, did not.[82] In addition, inner areas of London and Birmingham experienced serious decline in their industrial base in these years. In London, for example, manufacturing employment declined from 1.43 million to .94 million (see also Table 6.3).[83] The next chapter will be specifically devoted to the inner city and to

Table 6.2: Gross Domestic Product, Factor Cost: Current Prices — Regions of the United Kingdom, 1966-74

	1966	1972	1973	1974
United Kingdom	100	100	100	100
Northern Ireland	67.9	72.7	74.0	74.0
Scotland	89.1	90.9	92.8	93.4
North	84.1	87.8	88.8	90.1
North-West	95.7	96.2	95.9	94.5
Yorkshire and Humberside	96.7	91.9	91.5	93.0
South-East	114.7	116.2	115.8	116.6

Source: *Economic Trends* (Central Statistical Office, 12/76).

Table 6.3: Changes in Population and Economic Activity in the Inner Areas of the English Conurbations

	London	Tyneside	SE Lancs	Merseyside	West Mids
% change in population 1961-71	−13.5	−15.0	−16.0	−17.0	− 5.9
Net migration 1961-71 as % of 1961 population	−19.5	−18.6	−22.2	−24.5	−13.7
% employment change in manufacturing industry 1971-3	−15.4	− 4.5	− 7.0	− 7.4	− 7.3
% change in economically active males 1961-70	−13.5	−12.9	−18.4	−14.5	− 7.3

Source: Derived from Department of the Environment (1976), reproduced from J.S. Foreman-Peck and P.A. Gripaios, 'Inner City Problems and Inner City Policies', *Regional Studies*, vol.11 (No.6), 1977, p.404.

governments' changing perceptions of their problems. But for now it is important to ask what relationship, if any, exists between inner city decline and regional policy.

Unfortunately, far too little research has been conducted in this area. What evidence we do have, however, suggests that regional policies based on creating employment in manufacturing industry located in broadly defined areas have been highly insensitive to what is a complex pattern of industrial change. In an important article published in *Regional Studies* in 1977,[84] Alan Townsend, using some new evidence and summarising relevant research findings so far established, comes to the following conclusions:

(a) It is all too easy to overgeneralise about the decline of cities and regions. While manufacturing industry has declined rapidly in almost all inner cities, so have many service sector industries. In Newcastle, for example, population decline in the insured population from 180,600 in 1966 to 157,400 in 1971 was only *half* accounted for by a loss of manufacturing jobs. A whole range of non-manufacturing jobs, notably in wholesaling and transport have also declined rapidly.[85]

(b) At the same time, it is difficult to attribute the decline of jobs in Inner London and Birmingham specifically to regional policy. Most of the decline is attributable not to firms transferring but to them closing. Of those that transferred from Inner London between 1960 and 1974 only 9 per cent moved to the Assisted Areas.[86] Within the Assisted Areas most industrial development has consisted of *new* externally generated investment rather than transfers from other parts of the country or investment deriving from local resources.[87]

(c) Throughout the country, local physical planning powers together with the operation of the IDC system have channelled new investment away from inner areas and towards nearby suburban, New Town and green field sites. As a result, the 'outer' South-East and East Anglia remain highly favoured areas[88] — especially given the difficulties equivalent locales in the Assisted Areas continue to experience in attracting transferring plants and in generating locally derived industrial growth.

(d) Since 1966, the indiscriminate nature of regional aid has compounded the problems of the inner areas in the Assisted Areas. With 50 per cent of the Scottish population, Strathclyde attracted 58 per cent of the firms moving to Scotland and 66 per cent of resulting jobs in 1963. By 1973 these figures had dropped to 35 per cent and

38 per cent respectively.[89]

(e) A failure to co-ordinate housing and transport policies with regional policies has led to undesirable social consequences — especially in Scotland and the North of England. In cities such as Glasgow and Liverpool vast new council estates have been built on green field sites with poor communications with the central business areas, and often geographically removed from new industrial development.[90]

Townsend's specific recommendations are for a continuation of aid to the Assisted Areas (except perhaps Eastern Scotland) as their structural industrial problems remain acute. IDC policy, however, should be modified to aid inner areas — including London — and further investment in the outer South-East and East Anglia should be strongly discouraged.[91] Even if all these were implemented — and as the next chapter will show, the Government is moving in these general directions — vast problems remain. It may be, for example, that it is not skilled manufacturing employment that is needed in areas of high unemployment but unskilled and service jobs.[92] Certainly the Government instruments needed to respond effectively to what is a highly complex pattern of industrial change will have to be very sophisticated indeed.

Conclusions

It would be misleading to characterise post-war regional policy as a complete failure. Some have argued for example, that Government policies, while not solving unemployment and not ending regional imbalance, have been better than no policies at all.[93] In other words, if there has been a lessening of regional unemployment disparities it has been a result of government policies. This view is supported by a number of studies. Moore and Rhodes have argued that something of the order of 250,000 and 300,000 new jobs were created by government policies since 1966 in the Assisted Areas.[94] A study by Ashcroft and Taylor has disputed these figures, arguing that only something of the order of 90,000 jobs were so created, with private investment decisions and the general state of the economy being of more significance than government policies in generating employment opportunities.[95] Chisholm has supported this latter interpretation arguing that government policies have been continuously subject to change thereby undermining their possible impact because they have required at least four years to have any effect.[96] It seems likely, indeed, that the evidence of regional revival in eastern Scotland and northern England is explainable not by deliberate government policy so much as by a changing industrial structure including the fortuitous growth and revival of energy-based developments.

Moreover, as judged by the employment criterion — the most important criterion according to politicians from all political parties — regional policy has failed. For although the differentials have narrowed somewhat, the traditionally declining areas continue to experience substantially higher rates of unemployment than the average rates prevailing in the South-East and Midlands. Short term economic factors undoubtedly reduced the effectiveness of many of the measures. Frequently, fluctuations in the fortunes of the economy resulting from the effects of balance of payments crises have increased unemployment and obliged governments to abandon longer term strategies in favour of short term palliatives. But it would be wrong simply to explain away regional policies in terms of the influence of 'stop-go' policies. The employment-relief bias owes much to domestic political circumstances, and the measures adopted have often been ill-suited to the main purpose of reducing unemployment in those areas most at risk.

While the probable link between employment policies and elections was noted earlier in the chapter, we should be wary of being over-deterministic in this area. Certainly, specific laws cannot easily be linked to specific elections and their outcomes. Many of the most important policy innovations have occurred early in the terms of governments or when governments could not predict the timing of the next election (1945 Distribution of Industry Act, 1966 Industrial Development Act, 1972 Industry Act). Moreover, regional aid takes time to produce meaningful effects on employment (if these can be measured). It is highly unlikely that unemployed or potentially unemployed individual voters will suddenly look favourably on a government because it announces a new form of regional aid which is technical in language and produces no immediate change in local employment prospects. It is much more likely that governments (and especially Labour Governments), dreading the long term consequences of chronic regional unemployment, have adopted rather vague strategies for creating employment opportunities in the hope that a restructuring of industries in the regions would also occur. Of course some differences between the parties exist. Generally, Conservatives have favoured selective tax-incentive aid to profitable firms, while Labour has favoured indiscriminate aid in the form of investment grants. But while the parties have differed over the scope and methods of state intervention, they have usually agreed on the main goal of regional policy — the reduction of unemployment differentials. More importantly, notwithstanding Labour's hesitant steps towards more comprehensive planning in 1964 and (to a much lesser extent) in 1975, neither party has actually adopted long term economic planning policies involving the co-ordination of employment, investment and physical planning. We cannot, of course, predict what the possible results of such a policy might have been, but we can point to the undesirable consequences of the policies which have been implemented.

The failure to co-ordinate local physical and national economic planning has, as we saw, resulted in highly insensitive policies. Inner cities (often the areas with the highest rates of unemployment) both in the regions and in the Midlands and the South-East have suffered from the application of IDC policies favouring suburban and New Town sites. At the same time, housing and transport policies have frequently been completely unrelated to employment policies. Indeed, the creation of massive housing estates such as Easterhouse in Glasgow, without reference to the type and quantity of jobs available through industrial location policy, stand as monuments to the failure of British planning policy. One wonders if recently mooted cut-backs in the steel industry have been assessed in terms of their likely impact on DOE regional housing, land use and local government functions.

The blame for these failures must be attributed both to central and local governments. Local authorities have been important in bargaining for additional regional aid or pleading for inclusion in the regional programmes, but until recently they have not provided central governments with alternative and more sensitive policies. Not until unemployment levels had risen to record post-war levels and the failure of existing policy become obvious, did regional and local reports start to argue for a reassessment of industrial location policy in favour of inner cities and small declining cities.[97] If inner areas are to be given special help it will either mean substantially increased government expenditure or the redistribution of resources from better-off areas. Both are politically difficult courses to take — and opposition from richer areas (and in the case of Scotland from the SNP) to the latter alternative is likely to be considerable.

As noted several times already in this book, bureaucratic resistance to integrated planning at the national level has been considerable, and this applies with some force to the integration of physical and economic planning which would fundamentally alter existing departmental responsibilities and boundaries. It is clear that the creation of a planning ministry would arouse the institutional might and opposition of well entrenched organisations like the Treasury and the DOE. It is now widely accepted that the failure to create a planning ministry in 1945, and the short and stormy life of the DEA in the mid-1960s owe much to the opposition of existing bureaucracies. Added to the defence of bureaucratic boundaries and routines, the fact that an integrated planning system, as ideally desired by Barlow, would have meant a positive state role would also tend to go against the grain of civil service advice and proclivities. The British civil service has been described as less sympathetic to state interventionism compared with some European bureaucracies.[98] This may well be an understatement of a service which has the preservation of a limited regulatory state role premised on financial rectitude and limiting public expenditure as its dominant tradition.[99] Given these broad tendencies it is not surprising that a more interventionist and positive state role has not been developed for regional or national economic policies.

At the national level, at least, interest groups appear to have had a remarkably small effect on industrial location policies. There are, in fact, few if any regional interest groups in Britain. The Regional Economic Planning Boards and Councils set up in 1964 might be seen in this light, but it is clear that they have had only a marginal role to play in government decision-making. The problem for the Boards and Councils has been that they have been trapped without effective powers between local and central government responsibilities. It is hardly surprising that they have degenerated into 'talking-shops'.[100] At the national level, both the CBI and the TUC have been in favour of regional policies and they have worked through the NEDC to try and encourage unemployment assistance and regional revival. They have not, however, provided governments with clearly thought out alternatives to existing policies.

Industrial location and regional policies in Britain are now under review and the 1977 White Paper, *Policy for the Inner Cities*, specifically calls for greater emphasis on the intra-regional distribution of industry.[101] But many of the old problems remain. Government still lacks the sort of highly sophisticated instruments needed to permit responsive and effective state intervention. At the least, both comprehensive information on the relationship between labour, housing and land markets nationally and locally, *and* the administrative machinery, economic resources and political will to act on such information, are needed if intra and inter-regional inequalities are to be dramatically reduced. However, in spite of the recent partial reappraisal of policy, the political and economic constraints which have narrowed the focus of industrial location policy over the last 30 years remain, so we have little cause to think that a comprehensive reappraisal of policy will occur.

Notes

1. Manuel Castells, *The Urban Question* (London, Edward Arnold, 1977).
2. Graham Hallett, Peter Randall, E.G. West, *Regional Policy for Ever?* (London, Institute of Economic Affairs, 1973), p.19.
3. On this view see in particular, Stuart Holland, *The Socialist Challenge* (London, Quartet Books, 1975), and Stuart Holland, *Capital Versus the Regions* (London, Macmillan, 1976).
4. Leslie Hannah, *The Rise of the Corporate Economy* (London, Methuen, 1976), pp.142-61.
5. For further elaboration see Holland, *Capital Versus the Regions*, pp.127-95; Stuart Holland, *The Regional Problem* (London, Macmillan, 1976), pp.21-41; and A.R. Townsend, 'The Relationship of Inner City Problems to Regional Policy', *Regional Studies*, vol.II (1977), pp.225-51.
6. Nigel Harris, *Competition and the Corporate Society* (London, Methuen, 1972), pp.48-61.
7. C.L. Mowat, *Britain Between the Wars* (London, Methuen, 1956), pp.470-5.
8. These were granted by the Industrial Transference Board of the Ministry of Labour. For further elaboration, see Hallett, *Regional Policy*, p.19.
9. Ibid., p.22.
10. D.F. MacDonald, *The State and the Trade Unions* (London, Macmillan, 1960), pp.97-117.
11. Nigel Harris, *Corporate Society*, pp.48-61.
12. Hallett, *Regional Policy*, p.23.
13. For an overview, see Margaret Cole, *The Story of Fabian Socialism* (London, Mercury Books, 1963), and W. Ashworth, *The Genesis of Modern British Town Planning* (London, Routledge and Kegan Paul, 1970).
14. *Royal Commission on the Distribution of the Industrial Population*, Cmd.6153 (HMSO, January 1940).
15. For more detailed appraisal, see Peter Hall *et al.*, *The Containment of Urban England: Volume 2: The Planning System: Objectives, Operations, Impacts* (London, Allen and Unwin, 1973), pp.35-71.
16. Hallett, *Regional Policy*, p.24.
17. Ibid., p.24.
18. *Royal Commission*, Cmd.6153, pp.208-32.
19. For further discussion of these issues, see J.B. Cullingworth, *Environmental Planning, 1939-1964: Volume 1, Reconstruction and Land Use Planning, 1939-1947* (London, HMSO, 1975), pp.53-74, and Peter Ambrose, 'The British Land-Use Non-Planning System' (Paper to inaugural meeting of the Conference of Socialist Planning, London, 19 February 1977).
20. J.B. Cullingworth, ibid., pp.251-8.
21. *Employment Policy*, Cmd.6527 (London, HMSO, 1944).
22. Jacques Leruez, *Economic Planning and Politics in Britain* (London, Martin Robertson, 1975), pp.28-48.
23. For further discussion of these powers see Hallett, *Regional Policy*, pp.26-7.

24. Peter Hall, *Urban England*, pp.109-10.

25. Gavin McCrone, *Regional Policy in Britain* (London, Allen and Unwin, 1973), pp.112-3, offers suitable statistical evidence to support this point.

26. For further elaboration of this point see, David Howell, *British Social Democracy* (London, Croom Helm, 1976), pp.135-77, and Leo Panitch, *Social Democracy and Industrial Militancy* (London, Cambridge University Press, 1976), pp.235-59.

27. Leruez., *Economic Planning*, pp.28-48.

28. Hallett, *Regional Policy*, pp.28-9.

29. On the perennial role of the Treasury in fostering these approaches, see Samuel Britain, *Steering the Economy* (Harmondsworth, Middx., Pelican, 1971).

30. McCrone, *Regional Policy*, pp.112-15.

31. S. Jenkins, *Landlords to London* (London, Constable, 1975), pp.211-17.

32. Hall, *Urban England*, pp.125-7.

33. Hallett, *Regional Policy*, pp.29-30.

34. Bill Simpson, *Labour: The Unions and the Party* (London, Allen and Unwin, 1973), pp.105-15.

35. McCrone, *Regional Policy*, pp.115-16.

36. Hallett, *Regional Policy*, pp.32-3.

37. For a critique of this approach, see T. Wilson, 'The Economic Costs of the Adversary System', in S.E. Finer, *Adversary Politics and Electoral Reform* (London, Anthony Wigram, 1975), pp.104-11.

38. For a discussion of the relative merits of 'growth point' theories see Hallett, *Regional Policy*, pp.77-82.

39. For a critique of these arguments, see Stuart Holland, *Capital Versus the Regions* (London, Macmillan, 1976), pp.162-95.

40. Andrew Shonfield, *Modern Capitalism* (London, Oxford University Press, 1969), pp.151-75.

41. Vera Lutz, *Central Planning for the Market Economy* (London, Longmans, 1969), pp.3-23.

42. Michael Shanks, *Planning and Politics* (London, Allen and Unwin, 1977), pp.17-26.

43. G. Manners, D. Keeble, B. Rodgers, K. Warren, *Regional Development in Britain* (London, J. Wiley & Sons, 1972), pp.7 and 59.

44. As Shanks argues, *Planning and Politics*, pp.20-21, Macmillan faced serious intra-party opposition.

45. McCrone, *Regional Policy*, p.26.

46. For further details see Maurice Wright and Stephen Young, 'Regional Planning in Britain', in Jack Hayward and Michael Watson (eds), *Planning, Politics and Public Policy* (London, Cambridge University Press, 1975), p.237.

47. McCrone, *Regional Policy*, pp.208-09.

48. Nigel Harris, *Corporate Society*, pp.242-6.

49. Hallett, *Regional Policy*, p.32.

50. Maurice Wright and Stephen Young, *Regional Planning*, p.237.

51. Hugh Heclo and Aron Wildavsky, *The Private Government of Public Money* (Los Angeles, University of California Press, 1971), pp.209-10.

52. Leruez, pp.170-97.

53. *Royal Commission on Local Government in England*, Cmnd.4040 (London, HMSO, 1969), and *Royal Commission on the Constitution: 1969-1973*, Cmnd.5460 (London, HMSO, 1973).

54. Leruez, *Economic Planning*, pp.154-63.

55. Ibid.

56. Manners *et al.*, *Regional Development in Britain*, pp.59-60.

57. For a list of these studies, see Brenda White, *The Literature and Study of*

Urban and Regional Planning (London, Routledge and Kegan Paul, 1974), pp.110-22.

58. On the role of the Left in the Labour Party, see David Coates, *The Labour Party and the Struggle for Socialism* (London, Cambridge University Press, 1975), pp.97-129.

59. Peter Hall, *Urban England*, pp.125-39.

60. A.R. Townsend, 'The Relationship of Inner City Problems to Regional Policy', p.230.

61. *The Intermediate Areas: Report of a committee under the chairmanship of Sir John Hunt*, Cmnd.3998 (London, HMSO, April 1969).

62. Cmnd.?

63. T. Wilson, 'The Economic Costs of the Adversary System', p.108.

64. For general discussion of these trends see Solomon Barkin (ed.), *Worker Militancy and Its Consequences* (London, Praeger, 1975), pp.1-38.

65. For an overview, see Andrew Glyn and Bob Sutcliffe, *British Capitalism and the Profits Squeeze* (Harmondsworth, Middx., Penguin, 1969).

66. Jock Bruce-Gardyne, *Whatever Happened to the Quiet Revolution?* (London, Knight, 1974).

67. For an excellent account of industrial relations in this period, see Michael Moran, *The Politics of Industrial Relations* (London, Macmillan, 1977).

68. For a general discussion of this subject, see Hallett, *Regional Policy*, pp.40-43.

69. *The Labour Programme: 1973* (London, Transport House, Smith Square, London, 1973).

70. The 1975 Act gave the NEB £275 million to intervene in areas of high unemployment, and ship-building and off-shore platform credits were raised from £1,400 million to £1,800 million. The 1976 Act provided a potential increase of £1,050 million. It is also worth noting that the 1975 Scottish and Welsh Development Agency Acts gave these Agencies powers similar to the NEB in their respective regions. See also, J. Winkler, 'Law, State and Economy: The Industry Act 1975 in Context', *British Journal of Law and Society* (1975), pp.103-28.

71. Shanks, *Planning and Politics*, pp.74-6.

72. *Employment News* (The Department of Employment Newspaper), no.26 (October, 1975).

73. Ibid.

74. Ibid.

75. *Employment News*, no.28 (January 1976).

76. *Employment News*, no.30 (March 1976).

77. *Employment News*, no.32 (May 1976).

78. *Employment News*, no.36 (September 1976).

79. *Employment News*, no.39 (December 1976).

80. *Employment News*, no.42 (March 1977).

81. See A.R. Townsend, 'Inner City Problems', p.239.

82. Ibid., p.238.

83. Ibid., p.244.

84. Ibid.

85. Ibid., p.234.

86. Ibid., p.244.

87. Ibid., p.241.

88. Ibid., p.246.

89. Ibid., p.238.

90. Ibid., p.229.

91. Ibid., pp.248-9.

92. See Northern Region Strategy Team, 'Causes of the Recent Improvement in the Rate of Unemployment in the Northern Region Relative to Great Britain', *Northern Region Strategy Team, Technical Report, No.11*, Newcastle upon Tyne, 1976.

93. Peter Hall, *Urban England*, pp.125-39.

94. Barry Moore and John Rhodes, 'Regional Economic Policy and the Movement of Manufacturing Firms to Development Areas', *Economica*, vol.43 (February 1976), pp.17-31.

95. Brian Ashcroft and Jim Taylor, 'The Movement of Manufacturing Industry and the Effect of Regional Policy', *Oxford Economic Papers* (29 March 1977), pp.84-101.

96. Michael Chisholm, 'Regional Policies in an Era of Slow Population Growth and Higher Unemployment', *Regional Studies*, vol.10 (1976), pp.201-13.

97. For example, *The Strathclyde Regional Report (1976), Merseyside Structure Plan, Stage One Report* (1975), and *Tyne and Wear Structure Plan, Report of Survey* (1976) called for a reappraisal of policy. For full references, see Townsend, 'Inner City Problems'.

98. John A. Armstrong, *The European Administrative Elite* (Princeton, Princeton University Press, 1973), pp.299-318.

99. Heclo and Wildavsky, *Private Government*, pp.1-128.

100. Leruez, *Economic Planning*, pp.162-3.

101. *Policy for the Inner Cities*, Cmnd.6845 (HMSO, 1977), para.50.

7 POLICIES TOWARDS THE INNER CITIES

> At Social Services Committee we had another discussion of
> this extraordinary community experiment idea the Home
> Office has put forward, drafted by Derek Morrell. He made
> a curiously Buchmanite kind of religious speech about action
> changing lives and I suddenly heard him saying, 'There must
> be a second revolution in the welfare state, a second
> revolution.' I was more amazed than ever that the official
> paper had been accepted without a word of criticism from
> any other Department, though it's an astonishing mix-up of
> sociology and mystical religion. Then came a very dramatic
> moment. Jim [Callaghan] suddenly said, 'We must stop all this bloody
> religious nonsense.' Had the Home Office put this idea forward
> without taking him into their confidence? No, I fancy he had
> liked the paper when he first read it and it wasn't until he
> heard Morrell's mystical explanation that he was a smart
> enough politician to see that this wouldn't go down in that
> form, or help him in his battle between the Home Office and
> social services Departments. Jim said he would produce a paper
> of his own and I gather that his intention is to keep Morrell
> out of it as far as he can. (Richard Crossman, *Diaries of a
> Cabinet Minister*, vol.III, 1978)

In one sense, the fact that British governments have found it necessary
to pursue policies specifically directed at the problems of the inner
cities is evidence of the inadequacy of other urban policies. After all,
as broadly conceived in the post-war period, planning, land-use and
housing policies should have solved the 'urban problem' — at least as
then defined. In 1945, overcrowding in the big cities, unplanned urban
sprawl and serious regional imbalance were the dominating urban
problems. Today, judging by official statements and public concern,
the focus of attention has shifted quite dramatically. Instead of
overcrowding, inner city depopulation and decline are apparently the
problem. Instead of dispersing people and jobs from the cities,
politicians now talk of providing means to direct investment back to
inner areas.

Before explaining why this apparent transformation has occurred,
it is important to clarify what is meant by 'policies towards the inner

city'. To a greater or lesser extent, *all* urban policies involve the inner city, and concern with the problems of central cities has been with us at least since the Industrial Revolution. Why, then, single out inner city policies for special analysis? Primarily because since the mid-1960s governments have, for the first time, initiated policies specifically and exclusively designed to solve inner city problems. The post-war policies of containing urban growth, correcting regional imbalance and dispersing population from the overcrowded cities were also 'inner city policies' but at no time did governments perceive these as quite separate and distinct from other urban policies. Indeed, recent inner city policy initiatives are distinctive in another sense: they have been designed exclusively as *urban* policies. As earlier chapters have emphasised, although planning, land-values and housing policies have been *primarily* concerned with urban areas (and have been perceived as primarily urban policies) they have by no means been exclusive to urban areas.

For these reasons, inner city policies do justify separate treatment. Moreover, many of these policies touch on aspects of urban life — education, race relations, social services — which conventional urban policies ignore. As will be shown, in no way have inner city policies represented comprehensive reforms in these areas but they have helped focus attention on problems which have not normally been considered in the mainstream of urban policy.

The 'Rediscovery' of the Inner City, 1965-73

It is impossible to discuss the evolution of policies towards the inner cities without referring to the question of race and immigration. Between 1951 and 1966 Britain's non-white population increased from an estimated 74,500 to 595,100,[1] and the vast majority of these new immigrants settled in inner city areas or in areas whose housing stock was old and deteriorating. These new populations were also highly concentrated in certain streets and neighbourhoods. Slowly but surely during the 1960s public interest in immigration and its consequences increased. Until 1965, governments did not, however, make any special provision for the social and economic needs of immigrants. Instead, debate tended to be focused on the question of immigration control. At the same time, it was increasingly obvious that Britain's new minority populations were experiencing acute problems in housing, education and employment — many of them deriving from racial discrimination. Britain's first 'inner city' policies were, therefore, in reaction to the changing racial composition of inner city areas.

(a) *Compensatory Education*

In the context of a total absence of planning for immigrants, it is not surprising that one of the first areas perceived to be 'in trouble' as a result of immigration was education. With higher than average birth *like rabbits* rates among minorities and given their spatial concentration, the number of immigrants in certain primary schools rose dramatically during the early 1960s. As Rose *et al.* have shown in their comprehensive survey of race relations policy in the 1960s, official reaction to increasing numbers of non-white pupils, many of whom had difficulty with English, was two-fold in nature. First, following the publication of the Second Report of the Commonwealth Immigrants Advisory Council in 1965, and a White Paper on immigration in 1965, the Government accepted the need to 'disperse' non-white students on the grounds that both they and (more significantly) white students would suffer from high non-white concentration. Second, the White Paper and a subsequent section of the 1966 Local Government Act proposed that local authorities with 'substantial numbers of immigrants from the Commonwealth whose language or customs differ from those of the community' [3] receive special grants to employ the extra staff needed to cater for language problems in schools. These broad policy directives represent two of the most frequently proposed 'solutions' to racial disadvantage: dispersal and positive discrimination measures. As it turned out, the dispersal alternative was rejected by many local authorities including Inner London and Birmingham. Its implied use of busing was unpopular, and opposition to the general principle of dispersal came from white and non-white communities alike.[4]

More important for our purposes was Section 11 of the 1966 Local Government Act with its special grants for teachers of English. In many respects this provision represented a radical departure from existing policy. Area-based positive discrimination measures were quite new in British social policy, and as we shall see, they gained in influence throughout the 1960s. This said, the 1966 Act was a very minor affair, involving disbursements of just £1.4 million in 1967/8. There was, moreover, no recognition in the Act of the relationship between educational disadvantage and other problems affecting racial minorities, no reference was made to a *general* problem of urban deprivation, and administration of the law was left to the Department of Education and Science, hardly a department centrally involved in urban policy.

There seems little doubt that Section 11 owed its existence largely to an expert report (the 1964 Commonwealth Immigrants Advisory

Council Report) and when introduced in Parliament it was welcomed by all political parties. Expert opinion was also instrumental in producing the second major positive discrimination initiative in this period, the Educational Priority areas (EPAs) of 1967 and 1968. Reporting in 1967 the Plowden Report called for the creation of priority areas where children with serious disadvantages resulting from their home backgrounds would receive compensatory education.[5] Plowden's proposal would have involved fairly massive expenditure as it called for schools in deprived areas to be as good as the 'best in the country'. As it turned out only elements of the proposal were adopted, including a £16 million building programme started in 1967, a special allowance for teachers working in deprived areas, and the initiation of action-research teams in four EPAs. Again, the programme was confined to education, but in contrast to the 1966 Act, it was not concerned only with the problems of racial minorities. It was an area-based positive discrimination programme which used (for the first time) a relatively sophisticated formula for determining to which schools the special teachers allowance should apply. The formula included:

(i) the social and economic status of parents of children at the school;
(ii) the absence of amenities in the homes of children attending the school;
(iii) the proportion of children in the school receiving free meals or belonging to families in receipt of supplementary benefits under the Ministry of Social Security Act 1966,
(iv) the proportion of children in the school with serious linguistic difficulties.[6]

Obviously, this formula recognised the existence of area-based deprivation, although there was nothing in the arrangement to suggest that the schools themselves were at fault or that the schools affected would be found in large, geographically contiguous areas. On the contrary, the implication was that educational deprivation resulted largely from the characteristics of *individual families* living in 'pockets' of general social and economic deprivation. Such people were, according to the Plowden Report, caught in a 'vicious circle' of poverty. By improving primary education dramatically, this 'circle' could be broken, and, the Report argued, the downward spiral of poverty arrested. That this analysis owes much to the 'culture of poverty' thesis is obvious, and as we shall see, similar sentiments were to manifest themselves again and again during the late 1960s.

(b) *The Urban Programme*

Both Section 11 of the 1966 Local Government Act and the EPA initiative were conceived quite independently of what is normally considered 'urban policy'. However, changes were afoot in this period in the more traditional areas of urban policy. In particular, housing policy was slowly being adapted to deal with the specific problems of inner city areas. The Milner Holland Report on housing in London and the Denington Report on older housing (see pp.132-3) both pinpointed the acute situation in the inner cities and pleaded for the designation of areas deserving of special help and attention. In 1968, the White Paper, *Old Houses into New Homes*, echoed these views and called for a shift from wholesale clearance to rehabilitation. In one important sense the shift from renewal to rehabilitation and the recognition that certain areas had particularly acute housing problems was an admission that the post-war policy of 'decrowding' and dispersing population from overcrowded cities was partly based on false assumptions. Decay and disadvantage were, according to the post-war philosophy, synonymous with overcrowding, yet in the inner cities the former seemed to be increasing *while the dispersal policies were being implemented.* But a cautionary note is in order here. It would be quite wrong to imply that within the Ministry of Housing and Local Government there existed an awareness of inner city decline caused by rapidly shifting patterns of industrial investment. We now know that changes in the location of industry have been critical in determining the fate of inner cities. This was not appreciated within government circles in the mid and late-1960s, however. On the other hand, local governments and civil servants could hardly not notice the growing inequalities in British cities, and this explains the hesitant moves in housing towards providing special help for areas perceived to be in greatest need.

But these changes in the housing policy agenda occurred quite independently of the major initiative in urban policy in this period: the creation of the Urban Programme in 1968. During 1967 and 1968, public debate on race and immigration reached a new level. New and controversial legislation on the one hand to control immigration and, on the other, to provide Britain's racial minorities with stronger protection against discrimination was before Parliament. In this charged atmosphere, Enoch Powell, long a critic of the existing immigration arrangements, delivered his notorious 'rivers of blood' speech on 20

April 1968. Powell's warning that continued immigration would destroy the 'fabric' of British society had several immediate political consequences. For one thing, it had a profound influence on the subsequent immigration debate in Parliament.[7] For another, it almost certainly inspired the Prime Minister, Harold Wilson, to announce on 5 May 1968 that:

> We have decided to embark on a new and expanded Urban Programme. . .Many of our big towns face tremendous problems, whether in housing, whether in health and welfare, and even where there is virtually no immigrant problem. Expenditure must be on the basis of need and the immigration problem is only one factor, though a very important factor, in the assessment of social need. . .[8]

The programme that followed was hardly comprehensive, however, and drew more on the Plowden experience than on the experience of traditional urban policy areas. Two days after Harold Wilson's announcement, an inter-departmental working party was established which effectively determined the nature and scope of the Programme. Few specific details had been provided by the Prime Minister — although presumably because of the relationship between the Programme and immigration, he had said it could be administered by the Home Office. Seeking to avoid claims that the Programme was designed solely to solve racial problems, the working party decided to define the Programme's scope not only in terms of immigrant problems but also in terms of spatially determined 'multiple deprivation'. Therefore, drawing on the recommendations of the Plowden Report, and following the experience of the 1966 Local Government Act, the working party decided on a programme consisting of positive discrimination measures which would be available to local authorities within whose jurisdictions existed pockets of multiple deprivation. The chairman of the working party, Derek Morrell, was, moreover, simultaneously working on the possibility of introducing 'action research' projects based on the American community action experience. These, which were eventually to become the Community Development Project also approached the problem of urban poverty on the currently popular assumption that the inhabitants of specific areas experiencing multiple deprivation could be 'lifted' out of their poverty via 'self help' and positive discrimination measures.[9] There is little evidence suggesting that support and pressure for community action and participation existed outside the Home Office. CDP was very much an internally generated policy propagated in particular by Derek Morrell who was influential in spreading the concept both to the CDP and to the Seebohm Report on the personal social services on which he was also working at that time.

Designating *areas* for special treatment had the additional advantage of providing potential limits to the extent of government involvement. It soon became clear that the programme would have to be small in spending terms; given a suitable definition of deprivation, therefore, the Home Office could limit assistance to a strictly limited number of small areas. When the Urban Programme was announced by the Home Secretary in Parliament on 22 July, this emphasis on deprivation experienced by particular areas, which had been absent in the Prime Minister's original speech, was stressed:

> There remain areas of severe social deprivation in a number of our cities and towns — often scattered in relatively small pockets. They require special help to meet their social needs and to bring their physical services to an adequate level.[10]

The criteria eventually employed to decide which areas should receive help, were, however, remarkably vague. Circular No.1 issued in October 1968[11] asked local authorities to apply for aid under the Programme for areas which showed high incidences of overcrowding, large families, unemployment, poor environment, concentration of immigrants and children in trouble or need of care. As Edwards and Batley note in their comprehensive study of the Programme:

> The list owed much to the Plowden experience, but no cut off points were established and no definitions offered for each of these conditions. It was very much up to local authorities to decide how to respond.[12]

The fact that local authorities were requested to send in their requests for funds reflects the general lack of direction which characterised the early days of the Programme. Also symptomatic of this vagueness was the haphazard way in which the Programme's objectives were defined. Mention of education, housing and health in the Prime Minister's speech automatically involved the Department of Education and Science, the Ministry of Housing and Local Government and the Ministries of Health and Social Security. Originally the Department of Employment and Productivity was involved but it soon withdrew and although housing was recognised as a major influence on deprivation, the potential costs of incorporating housing aid meant that (with the exception of housing advice centres) the Urban Programme failed to develop in the housing area.[13] What eventually transpired, therefore, was a programme which:

> depended more on the individual Departments' views about gaps in their particular services than on a collective view about the purposes of the new programme. Given the haste with which the Urban Programme was conceived, and given the involvement of the whole range of Government Departments with their separate commitments, it is, perhaps, not surprising that what emerged was an inclusive list without any priority ordering.[14]

The Programme was given status as a special grant funded out of the Rate Support pool, providing for 75 per cent of the costs of projects, the remaining 25 per cent having to be provided by local authorities. At least until 1971, funds allocated did constitute *additional* spending. This fact, together with the generally rather untidy arrangements of a programme involving several departments in a multiplicity of areas, inspired the opposition of the Treasury, and from 1972 spending on the Programme was taken into account during local/central government negotiations over the size of the Rate Support Grant.[15] Since 1972, therefore, local governments have had to be prepared to redistribute funds from other spending areas in order to qualify for assistance under the Programme.

Most of the projects funded during the first four years of the Programme involved nursery education, day nurseries, child care and community work.[16] By 1975, total expenditure over the seven years reached £55.5 million.[17] The Programme was, then, very small in relation to total expenditure in the urban policy area, and it also continued the logic of the 1966 Local Government Act and of Plowden, by stressing positive discrimination measures in education. Originally, the Programme concentrated on the problems of immigrant communities. Since 1972, however, there has been a move away from the immigrant and education focus and towards the funding of voluntary organisations operating in deprived areas, whether immigrant or not.

That the Programme is perceived both by local and central governments as one designed to fill in 'gaps' or to speed up existing programmes seems indisputable. This is acknowledged by an official

Home Office statement in 1972 which stressed that:

> The Urban Programme is not intended to do the work of the major
> social services like education or health; it does not build primary
> schools, houses or hospitals. It tries, rather, to encourage projects
> which have a reasonably quick effect and which go directly to the
> roots of social need.[18]

In historical perspective the Urban Programme appears an odd policy
initiative. It was almost completely unrelated to other aspects of urban
policy; it was run by the Home Office rather than the Ministry of
Housing and Local Government or (latterly) the DOE, the two agencies
most centrally involved with urban problems. Moreover, an analysis of
the Programme by the authors showed that neither interest groups nor
political party conflict played a significant role in its genesis and
implementation.[19]

When James Callaghan announced the initiative in Parliament it was
welcomed on all sides, and at no time down to 1975 was there any
evidence of party rancour or disagreement over the principles of the
Programme. In fact, the ideas behind the Programme were as at home
in the Conservative as in the Labour Party for they embodied notions
of selectivism rather than the universalism which was such a powerful
influence on Labour's post-war urban and social policies. As
Conservative Home Secretary in the period between 1970 and 1974,
Robert Carr reinforced the Programme and took upon himself the job
of co-ordinating minister of all positive discrimination policies. He also
established the Urban Deprivation Unit in the Home Office at this time
to undertake analysis of the various programmes.

The groups traditionally involved in urban policy — housing,
transport, planning — were almost completely uninvolved in the Urban
Programme. Perhaps this is not surprising given what we know about
the TCPA, the TPI, the RIBA and the RICS (see p.5). In
essence, these groups were more concerned with defending their
professional interests in relation to legislation directly affecting them
than with a programme which by no stretch of the imagination
appeared related to the broad issues of planning, housing and land use.
This is not to say that groups such as the TCPA have been unconcerned
with urban problems. It is just that it has viewed the main problem as
overcrowding and urban sprawl which would best be solved by planned
dispersal to new and growth towns. As a result, the TCPA has been
preoccupied with the growth sector of urban change, rather than with

the social problems characteristic of inner city decline.[20]

At the same time, in 1968 few groups had been formed specifically to champion the cause of the inner city poor and without such a lobby mass pressure from below to solve urban problems was unlikely. On the contrary, the Urban Programme was almost entirely the product of elites and elite perceptions of what the 'urban problem' was. At the national level, Home Office civil servants inspired by currently popular ideas about poverty were critical in determining the shape of the Programme. Positive discrimination was also enshrined in public policy via the Seebohm Report which was published in 1969. Local governments and their associations were also important in negotiating the detail of the Programme. It was they who resisted government attempts to divide costs on a 50/50 basis and insisted instead on a 25/75 distribution.[21] They were also partly responsible for acquiring for local authorities the right to vet individual schemes and therefore the ability to hold grant recipients directly accountable to local rather than central government.[22]

(c) *The Community Development Project*

By espousing area based positive discrimination measures, the Government was making at least the implicit assumption that poverty was residual; that there were some individuals who had escaped the all embracing net of the welfare state and were therefore in need of special help. Such an analysis accepts the basic structure of society and implicitly blames poverty on the personal characteristics of the poor themselves. The 1966 Local Government Act, the EPAS and the Urban Programme all made this assumption, although it was rarely made explicit. However, the fourth experiment in this area, the National Community Development Project was much less ambiguous about its immediate and long term objectives. Introduced in 1969, it was announced as a 'neighbourhood based experiment aimed at finding new ways of meeting the needs of people living in areas of high social deprivation'.[23] To this end, twelve CDP teams were established between 1969 and 1972 in areas perceived to be suffering from severe urban deprivation. As with the American Community Action Projects established under the 1964 Economic Opportunity Act, the CDP's main objective was to encourage self-help and participation by local residents in the hope of improving communication with and access to local government and its services. Each CDP programme consisted of a team working with the local authority, and monitored by a local university or polytechnic. Much has been written about the 12 schemes and their experience[24] and this is not the place to record their progress in detail. However, it is important for our purposes to point to the rather extraordinary circumstances surrounding the inception of the scheme. As with the Urban Programme, the CDP was almost entirely the product of the Home Office. Derek Morrell was the prime mover within the bureaucracy; his vision of the future and of the problems besetting British cities was instrumental in determining the organisation and objectives of the CDP. He was in fact, working on the idea of community action at the time of the Urban Programme announcement, and when launched, the CDP was funded under similar arrangements: 75 per cent Home Office, 25 per cent local authorities. (The research aspect of the CDP was funded 100 per cent by the Government.) No doubt the decision to launch the CDP was helped by the Urban Programme initiative and the two programmes were linked administratively. The major distinction between the two schemes was the CDP's emphasis on action research and participation. As Derek Morrell put it in reference to the Hillfields (Coventry) CDP:

The whole project is aimed against fragmentation. . .The starting point of the project is that ours is a fragmented, disintegrating society. But the project aims at evolutionary changes, not revolution. Depersonalisation is another problem. The technical juggernaut is taking over and we are no longer the masters. The most difficult step will be how to discover to perform the crucial task of raising the people of Hillfields from a fatalistic dependence on 'the council' to self-sufficiency and independence.[25]

As with the other initiatives, political parties and interest groups played virtually no role whatever in the genesis of the CDP. Also, as with the Urban Programme, local authorities were important during implementation. This is hardly surprising given the central role ascribed to local co-ordination in the CDP organisation. But unlike the Urban Programme, the local projects were designed specifically to improve the local 'service delivery system', so local governments, rather than being the mere recipients of central government largesse, were actually expected to become more responsive to the needs of citizens. Almost without exception, the individual CDP teams experienced considerable resistance from authorities required to improve their services. As in the case of America's Community Action Projects,[26] hierarchical local government bureaucracies set in established values and procedures could not accommodate these new demands. Of course, as originally conceived, the CDP teams were not meant to conflict with local governments. But given their brief, it was virtually inevitable that they would. In sum:

(i) They were assigned to work in areas described as severely deprived. Yet at the ground level it became obvious to most of the teams that the designated areas were often no more or less deprived than surrounding areas.

(ii) Hence the target areas, while containing many poor people, were often not dominated by the poor. It was clear that if poverty was the problem, a strategy much more geographically inclusive and radical in its approach would have to be adopted.[27]

(iii) Because of the reliance on an official (if vague) definition of deprivation which emphasised the characteristics of *individuals*, project workers were expected to concentrate on improving access to the social services. However, some teams saw that the fundamental problem of deprivation was related more to patterns of commercial and industrial development than to poor social service provision.[28]

(iv) Thus convinced, many project workers challenged the very processes whereby local governments allocate resources to areas and individuals, rather than, as their brief required, sought to improve the *efficiency* of allocation.[29]

(v) In those instances where teams did attempt to improve target populations' access to services (as in the case of the Southwark CDP), the hierarchical and highly stratified nature of local government prevented meaningful results from being achieved.[30]

It now seems almost certain that the closure of the CDP Information and Intelligence Unit in 1977, together with the decision not to pursue similar projects in the future, was precipitated by the highly critical stand taken by most of the teams. After 1974, the Home Office let individual local authorities decide the fate of their CDPs. As Andrew Milnor has put it:

When dominant interests decided to go headhunting the Home Office did little to protect their own projects, and by 1975 had gone so far as to suggest that local authorities might wish to reconsider their commitment. When the time came to unburden itself of the projects the Department did not step in to preserve this or that aspect, but allowed the local authorities to decide what would be kept and what thrown away. The need to sustain relationships between central administration and local authority meant the sacrifice of CDP teams and the termination of their efforts in experimental social policy.[31]

(d) *Other Initiatives to Combat Urban Deprivation*

By 1972, some disquiet at the fragmented nature of the various positive discrimination programmes existed. Outside government, Shelter, the charity and publicity group formed specifically to represent homeless and badly housed people, criticised the programmes for their failure to attack 'fundamental' causes of inequality. The report of the Shelter Neighbourhood Action Project (SNAP) which had been set up in an inner area of Liverpool to help the local authority implement the 1969 Housing Act (see p.136) concluded: 'The really intractible nature of urban deprivation is that to solve one problem is but to succumb to another and, since public action is always conceived in a fragmented fashion, resulting programmes have not been relevant to the real circumstances of the inner city.'[32] Possibly in response to such criticisms, several new initiatives were launched in this period both by the Home Office and by the Department of the Environment.

In November 1972, Robert Carr, the Home Secretary, announced the creation within the Home Office of an Urban Deprivation Unit. The aims of the Unit were two-fold: first to improve co-ordination between the various Home Office programmes concerned with urban deprivation; and second, to conduct research into the nature of urban deprivation. As far as the civil servants on the ground were concerned, these twin aims were closely related. A Unit report calling for a major research study of deprivation put it thus:

Urban deprivation is a complex phenomenon straddling departmental responsibilities and local authority boundaries. Tackling it more effectively must therefore involve the co-ordination of large numbers of separate policies and agencies at all levels of Government. This in turn requires a clear understanding of the nature of the problem and of the limitations of different forms of government action in dealing with it. The objectives of this study are:
(i) to analyse the problem of urban deprivation;
(ii) to produce a framework within which a comprehensive programme or set of policies for tackling it can be developed, and
(iii) to consider arrangements for carrying out this programme and for monitoring progress.[33]

246 Policies Towards the Inner Cities

A parallel move within the DOE involved the creation of the Inner
Area Studies (IASs). During the budget debate in March 1972, Peter
Walker, Secretary of State for the Environment announced that the
Department would develop a 'total approach to the urban environment',
through studies to be undertaken in six towns and inner city areas.[34]
Two types of studies were to be contracted with professional
consultants. One would primarily be concerned with the management
of towns and how the new district authorities' decision-making
structures could deal with 'urban environmental problems'. Oldham,
Rotherham and Sunderland were selected for analysis. The other three
studies (the Inner Area Studies) would look at the 'environmental
problems of three inner city areas [Liverpool, Birmingham and
Lambeth] and the possible courses of action to deal with them'.[35]
The main objective of the latter studies was to 'provide lessons on the
powers, resources and techniques which the Department and local
authorities will need to deal with the problems of our inner areas
generally'.[36] In some respects, the Inner Area Studies were distinct
from the innovation of the 1960s. First, they were a product of the
DOE, the agency responsible for 'mainstream' urban policy in housing,
planning and transport. Second, at least in their rhetoric, they
recognised the interconnectedness of the problems and policies affecting
urban areas. A 'total approach' strongly suggests the need to relate the
specific problem of urban deprivation to other factors affecting urban
society. Third, they recognised the dearth of knowledge about exactly
what was going on in inner city areas. Both the EPAs and the Urban
Programme made certain *a priori* assumptions about the nature of urban
problems and poverty which were essentially ideological in nature.
Having diagnosed the urban problem as one deriving from the
inadequacies of individuals, these programmes then went about looking
for indicators of 'deprivation'. Quite apart from the problems of
constructing indices of deprivation (which are legion[37]) very little
research had been conducted in the mid-1960s into the nature of urban
problems. The brief given to the Inner Areas Studies' consultants was
wide and included some 'action research' elements, but the main thrust
of the studies was in research. Of course, all research makes *a priori*
assumptions, and the studies' area focus was very similar to earlier
initiatives. However, the emphasis on a 'total' approach suggested that
such things as employment levels and population changes would be
examined. Perhaps surprisingly, this was novel, even as late as 1972.
The Urban Deprivation Unit was also an advance on the 1960
programmes because of its emphasis on research and its ambition to

co-ordinate existing programmes.

It would, however, be quite misleading to characterise these changes as revolutionary. Rather than the IASs and the Urban Deprivation Unit being radical policy departures, they were designed to improve the efficiency of existing programmes. The area based focus remained, and there was nothing in either initiative that challenged the need for positive discrimination as the *primary* means whereby deprivation could be removed. Certainly, an increased appreciation of the complexity of urban problems was present, as the emphasis on research reflects. In sum, these innovations under a Conservative government in no way challenged the assumptions of the 1960s – although, as with the CDP, there was the potential that, once implemented, they could lead to radically different perceptions of the nature of urban problems.

The IASs and the Urban Deprivation Unit were novel in another respect. Both had as broad aims the integration of existing programmes and policies – not, it should be added, in order to reduce costs, but rather to expedite more efficiently the objectives of the Labour programmes of the 1960s. In fact, during the 1970-74 period, expenditure on inner city programmes rose quite rapidly – even if it remained small in relation to spending on traditional policies.[38] Nothing, indeed, better demonstrates the almost complete absence of party controversy over inner city policies, than does Conservative policy between 1972 and 1974. Robert Carr, the Home Secretary, together with Peter Walker at the DOE were, if anything, more enthusiastic about combating urban deprivation than were their Labour predecessors.[39]

It may be that the Conservatives were reacting to outside criticism of existing programmes but it should be stressed that there was little criticism of the fundamental principles underpinning the CDP, the EPAs and the Urban Programme. When, for example, A.H. Halsey published the first report of the EPA action research experiments in 1972, positive discrimination in education was hailed as a major advance for the educationally disadvantaged.[40] The Halsey Report accepted that the EPAs were of limited value in combating the general problem of poverty, but it considered that with some administrative improvements, the EPA concept had great potential.[41] In fact, the most notable characteristic of this period was neither criticism of nor praise for the various experiments, but a near absence of comment on them. They were, it is true, relatively recent innovations in 1972, but the experience of similar American projects had been widely publicised.[42] It is surprising, then, that the British experiments aroused so little debate.[43]

The period between 1965 and 1975 witnessed major innovations in inner city policy all of which made certain assumptions. Urban problems were perceived largely in terms of multiple deprivation experienced by individuals concentrated in certain 'pockets' or 'blackspots' of urban decline. Although initially race and racial problems were a major spur to the creation of the programmes, this issue tended to recede in importance as an appreciation of the extent to which 'multiple deprivation' affected many white populations — often in cities like Glasgow and Newcastle where the minority population was small. Political party debate played virtually no part in shaping this new policy agenda. It is true that the original decision to introduce the Urban Programme was highly political, inspired as it was by a desire to douse the flames aroused by Enoch Powell's 'Rivers of Blood' diatribe. However, it is difficult to find quite such dramatic evidence supporting a claim that the other experiments were primarily politically motivated. Instead — and this is also true of the final form of the Urban Programme — civil servants and politicians influenced by currently popular ideas concerning the nature of poverty and urban society were instrumental in adding positive discrimination to the policy agenda. Also important in all the experiments were the values and interests of the myriad local authorities who were responsible in most cases for administering the programmes at the ground level. Perhaps the most remarkable feature of the experiments was their almost total administrative isolation from mainstream urban policies in housing, land-use planning and transport. If evidence is needed to support the view that policy makers perceived urban problems in terms of a culture of poverty, then this isolation is it. For the post-war policies of industrial location, dispersal and slum clearance carried on quite merrily between 1965 and 1974 and were generally considered *unrelated* to the positive discrimination experiments.

Government and the Inner Cities 1974-8: Policy Renewal or Policy Confusion?

The entrance of the DOE into the positive discrimination arena in 1972 represented the first stirrings of a major change in policy. As the agency responsible for most urban policies its administration of the Inner Areas Studies had at least the potential for linking urban deprivation programmes to housing, planning and transport. Moreover, the 1969 Housing Act had, through the creation of the General Improvements Areas (GIAs) provided for the concentration of rehabilitation grants in

certain declining inner city areas. This logic was extended by the 1974
Housing Act which established the more comprehensive Housing
Action Areas (HAAs). As was revealed in Chapter 4 both these
programmes have experienced problems and neither can be considered
dramatic changes in policy. However, they *were* the first attempt to
link area based positive discrimimation to a major urban policy area,
and they reflect a general shift in thinking towards the inner city which
had begun during the late 1960s and early 1970s.

The first element in this shift was a growing belief that the attack
on urban deprivation had to be 'comprehensive'. Hence the 1972
reference to a 'total approach to the Urban environment', and the wide
brief given to the IASs. On 1 July 1974 yet another programme was
announced: the 'Comprehensive Community Programmes'. Speaking
in the House of Commons Roy Jenkins, the Labour Home Secretary,
heralded these as:

> a new strategy for tackling the problems of those living in the most
> acutely deprived urban areas. It involves the preparation and
> subsequent implementation by selected local authorities in
> collaboration with all those concerned, of comprehensive
> community programmes containing an analysis of the needs of the
> area considered as a whole and proposals for meeting them. Those
> programmes are to be developed through a series of trial runs, and
> financial arrangements will be discussed with the local authorities.[44]

Again, the rhetoric shows how thinking had shifted towards the belief
that the success of positive discrimination depends on a total or
comprehensive approach. How this could be achieved by the Home
Office whose programmes touched on urban areas quite marginally in
comparison with the DOE or DHSS, was not explained. As it turned
out, the CCPs were not really a new national programme at all (only in
Gateshead and Motherwell were CCPs actually launched) but instead
were a pilot research project designed to discover the best way
government could use its resources to combat urban deprivation. One
important result of this research effort was a review of urban
deprivation policies by the Institute for Local Government Studies
at the University of Birmingham.[45] As might have been expected, this
report showed that local government officials gave low priority to the
various urban deprivation experiments, partly because of the difficulty
in defining deprivation, but also because of the near absence of
co-ordination between programmes, and the fact that few of them

(the Urban Programme being the main exception) involved much expenditure.[46] Also not surprisingly, officials considered slum clearance and area improvement (HAAs and GIAs) much more important in affecting deprived areas.[47] Both involved considerable expenditure, and slum clearance could completely transform — and sometimes destroy — inner city communities. It could be argued that of all the problems local citizens encounter in their dealings with government and private interests, housing and clearance issues are the most serious and the most extensive. For example, during the year August 1973 and July 1974, the Southwark CDP Information and Advice Centre received 407 callers with problems associated with redevelopment, 366 with landlord/tenant difficulties and 241 with home loss. Together, these represented more than 40 per cent of all grievances; the next most important issue, Social Security accounted for just 17 per cent of the total.[48]

Neither the DOE's innovations nor the CCPs represented a radical departure from past policy. All were founded on the assumption that area based positive discrimination measures were the most suitable weapons for combating individually defined deprivation. However, the new 'holistic' approach did reflect disquiet with the effectiveness of the separate experiments, even if, in practice, taking a comprehensive view changed very little.

The second element in the shift in thinking characteristic of this period was the generation of a large volume of research — much of it deriving from the experiments themselves — offering a fundamental critique of successive governments' strategy towards the inner city. Very generally, this research consisted of two distinct critiques:

(a) A radical critique deriving mainly from the experience of the CDP teams. As earlier noted this was based on a general analysis of the role of capital investment in urban areas, and of the relationship between capital and the state. To a greater or lesser extent this work employed a Marxist framework and it paralleled work being conducted by academic Marxist urban sociologists, particularly those contributing to the annual conferences on urban society organised by the Centre for Environmental Studies.[49]

(b) A liberal critique deriving from a variety of sources in and outside government. A major part of this work concluded that the economic base of many cities or parts of cities was rapidly being eroded. One of the first claims to this effect, *The Inner City*, was published by Graham

Lomas in 1974.[50] Lomas's study concentrated on London and found that certain areas of Inner London were experiencing serious economic decline. However, other areas were prospering and, within the declining neighbourhoods, government housing and employment policies had aggravated labour and housing shortage and accelerated the decline.[51] Debate on the nature and extent of decline in London continues[52] — although the census figures show indisputably that there has been a rapid and accelerating decline in skilled jobs in manufacturing industry in the city. In 1975 the Greater London Council added its own not inconsiderable weight to the debate, and in a publication, *London: The Future and You*, pleaded for a redirection of industrial investment back to the inner city.[53] Also in 1975, a Fabian Society pamphlet criticised existing policies for accelerating the retreat of industry from the inner cities to New Towns and growth towns, and also condemned area-based approaches to the inner city.[54] David Eversley and others specifically attacked the New Towns' failure to take the old and disadvantaged and their tendency instead to take young white skilled workers.[55] Evidence of the effects of housing policy on the disadvantaged and particularly on racial minorities also came to light in 1975 and 1976.[56] *The Economist* devoted a special section in January 1977 to the particular plight of London.[57] Finally, when the Inner Areas Studies were published in 1977, they stressed the serious industrial and housing problems of Liverpool, Lambeth and Birmingham, rather than inadequate social services and other individual-related problems.[58]

Not all informed opinion was ranged against existing policies. Many planners continued to support dispersal and the expansion of New Towns, although they recognised that much needed to be done to make the inner cities attractive for their remaining populations.[59] Professional planners reacting to what they saw as a new orthodoxy defended dispersal by arguing that it was complementary to rather than competitive with inner city rejuvenation. They accepted central city population decline as inevitable and saw the government role as one of planning the dispersal to New Towns and growth areas in an orderly fashion while also encouraging inner area renewal.[60] Moreover, the Lambeth Inner Area Study accepted this reasoning arguing that population pressure *still* existed in some parts of London, if not in Liverpool and Birmingham.[61]

Official reaction to what by 1976 was an intensifying debate came with statements by the Prime Minister and by Peter Shore, Labour's

Secretary of State for the Environment to the effect that the
Government was about to reappraise its policies towards the inner city.
At a *Sunday Times* sponsored conference significantly entitled 'Save
Our Cities', Peter Shore repeated this pledge, and stressed the need for
renewed industrial investment in inner areas, as well as improved
housing and other services.[62] Mr Shore continued:

> There is to my mind one outstanding conclusion from all the
> research and development work of the past few years, from the
> Community Development Projects, the Urban Programme, the
> Comprehensive Community Programmes and above all the Inner
> Area Studies, and it is this.
>
> If we are to make real headway in improving the conditions of
> our inner city areas we must use the main programmes of central and
> local government. We need to get an inner city dimension into those
> programmes, at central and local level alike. By main programmes
> I mean education, social services, housing, transport, planning,
> industry, manpower and the various environmental services. We
> cannot rely solely, or even mainly, on extra initiatives such as the
> Urban Programme or [sic] Educational Priority Areas. These provide
> valuable topping up, and help to ameliorate problems. But if we are
> to get to grips with the underlying economic and social forces, we
> must deploy the major instruments of public policy.[63]

The Government's precise plans for the inner city were published as a
White Paper June 1977.[64] Drawing largely on the research generated
by the various urban deprivation experiments and especially the Inner
Area Studies, the White Paper pointed to the serious economic decline
experienced by many cities. Semi and unskilled men were greatly
overrepresented in inner Birmingham, Manchester and Glasgow,[65] and
between 1966 and 1976 population decline in these cities and also in
Liverpool, Inner London, Nottingham and Newcastle ranged from 22
to 8 per cent.[66] Economic and population decline was accompanied,
the document added, by physical decay and widespread social
disadvantage, and the main aims of policy should be to raise the
economic and social status of inner city areas and their inhabitants. To
this end several important initiatives were proposed. Existing
programmes and policies were to be organised so as to help inner areas;
housing policy was to be geared to employment opportunity and
mobility; the delivery of social services was to be co-ordinated more
effectively at the local level; and the rate support grant further adjusted

to take account of the needs of inner areas. Economic policy, especially industrial location, was also to be revamped so that, after the Assisted Areas, inner city areas would take precedence in the granting of Industrial Development Certificates (IDCs). Significantly, New Towns would have to take second place to the declining cities. In addition, the powers of local authorities to assist industry were to be extended and the objectives of the Location of Offices Bureau (LOB) changed so as to assist location in inner areas — the precise opposite of its original brief!

The White Paper also proposed the revamping of existing inner city programmes, including the transfer of the Urban Programme, the Urban Deprivation Unit and the CCP to the DOE, and an expansion of the Programme brief to include industrial, environmental and recreational matters as well as social projects. Funding for the Urban Programme was to be increased from £30 million in 1976/7 to £125 million in 1979/80, and the CCP experiments were to be maintained as an information gathering exercise for central and local governments. Finally, the White Paper proposed the creation of special local/central government 'Partnerships' for some of the larger cities. This novel proposal involved setting up joint machinery to analyse inner area needs, draw up a programme and oversee its implementation.[67] For Scotland, the document proposed special help, including support for the Glasgow Eastern Area Renewal project by increasing Urban Programme funds from £6 million to £20 million between 1976/7 and 1980/81.[68]

There can be no doubt that the White Paper represented an important change in policy. Area based positive discrimination measures with a primarily social service orientation were effectively dropped, and replaced with an emphasis on administrative co-ordination and economic revival. Mainstream urban policy including housing, planning, and industrial location were in principle to be linked to inner city decline for the first time, and the post-war policy of dispersal, while not discarded, was accorded lower priority than ever before.

Some planners have reacted to these broad initiatives with some anguish. Already under attack from all sides for the redevelopment follies of the 1960s, many planners long committed to the post-war planning paradigm, considered the general trend against dispersal as a denial of all they held dear.[69] On closer examination, however, *Policy for the Inner Cities* looks much more like the murmurings of a policy reversal rather than a full scale retreat from the *status quo*. Little in the way of extra resources was promised for the inner cities and, although modifications in planning and dispersal policies were mentioned, how and to what extent these would occur was not clear. As for administrative co-ordination little detailed guidance was provided, either for the proposed central/local partnerships or for the co-ordination of housing, transport, planning, employment and industrial location policy. When it is remembered that the IDC system is administered by the Department of Trade and Industry, urban transport by the Department of Transport, and housing and planning by rather distinct sections within the DOE, the formidable character of the co-ordination problem is revealed.

At the time of writing, it is still uncertain what the Government intends, although on 8 November 1977 and in line with the White Paper, Mr Shore announced to Parliament his intention to increase urban aid to £125 million by 1979 and to establish central/local partnerships in Liverpool, Birmingham, Manchester/Salford, Lambeth, Hackney, Islington, the London Docklands, Newcastle upon Tyne and Gateshead.[70] In addition, housing resources have been further redirected towards inner city areas.[71] Interestingly, the Conservative reaction to these initiatives has been to complain that they are insufficient. Generally, the Conservatives have welcomed the principles underpinning the policies, and in November 1977, Michael Heseltine, Opposition spokesman on the environment declared that: 'The sums of money Mr Shore is offering are so small and so spread over the years in relation to the scale of the problem that he is giving a false impression in suggesting that there are any real solutions to the problem.'[72] It is true that the Conservatives pleaded for less centrally directed subsidies and more incentives for private industry to invest in the inner city[73] but according to the White Paper such incentives were a part of official policy. In sum, the Conservatives accepted totally the wisdom of redirecting resources back to inner areas — even if they disagreed with some of the means to this end being employed by Labour.

For students of the public policy process the 1976/7 policy reappraisal offers fertile ground for analysis. As with all the inner city initiatives, inter-party politics appeared to play a minimal role. Instead, government reacted to the large volume of research generated in the period between 1970 and 1975 which pointed to the deteriorating relative position of the inner city and to the inadequacy of existing policies. Neither were interest groups crucial in precipitating the reappraisal. Although such organisations as Shelter and the Child Poverty Action Group generally welcomed inner city reinvigoration, there is no evidence to suggest that the Government was responding to their specific demands. A slightly more cynical interpretation of the reappraisal involves political and especially electoral considerations. There are two positions here. First, it has been argued that the new emphasis on the inner cities was government's reaction to increasing urban unrest — especially over racial questions. Certainly between 1975 and 1977 the political salience of race increased perceptibly. Racist political parties gained support, particularly at the local level,[74] and violent confrontations between the police, minorities, fascist and left wing groups began to occur.[75] With unemployment among racial minorities increasing much more rapidly than among the population as a whole (between 1974 and 1977, total unemployment increased 120 per cent, but among racial minorities the increase was 350 per cent)[76] and given the concentration of minorities in inner city areas, this seems a reasonable thesis. However, important caveats to any such claim must be made. The most disadvantaged urban areas are not always those with high concentrations of minorities. Indeed, Glasgow, Gateshead, Newcastle and even Liverpool, all cities which have received government aid under the various programmes, have few non-whites in comparison with London and Birmingham. Even within the latter cities, areas of great disadvantage do not always coincide with high minority concentration.[77] Irrespective of race there is, moreover, little evidence that social and political protest has been at a high level within the most run down inner city areas. Also, if, as some radical commentators have claimed, the motives of government have been to manipulate rebellious and disadvantaged masses into political quiescence rather than simply to improve their objective living conditions and life chances, then the 1976 and 1977 initiatives seem sadly misguided. No sensible observer inside government or out could expect the limited measures announced in 1977 to transform the inner city, or radically to improve the economic position of racial minorities. On the other hand, announcements to the effect that government intends to 'rescue' the inner cities might well have the effect of raising the political salience of the 'urban question' including the status of racial minorities. Consequently, the 1976/7 'reversal' far from clamping down on potential or actual unrest, may have just the opposite effect.

The second possible political motive behind the new policy is electoral. Central cities have long been Labour strongholds, and their relative neglect perhaps reflects the complacency with which central and local party organisations have regarded them. Moreover, rapidly declining populations will, following a redistribution of seats, dilute this Labour strength by incorporating present central city constituencies into larger, more complex constituencies. In addition, the Scottish National Party has demonstrated its ability to capture a central Glasgow seat,[78] and similar threats to all the urban Labour strongholds in Scotland exist. So, by redirecting resources to the inner cities, and by arresting population loss, Labour could be protecting an established strength. No doubt this is a reasonable assumption, but it seems unlikely that the Government was motivated primarily by electoral considerations. In the cities named under the 'partnership' arrangements not that many constituencies are, in fact, involved, and in any case, Shore's new policy is very much a long term affair. In a political climate where electoral calculations are made in terms of months and weeks, it seems almost bizarre to claim that a Labour Government would announced a major new urban policy in the (anyway doubtful) hope that it would be electorally useful some years distant. Finally, as mentioned in Chapter 2, personnel changes may have been a factor in explaining the policy renewal. Peter Shore was certainly more sympathetic to a reappraisal than was Anthony Crosland who had long been a supporter of the post-war urban containment and population dispersal principles.

What is certain is that local authorities and their associations will be critical in determining the future shape of inner city policy. The Government has already involved some of them directly via the central/local partnerships and, following the experience of the Urban Programme, the CDPs and the IASs, it now looks as though the Government is convinced of the need for a major role for the authorities in all inner city programmes.

Conclusions

Recent developments in urban policy may signify a break from the basic principles of decrowding and dispersal established after the War. Surprisingly, the major vehicle for recent changes was the initiation of some rather disjointed and ill-thought out positive discrimination programmes during the mid and late-1960s. Rather than these being part of a fundamental critique of urban policy, they were viewed by idealistic civil servants as a supplement to social and educational services which in some geographically defined areas had proved inadequate in combating poverty. Defining urban problems in terms of individual-related area deprivation was a highly *convenient* policy to pursue at the time. Expenditure need not be great and, more important, existing power relations in urban society need not be challenged. Any government offered the opportunity to solve a persistent social problem at such low economic and political cost is likely to take it.

As it turned out, the area based positive discrimination measures conceived by the Home Office and (to a lesser extent) the DOE, completely misunderstood the nature of the urban problem, and it was not until after a long and painful education induced by the experience of the programmes at the ground level that government was obliged to reassess its strategy. The currently popular diagnosis based on an analysis of changes in industrial and commercial investment is almost certainly on stronger ground, although much uncertainty about the fate of recent initiatives remains. It may be, for example, that government sponsored industrial investment in the inner city will benefit some social groups rather than others, that young skilled white workers will be attracted back to the city only to displace the disadvantaged. Calls for labour intensive small scale industry in the inner city may be of greater help to the disadvantaged, but no one is exactly sure what this means. Most labour intensive small scale industry uses cheap labour, perhaps then, the Government's encouragement of small business will result in the creation of sweat shops.[79] All this assumes, of course, that investment *can* be attracted to the inner city. Treasury opposition to large scale subsidies might prevent this, as might electoral and local authority opposition from the more prosperous parts of society and from rural areas. Rest assured that any subsidies will have to be large. The experience of the Assisted Areas demonstrates the severe limitations on the state's ability to direct private investment in a mixed economy — and in many respects suburban locales within the Assisted Areas are in a more favourable position than are the inner cities. They have a pool of skilled labour, low land costs and (generally speaking) a relatively 'easy' housing market. Depressed inner city areas lack most of these. Planners and other professionals remain, moreover, resolute in their opposition to a total reversal of post-war policy and a denial of the New Towns ideal. Further, the Government's selection of certain inner areas for special help under the partnership arrangements, still has an arbitrary element to it. Many impoverished communities have been left out, as have all those individuals (a majority of the poor) whose condition cannot be defined in spatial terms.[80] Perhaps, indeed, the planners are right in fearing that the Government might abandon the New Towns ideal. As was noted in Chapter 2, the New Towns represent one of the few at least partial successes of post-war planning policy. The need for planned urban growth remains — including further growth in some New Towns. However, whether, given existing administrative structures and economic and political constraints, this can be reconciled with the revitalisation of the inner cities, remains to be seen.

Of all the areas covered in this book, inner city policies have been the most 'internalised'. Party politics and ideology and external pressure from interested groups have played minimal roles in comparison with the housing, land-use planning and values, transport and regional economic policy areas. Instead, certain ideas about poverty and urban society, together with the results of mainly internally generated research have been of paramount influence. This said, events since 1975 are likely both to increase the political salience of the inner city issue and to result in its incorporation into mainstream urban policy. If, indeed, Peter Shore's White Paper really does represent a *reversal* of post-war policies and a desire to integrate housing, transport, planning and economic investment policies in inner cities, then the Pandora's Box will truly have been opened, and political and bureaucratic battles over resources and jurisdictions will be legion. Perhaps however, the cautious progress of the new inner city policy is evidence that the Government is aware of the costs of adopting a truly radical policy. As will be argued in the next chapter, to be effective, such a policy would require not only great political resources, but also the abandonment of the incrementalist and selectivist policies which have characterised Labour programmes since 1964.

Notes

1. E.J.B. Rose *et al., Colour and Citizenship: A Report on British Race Relations* (London, Oxford University Press, 1969), Table 10.1, p.97.

2. Ibid., Part III.

3. Quoted by Roy Hattersley, 2nd Reading of the 1966 Local Government Bill, H.C. Deb.729, para.1334.

4. Rose *et al., Colour and Citizenship*, pp.272-3.

5. *Children and Their Primary Schools: A Report of the Central Advisory Council for Education* (London, HMSO, 1967), ch.5.

6. Quoted in A.H. Halsey (ed.), *Educational Priority, Volume 1: EPA Problems and Policies* (London, HMSO, 1972), p.46.

7. Rose *et al., Colour and Citizenship*, pp.617-18.

8. Quoted in Clare Demuth, *Government Initiatives on Urban Deprivation*, Runnymede Trust Briefing Paper (London, 1977), p.3.

9. John Edwards and Richard Batley, 'The Urban Programme', unpublished manuscript, Beford College, London, 1976, ch.3. We are indebted to the authors for providing us with selected chapters from this study.

10. H.C. Deb.769, 22 July 1968, para.40.

11. Home Office, Urban Programme Circular, no.1, 4 October 1968.

12. Edwards and Batley, 'Urban Programme', ch.3, p.25.

13. Ibid., ch.3.

14. Ibid., p.25.

15. Ibid., pp.31-2.

16. H.C. Deb.847 (1972-73), Written Answers, p.122.

17. Quoted in Claire Demuth, *Urban Deprivation'*, p.4.

18. Quoted in Michael Meacher, 'The Politics of Positive Discrimination', in Howard Glennerster and Stephen Hatch (eds.), *Positive Discrimination and Inequality* (Fabian Research Series, no.314, London, 1974), p.4.

19. David McKay and Andrew Cox, 'Confusion and Reality in Public Policy: The Case of the British Urban Programme', *Political Studies*, vol.26 (December 1978).

20. See B. Foley, 'British Town Planning: One Ideology or Three?', *British Journal of Sociology*, vol.II (September 1960), pp.211-32; also, B. Foley, 'Ideas and Influence: TCPA', *Journal of the American Institute of Planners*, vol.12 (October 1960), pp.9-15.

21. Edwards and Batley, 'Urban Programme', p.31; *The Times*, 23 and 28 July 1968.

22. Ibid.; see also M. Adeney, '3M Given to Areas of Special Social Need', *Guardian*, 23 November 1972, p.4.

23. Quoted in Clare Demuth, *Urban Deprivation*, p.6.

24. See in particular the publications of the National Community Development Project, *Poverty of the Improvement Programmes* (1975); *Forward Plan 1975-1976* (1975); *Local Government Becomes Big Business* (1975); *Whatever Happened to Council Housing?* (1976); *Profits Against Houses* (1976); *The Costs of Industrial Change* (1977); *Gilding the Ghetto* (1977), all CDP Information and Intelligence Unit, London; also, N. Flynn, 'Urban Experiments Limited: Lessons from CDP and Inner Area Studies', paper before the CES Conference on Urban Change and Conflict, 4-7 January 1977, York University; Ray Lees and George Smith, *Action Research in Community Development* (London, Routledge and Kegan Paul, 1975); George Smith, 'Community Development: Rat Catchers or Theorists?', *New Society*, 14 February 1974; Alan Davis, Neil McIntosh, Jane Williams, *The Management of Deprivation: Final Report of Southwark Community Development Project*, Polytechnic of the South Bank, 1977.

25. Quoted in *Gilding the Ghetto*, p.12.

26. See Peter Marris and Martin Rein, *Dilemmas of Social Reform* (Harmondsworth, Middx., Penguin, 1974).

27. *Gilding the Ghetto*.

28. *Inter Project Report*, pp.48-9; *The Costs of Industrial Change*.

29. Ibid.

30. *The Management of Deprivation*.

31. Andrew Milnor, 'Central Government and Community Action: Britain's Community Development Projects', unpublished paper, State University of New York at Binghamton, 1977.

32. Quoted in Flynn, 'Urban Experiments', pp.11-12.

33. 'Urban Deprivation: A Preliminary Report' (Home Office Press Release, 25 July 1973), p.6.

34. DOE, Press Release, 9 June 1972.

35. Ibid.

36. Ibid.

37. See Sally Holtermann, 'Areas of Urban Deprivation in Great Britain: An Analysis of 1971 Census Data', *Social Trends*, no.6 (London, HMSO, 1975); John Edwards, 'Social Indicators, Urban Deprivation and Positive Discrimination', *Journal of Social Policy*, vol.4, no.3 (1975), pp.275-87; Peter Townsend, 'The Difficulties of Policies Based on the Concept of Area Deprivation', The 1976 Barnett Shine Foundation lecture, Queen Mary College, London, 1976, pp.15-17.

38. Expenditure on the Urban Programme increased from £7.1 million in 1970/71 to £16.5 million in 1974/5, quoted in Claire Demuth, *Urban Deprivation*, p.4.

39. Although it should be stressed that by the early 1970s general enthusiasm for positive discrimination had increased and this may have influenced Conservative politicians.

40. A.H. Halsey (ed.), *Educational Priority, Volume 1: E.P.A. Problems and Policies.*

41. Ibid., ch.14.

42. See Marris and Rein, *Social Reform.*

43. Although among the more radical critics of government social policy, disquiet was shown at the selectivist (as opposed to universalist) assumptions underpinning the experiments. See Muriel Brown, 'Inequality and the Personal Social Services', in Peter Townsend and Nicholas Bosanquet (eds), *Labour and Inequality* (London, Fabian Society, 1972).

44. Quoted in Claire Demuth, *Urban Deprivation*, p.8.

45. John Stewart, Kenneth Spencer, Barbara Webster, *Local Government: Approaches to Urban Deprivation*, Home Office, Urban Deprivation Unit, Occasional Papers No.1, 1976.

46. Ibid., Part.II

47. Ibid.

48. Alan Davies, Neil McIntosh, Jane Williams, *Management of Deprivation*, pp.32-3.

49. See *Gilding the Ghetto, The Costs of Industrial Change.* For examples of the work being done in Marxist urban sociology, see Chris Pickvance (ed.), *Urban Sociology* (London, Tavistock, 1976).

50. Graham Lomas, *The Inner City* (London Council of Social Service, London 1974).

51. Ibid.

52. See in particular, Chris Hamnett, 'Social Change and Social Segregation in Inner London, 1961-1971', *Urban Studies*, vol.13 (1976), pp.261-71; Peter Gripaios, 'Industrial Decline in London: An Examination of its Causes', *Urban Studies*, vol.14 (1977), pp.181-9.

53. GLC, *London: The Future and You – Population and Employment* (London, GLC, 1975).

54. Nicholas Falk and Hanis Martinos, *Inner City* (Fabian Research Series, no.320, Fabian Society, London, 1975).

55. David Eversley, 'Who Will Rescue Our Cities?', *Built Environment Quarterly*, vol.1, no.3 (December 1975).

56. Pat Niner, *Local Authority Housing Policy and Practice*, University of Birmingham, Centre for Urban and Regional Studies, Occasional Paper No.31 (1975); David Smith and Anne Whalley, *Racial Minorities and Public Housing* (London, PEP Broadsheet No.556, 1975). See also David H. McKay, *Housing and Race in Industrial Society* (London, Croom Helm, 1977).

57. 'London's Burning! London's Burning! A Survey', *The Economist*, 1 January 1977, pp.17-38.

58. The three towns studies (Oldham, Rotherham and Sunderland) were published in 1973, and summaries of the consultants final reports on Liverpool, Birmingham and Lambeth were published in January 1977. The full report appeared later in the same year: Graeme Shankland, Peter Wilmott and David Jordan, *Inner London: Policies for Dispersal and Balance: Final Report of the Lambeth Inner Area Study* (London, HMSO, 1977); Hugh Wilson and Lewis Womersley, Roger Tym and Associates, Jamieson Mackay and Partners, *Change on Decay: Final Report of the Liverpool Inner Area Study* (London, HMSO,

1977); Llewelyn-Davies, Weeks, Forestier-Walker and Bor, *Unequal City: Final Report of the Birmingham Inner Area Study* (London, HMSO, 1977).

59. See David Hall, 'The Fallacies in the Dispersal Debate', *The Planner*, vol.62 (November 1976), p.206; John Silkin, 'New Towns and the Inner City', *Town and Country Planning*, vol.44 (September 1976), pp.381-5; David Lock, 'Planned Dispersal and the Decline of London', *The Planner*, vol.62 (November 1976), pp.201-4.

60. Ibid.

61. *Inner London: Policies for Dispersal and Balance.*

62. Address by Peter Shore, Secretary of State for the Environment to 'Save Our Cities' conference in Bristol, 9 February 1977.

63. Ibid., p.6.

64. *Policy for the Inner Cities*, Cmnd.6845 (HMSO, 1977).

65. Ibid., p.2.

66. Ibid., p.17.

67. Ibid., pp.10-19.

68. Ibid., p.23.

69. See Hall, 'Dispersal Debate'.

70. *The Times*, Parliamentary Report, 9 November 1977.

71. 'Councils to receive £100 million more for housing in 1978-9, with emphasis on decaying urban areas', *The Times*, 5 January 1978.

72. *The Times*, 9 November 1977.

73. Ibid.

74. In the May 1976 local elections the National Front fielded 176 candidates and 80 of these polled more than 10 per cent of the vote, and in a July 1976 local by-election in Deptford, South London, the two main racist parties, the National Front and the National Party together polled 44 per cent, compared with 43 per cent for the successful Labour candidate, *Sunday Times*, 4 July 1976, p.6. Since 1976, however, these parties' showing in elections has deteriorated.

75. Generally, disturbances have been of two types: confrontations between the police and black youths, and between white racist groups and left wing protesters of all races.

76. Manpower Services Commission, *Review and Plan 1977*, quoted in *New Society*, 5 January 1978.

77. See Department of the Environment, *Census Indicators of Urban Deprivation*, Working Note No.8 (London, DOE, 1975) for the relationship between New Commonwealth residential settlement and indicators of urban deprivation.

78. In September 1973, the SNP captured Glasgow Govan from Labour – although they lost it to Labour at the subsequent February 1974 Election, David Butler and Dennis Kavanagh, *The British General Election of February 1974* (London, Macmillan, 1974), p.311.

79. Peter Hall has proposed the encouragement of small business run by racial minorities which would almost certainly result in the creation of sweat shops; the 'Inner Cities Dilemma', *New Society*, 3 February 1977, pp.223-5.

80. See Townsend, 'The Difficulties of Policies Based on the Concept of Area Deprivation', pp.7-20.

8 POLITICS, POLICY AND URBAN SOCIETY

> British society to-day exhibits a greater unwillingness to
> discover, to collect and to face up to the social facts of life
> than at any time during the last hundred years. . .Indeed, as
> the potentialities of the social sciences widen, the barriers to
> their effective utilization seem to become more formidable.
> Thus the paradox of better means to social knowledge and less
> inclination to use it. (O.R. McGregor, 'Social Facts and Social
> Conscience', *Twentieth Century*, 1960)

Has post-war British urban policy been a failure? It is all too easy to
answer this question with an unqualified affirmative, and in the light
of the foregoing chapters, readers may be surprised that we ask the
question at all. Government, however, is the art of the possible not the
ideal and any appraisal of this complex policy area must take account
of the very real economic and political constraints on policy makers in
modern industrial societies. According to many Marxist commentators,
political reformers working through the organs of the state are always
doomed to failure because the state at all times serves a master —
capital — whose interests are wholly incompatible with those of the
urban masses.[1] In the light of the continuing inequalities characteristic
of British and other Western cities this neat argument is quite
compelling. One of our main objectives, however, has been to
demonstrate that the state's role in urban society has been highly
variable and has changed according to historical period and, as
important, according to urban policy area. To say that the state's role
has been variable does not, of course, put an end to the matter because
much depends on the nature of state intervention and particularly on
the consequences of intervention for different social groups. In this
context, our final chapter has three main aims. First, to outline and
summarise the configuration of forces responsible for setting the policy
agenda in each of the areas covered in earlier chapters. By policy agenda
we mean the courses of action available for discussion and debate at the
central level, including 'feedback' from implementation experience.
Our second aim is to explain why the policy agenda has taken the
shape it has and to discuss the implications of this for different social
groups. In attempting the latter, we must dwell on the effectiveness of
and prospects for party government for, as we noted in Chapter 1,

parties are liberal democracy's main vehicles with the potential for
mobilising and articulating class interests and translating these into
policy.

The Chapter's final section is devoted to the specific question of
what can be done to forge a national urban policy and whether or not,
in the face of existing constraints, it is possible even to talk in such
terms.

The National Urban Policy Agenda, 1945-78

Drawing on the findings of Chapters 2 and 7, Table 8.1 shows the
particular configuration of influence on the policy agenda in each of
our policy areas. There is, obviously, an arbitrary element in such an
exercise; we have not been able to weight the role of various actors
and forces in a precise fashion. Nonetheless, our analysis did reveal
certain patterns and it is these which Table 8.1 attempts to represent.
Looking at each set of actors in the policy process in turn, the following
are worthy of note:

(a) Parties in Government

When discussing the role of party in government it is important to
distinguish between the extent of party competition in a particular
area and the extent to which, irrespective of competition, party and
party ideology have been important in shaping the policy agenda. It is
certainly possible for competition to be high, but to have little impact
on policy. Some may even argue, indeed, that this is the 'natural' state
of policy making in Britain, where party competition in the form of
sharply contrasting election Manifestos founders on the rocks of
internationally imposed economic constraints which effectively
standardise different parties' policies once in office.[2] Certainly, we
recorded many instances where macro-economic policies had thwarted
the best laid plans of governments — and especially Labour
Governments. While accepting this, Table 8.1 does not refer to those
macro-economic constraints which are largely unaffected by party
factors, for one of our central concerns has been to assess the
independent effect of party and other actors in the policy process.
Our reference to 'party in government' in Table 8.1 is, therefore,
confined to an assessment of the extent to which party competition
and party ideology have been important in shaping the policy agenda
and ultimately, therefore, who gets what in urban areas. In the two
areas where party factors have been critical, housing and land values,
party differences have also been high. However in industrial location

Table 8.1: Agenda Setting in National Urban Policy

Political actors	Policy Areas		
	Housing	Land values	Regional industrial location policies
Parties in central government	Strong party ideological influence, high level of party competition and high electoral salience	Strong party ideological influence, parties competitive, but electoral salience latent	Some party ideological role, but parties agreed on basic goals of policy, high electoral salience as an employment issue
Organised interests: professional and and economic	Highly active, but functionally fragmented. Have had little direct influence on policy	Gradually increasing involvement since 1945, with some reinforcing influence on policy	Some trade union and business role, but generally not a significant influence on policy
Organised interests: protest movements	Little involvement until late 1960s, increasing activity since, but little direct impact on policy	Little involvement or impact on policy throughout	Little involvement or impact on policy throughout period
Central government bureaucracies	Some inertial influence on policy especially vis à vis central/local relations	Important constraining influence on policy innovation in particular periods (1945-50, 1964-70)	Strong inertial influence on policy
Local government bureaucracies	Virtually sole influence in housing management matters, important role in all housing policy areas	Important constraint on change — especially between 1964 and 1970	A marked role in bargaining for central government aid

Table 8.1 *(contd.)*

Policy Areas		
Land-use planning and administration	Urban transport	Inner cities
Relatively small party role except in 1947-61 period, with the exception of local government reform near party agreement since. Low electoral salience	Small party role with partial exception of late 1960s. Low electoral salience (although higher since the rise of the car)	Virtually no party role or party differences. Low electoral salience
Critical in presenting policy alternatives post-1945. Some reinforcing influence since	Probable strong reinforcing influence between 1950 and early 1970s	Little direct involvement, throughout, although expert opinion important in influencing policy
Little involvement until 1960s, increasing activity of local community groups since with some reinforcing influence on policy	Considerable involvement since 1960s, with some direct influence on policy and strong reinforcement influence since early 1970s	No initial involvement, some since 1970 but with little impact on policy
Critical actors in certain periods (1945-47) and to a lesser extent 1961-78	Major policy role reinforced by economic interests	Critical actors throughout, with local authority feedback have shaped policies virtually undisturbed
Important influences on local government reform and some impact on underlying principles of land-use planning	Important negotiating and bargaining role vis à vis central bureaucracy, but essentially deferential to new (professionally conveyed) ideas	Important reactive role vis à vis central bureaucracies at the implementation level

policies, while party differences have been relatively small, we did discover that quite rigid party positions on the question of unemployment were crucial in shaping the policy agenda. In earlier chapters we often referred to the electoral strategies adopted by different governments in the various policy areas, and the relationship between party ideology and electoral strategy is a complex one. In locational policies, for example, Labour's devotion to employment rather than economic growth solutions almost certainly derives both from the ideological base of the Party and from rational electoral choice. Within the Conservative Party, it seems almost certain that the occasional deference to employment based policies was a function of electoral strategy. In housing, a mixture of ideology and electoral strategy was important in influencing policy in both parties. The Conservatives' ideological devotion to owner occupation was also, given their social base of support, electorally useful. Labour Governments had a strong ideological investment in public housing which they have also at least *perceived* to be electorally useful. As we will argue later, however, this perception may have been misplaced. In contrast to housing, land-values policy was characterised by a hiatus between the Labour Party's commitment to public ownership (or at least to a significant state role in taxing profits from land — which *all* sections of the Party adhere to) and the electoral costs of pursuing a dominant state role.

In three central areas of urban policy — land-use planning, urban transport and inner city policies — party politics and ideology played a small role in shaping the policy agenda. It is true that in urban transport policy in the late 1960s and (to a rather greater extent) in land-use planning between 1947 and 1961, party in government played some role, but the general picture is one in which party politics and ideology took second place to other actors in the policy process. When attempting to explain why these questions were largely without party influence or controversy, we can look to several obvious possibilities.

The first is that these areas involve what psephologists have called 'valence issues' — or issues on which everyone, including parties and the electorate, is agreed.[3] It is certainly the case that, judging by opinion polls and election surveys, these matters have not aroused intense feelings as have, for example, industrial relations, race relations or nationalisation. But, except within the very narrow paradigm of election studies, the valence issue explanation has little value. For, given full information and understanding, there are very few issues indeed on which all parties and interests are agreed. Of course all are agreed on the need to fight against vaguely defined problems such as poverty, ignorance and war. But our three areas of urban policy are hardly in this category. On the contrary, they are areas in which the political choices are many and complex and where the costs and benefits of pursuing different policies fall quite unevenly on different classes. This brings us to our second and related possible explanation for the low political and electoral salience of these issues: even if with full information — and parties are major vehicles for publicising issues and thus informing the public — there would be little agreement on these issues, perhaps little is at stake in terms of government expenditure or impact on the population compared with (say) industrial relations. Not so! Policies favouring car owners can penalise non-car owners not only by taxing them for benefits they may not receive but also by reducing their residential and labour mobility. Land-use planning is the supreme example of an issue which, in party political and electoral terms, has been largely apolitical, but which has a profound impact on resource distribution in urban areas. Inner city policies have the potential, at least, for a major redistribution of resources across classes and jurisdictions. It is interesting that it is in precisely these 'non-political' areas that protest movements — or political organisations not allied to established political parties or to economic and professional interest groups — have been the most vocal, if not the most successful, in shaping policy. It is also interesting to note that in those areas of housing policy such as slum clearance, renewal and local authority public housing management which have *not* been important party political issues, protest movements have been equally vocal.

Perhaps the reduced role of parties in some areas of urban policy making is explainable in terms of their being excluded from participation by the technicalities of the issues involved, or by the political power of other interests and groups. The technicality argument may have some credence in particular periods and with respect to some issues, but it cannot qualify as a total explanation. Few issues, after all, are more technical than land values or public housing finance, and yet these have been sources of fierce (if crude) party political conflict. It seems much more feasible to argue that when an issue is for some reason not a source of party interest or conflict, then politicians will fall back on technical arguments or expert advice to justify or support a particular policy position. The political power argument is relevant in this context. As Table 8.1 shows, civil servants in particular have been highly influential in presenting policy choices in inner city policies, urban transport and land-use planning. Possibly this is because through their control of information they have simply denied politicians the opportunity to perceive problems in political terms. Alternatively, as is often claimed in the literature, they may have established 'symbiotic' relationships with economic and professional interest groups and thus have either co-opted politicians or largely excluded them from participation in policy making.[4] These arguments are reminiscent of recent corporatist theories which assume that bureaucracies, organised groups and parties share the same interest in preserving the integrity of the state or advancing economic growth. As a result, politicians cease to respond to social classes and groups through competitive party politics and instead make decisions jointly with civil servants, experts and interested economic and professional groups.[5] But such reasoning does not tell us why there is such great variation in the extent to which politicians are prepared to take a leading role. The single most important explanation of this variation is, in fact, a very simple one: some areas of urban policy have been profoundly influenced by party ideology, while others have not.

As Chapter 4 demonstrated, housing has long been an item on the policy agenda and has neatly divided the parties in terms of policy position. Labour's devotion to public housing and the Conservatives' devotion to owner-occupation was forged during an era when the parties' bases of social support were quite distinct. In the 1920s and 1930s few working class people could even contemplate home ownership, and Labour's advocacy of council housing was both electorally rational and already enshrined in party doctrine. The Conservatives' advocacy of private home ownership was equally compatible with party ideology and party support. Land values policies too have long divided the parties along a distinct left/right ideological spectrum. Few issues could more fundamentally divide parties adhering respectively to socialist and capitalist traditions. Small wonder, then, that these two issues have been characterised by a high degree of party competition and party activity in government. Locational policies are in intermediate case. Between the wars, Labour was strongly committed to regional revival, and since 1945 both parties have sought this goal. However, the close link between industrial location and employment has, at one time or another, caused both parties to perceive locational policies in employment terms, and of course all political parties have promised to reduce unemployment (this broad aim *does* qualify as a valence issue). In the degree to which and the means whereby unemployment was to be reduced, party ideology has been important but not nearly so much as in the housing and land values areas.

In marked contrast, our three other areas of urban policy – land-use planning, urban transport and inner city policies – are all relatively *new* areas of policy. None were specifically mentioned in party Manifestos until after the Second World War. At first sight they may appear largely technical areas in which distinctive party positions would be difficult to calculate. But as we emphasised, all three fundamentally affect resource distribution and the spatial form of urban areas and the policies pursued since 1945 have affected different social groups in a highly variable fashion. We have no reason to suppose that these areas are actually or potentially more or less 'important' than housing or land-values policy. Both their low party political salience and the relatively high salience of other areas is, we contend, largely a function of the failure of the parties to adapt their philosophies and programmes to rapidly changing economic and social circumstances. In areas such as housing and land values (and also industrial policy), parties in power have tended to fall back on established ideological positions dating from earlier historical periods but which later, in the context of changed circumstances, may have little value either electorally or in achieving broad aims of party policy such as equality or economic efficiency. Take housing: as an issue it has constantly been perceived by politicians as electorally important, and opinion polls have repeatedly shown that the electorate consider it a significant issue. Yet there is little evidence that the electorate divide conveniently on a public *v.* private housing dimension. What evidence there is suggests that the public are interested in access to good housing at low cost.[6] However, Labour's continued adherence to the *principle* of public ownership is not necessarily electorally rational. Moreover, when it comes to reconciling Labour's commitment to public ownership with broad principles of equality in housing provision it is quite obvious that the two need not – and indeed have not – been synonymous.

On the contrary, there is mounting evidence that rather than British council housing having reduced inequalities, it may well have increased them – especially when it is remembered that one major consequence of council housing policy, class segregation, has profound implications for occupational and educational opportunities as well as access to a whole range of other services.

Land-values policies have also been affected by obsolete ideological precepts – although in a rather different way from housing. Labour's failure to nationalise land had many causes, but one important barrier to nationalisation was Labour Governments' conviction that such a course would be electorally damaging. However, in the absence of debate on what precisely nationalisation was, it is difficult to know how the electorate might have responded. Certainly a radical solution to the land problem might be quite acceptable to most people so long as rights of owner occupation were fully protected. Labour Governments, convinced that profits from land speculation are inherently evil, have experimented with various interventions in the market, none of which have been carefully thought through in terms of their practicality and, more important, in terms of the fundamental *purposes* of reform. If the purpose of land legislation has been to control excess profits and curb inflation in the hope that non property owners and the disadvantaged will benefit, then the measures adopted have been singularly inappropriate. The Land Commission and the Community Land Act have had all the trappings of radical reform, but given existing economic and political constraints, there was (and is) little hope of these achieving the noble objectives of redistributing betterment from the advantaged to the disadvantaged.

In those areas where party controversy and activity have been low, the failure of the parties to adapt to changing circumstances has been rather more obvious. In the conclusion to their monumental study of planning in post-war England and Wales, Peter Hall *et al.* point to the most notable failure in British land-use planning:

> It is the lack of, and urgent need for, an explicit element in planning procedures for measuring the welfare impacts on different sections of the population. Some groups in our study proved to gain a great deal from planning policies and associated policies in related fields such as housing and transport. Other groups have lost; but the balance of gains and losses has often been surprisingly inequitable. There is an urgent need for procedures at all levels to incorporate an evaluation not merely of aggregate benefit against cost to society as a whole, but of specific gains and losses to different groups. This incidentally will demand that physical plans be increasingly integrated with general plans for social development at both central and local government level.[7]

Strangely, however, these authors do not discuss how, politically, these objectives might be achieved, and in particular what role political parties should play in remoulding the policy agenda. It is difficult to conceive of other agents who could, with the same force and effectiveness, place land-use planning in a framework which measures welfare costs and benefits. Post-war British planning has, of course, been underpinned by certain principles and purposes — dispersal and containment, regional revival, and decrowding. But, as Donald Foley has observed, these objectives have been defined almost solely in terms of an idealised spatial design of plan. Once a 'decent' and 'balanced' environment was achieved, our urban ills — and even our general societal ills — would vanish.[8] Both in the critical period of post-war reconstruction, and from the 1950s to 1970s, Labour and Conservative Governments concurred in this philosophy without really searching further into the economic, welfare and political consequences of policies. Explaining *why* they so concurred is difficult. It may be that they were diverted by issues which, on the face of it, seemed more important or which provided obvious sources of party competition. There may, indeed, be something in the argument that the *adversary* style of British party politics diverts energy into inter party debate *per se*, rather than into rational appraisal of contrasting goals and objectives.[9] Perhaps it was politically easier to defer to civil servants and experts in this apparently technical area. Foley and Hall point to a rather different explanation, however. They argue that within the elitist style of British decision making, there is an overriding faith in simple unitary solutions. As Foley puts it:

> It characteristically builds around seemingly self-evident truths and values and, in turn, bestows a self-justifying tone to its main propositions and chains of reasoning. . .While it may contain highly rational arguments, it is characteristically suprarational in its over-all spirit.[10]

That it is the job of political parties in government to avoid 'suprarational' decision making and instead to calculate the effects of policies on the economy and different social groups, seems obvious. It is also reasonable to assume that the parties' failure to do so in such key areas of policy as land-use planning must in fact reflect on the parties themselves as well as generally on decision making in British government.

Similar criticism can be made of urban transport planning and inner city policies. In both, politicians have tended to accept the wisdom of experts and civil servants, without thinking through the economic and social consequences of proposals. Governments have tended to react rather than to initiate and only very tenuous links between the policies adopted and the social base of support for the parties can be discerned.

Studies by Graham Wilson and Michael Moran of, respectively, agriculture and industrial relations, come to similar conclusions:[11] parties have tended to operate within outmoded conceptual frameworks, which have prevented *purposeful* policy making and have blinded them to the social, economic and political costs of pursuing particular policies.

(b) Organised Professional and Economic Interests

As Table 8.1 shows, with the partial exception of inner city policies, interest groups have been actively involved in all the areas under discussion. However, in very few instances was it possible to identify groups as the dominant actors in policy making. Instead, they frequently had a 'reinforcing' influence on policy. While this is a rather imprecise concept, interest group theory provides us with no better word for describing the tendency for politicians and bureaucrats to decide on courses of actions which involve the least political costs. Often this means concurring with the position of or information provided by vested interests, or using their arguments to support a particular policy option. Hence, professional planning groups have frequently found governments pursuing policies which were in broad agreement with their own objectives, and this coincidence of interest has reinforced policies by reducing the political opposition to government plans.

In urban transport and land-use planning, professional advice channelled through the civil service was crucial at particular times in presenting a narrow range of alternatives to policy makers (1935 to 1947 in land use planning; 1960 to 1966 in urban transport) but, in these instances, professional interests were working *within* government and were difficult to distinguish from civil servants. In the British context, at least, an important distinction exists between professional and economic groups. Within planning, this distinction becomes vital, for planners do not necessarily serve a particular economic interest. Rather, as the observations of Donald Foley suggest, they serve established paradigms of urban planning and change. These may in turn favour some economic interests more than others, but the link is indirect and diffuse. As we discovered earlier, many of the economic interests most centrally involved in urban policy — transport and property interests, manufacturing industry — have benefited from a succession of urban policies. Significantly, with the obvious exception of the very unusual post-war reconstruction period, there has been little relationship between the benefits accruing to different economic interests and the party political complexion of governments. Labour's sundry attempts to control land values generally failed. Because their subsidies have been largely indiscriminate, Labour regional policies have, if anything, been more attractive to industry than have Conservative policies. Since 1961, few differences in policy can be discerned in land-use planning and Labour's attempts to favour public over private transport in 1968 were feeble, to say the least.

Perhaps the most significant economic interest involved in housing, the builders, have benefited from Labour's efforts to build a maximum number of housing units in both public and private sectors, and policies favouring the former help the large corporate builders and penalise the small firms. Even though under Labour Governments public housing starts have increased, the owner-occupied sector has shown an inexorable increase in the post-war years. It would be difficult, therefore, to argue that estate agents, building societies and others linked to the sector have suffered as a result of Labour's housing policies.

But the 'success' of economic interests in urban policy probably owes little to lobbying or other efforts to infiltrate and pressure government. Recent revisions of the pluralist interpretation of interest groups in British politics show that interest groups do not play a highly intrusive role in government.[12] That so many economic interests are nonetheless protected is evidence of the *shared* values and interests between policy makers and groups, and, as will be argued below, in particular between civil servants and established economic interests.

(c) Protest Movements

Our study has not attempted to assess the position of protest movements in policy making in any comprehensive way, and much ignorance remains as to their precise role. It would, however, be a serious mistake to omit any reference to them, for in many policy areas their activities have increased rapidly in recent years. It has become fashionable to refer to citizens' efforts to protest government activities as evidence of *anomie* or a general disillusionment with capitalist society.[13] However, reconciling such an analysis with the wide range of activities which have characterised public protest in urban policy in recent years is very difficult, if not impossible. The literature on public participation reveals that groups of citizens have organised to protest government actions at a variety of levels and using a variety of methods.[14] Generalisation is, therefore, difficult, although we can point to two very tentative conclusions deriving from the experience of protest movements in urban policy. First, as could have been predicted with some confidence, protest based on middle class support has been notably more successful than protest by poor people. Even when the poor have been aided by national organisations such as Shelter or the Child Poverty Action Group, few dramatic results have been achieved. In contrast, mainly middle class efforts to to block the construction of urban motorways have sometimes been highly successful.

The second conclusion has important implications for the first: protest activities have been highest in those areas where political parties in government have generally failed to formulate policies in terms of welfare or other distributive criteria. This failure was seen most obviously in housing management, land-use planning and urban transport. It is but a short step to infer that the rise of urban protest is attributable not only to the massive structural changes wrought by modern industrial society in urban areas but also to a failure of political parties to respond to citizens' demands and needs by offering realistic alternatives based on coherent and purposeful party politics. Moreover, this failure is most serious for those social groups who are least able to wield political and economic resources outside of established party politics. Of course this almost always means the poor. Whether or not political parties, or parties working through bureaucracies, can become more responsive to citizens' needs and demands is a subject we will return to later.

(d) Central Government Bureaucracies

It has become an orthodoxy to attribute British civil servants with a major role in policy making. But civil service influence takes a variety of forms which are by no means equal in weight. A common claim is that civil servants have a 'filter' influence on policy; or through their monopoly of information they present to governments only those policies which defend existing practices and operating procedures. As such they act as a bulwark against new ideas and policies. In our study, considerable evidence supporting this view was presented but mainly concerning attempts at administrative reform rather than with regard to substantive policy. A desire to protect existing administrative jurisdictions is probably a universal characteristic of bureaucracies, and the stress on functional division of responsibility and on *community*

in British administration[15] has probably strengthened this tendency —
hence the opposition of civil servants in the post-war years to the
suggestion that a comprehensive planning ministry be created, and also
the coolness towards the DEA in 1965. Attempts at integration have
not always been resisted so fiercely, mainly because (as with the
creation of the DOE) functionally distinct bureaucracies can survive
intact within nominally integrated comprehensive agencies. Resistance
to administrative reorganisation has, then, been significant and as we noted,
the strict functional division of powers in British administration has often
prevented the formulation of comprehensive and integrated policies.

With regard to substantive policy innovations, the filter role of civil
servants has been much more ambivalent and difficult to identify. As
Heclo and Wildavsky note, civil servants do not explicitly conspire to
exclude certain policies from governments' purview. On the contrary,
they often go along with policies which are ill thought out or even
nonsensical.[16] A much more important channel of civil service
influence was through what we have called the 'inertial' effect. By this
we mean the role of civil servants is automatically enhanced when
governments offer little advice or guidance in particular policy areas.
Time and again in land-use planning, land values and transport policy,
governments have left the 'detail' of policy to civil servants. With
administrative discretion at such a high level, civil servants have
sometimes virtually ruled by default. This brings us full circle, for the
failure of governments to provide guidance is clearly related to the
failure of party in government and of party in opposition. With
governments and oppositions largely unconcerned with appraising
systematically the economic and social distributive effects of policies,
it is not surprising that governments have deferred to expert civil
servants. This tendency reached its apotheosis in inner city policies
where virtually the only initial guidance provided by the Government
in 1968 was a loosely worded speech by the Prime Minister. Small
wonder that civil servants opted for highly selective area based positive
discrimination measures given the lack of guidance from above and the
perceived low political and economic costs of limited positive
discrimination programmes. When left to their own devices, civil
servants will, in other words, opt for policies which are incrementalist
and which avoid challenging existing power relations. It is unlikely,
therefore, that established economic or political interests will lose as a
result of civil servants exercising discretion. This does not mean to say
that bureaucrats are explicitly working on behalf of economic interests.
It is simply to say that both have an interest in the maintenance of the

status quo.

Even the oft quoted secrecy and 'internalised' decision making style of the civil service is more a problem of British government than of the administration *per se.* After all, no bureaucracy *voluntarily* seeks diverse and conflicting opinion from a wide range of interests in society. Open government derives not from the values of civil servants or from the nature of rules and procedures, so much as from the willingness of governments to expose their policy formulation and implementation processes to public scrutiny. It may, as in some areas of policy making in the United States, take a particular configuration of political and electoral power or a specific 'political culture' to achieve this. On the other hand, to return to our earlier theme, political parties and their organisations have the potential for producing the same effect. In our broad areas of urban policy, it is apparent that they have failed to achieve this.

(e) Local Government Bureaucracies

Local governments have played a major role not only in implementing centrally directed policies, but also in bargaining with central government and, in some instances, in determining the shape of policy. That local governments perform these various functions is widely accepted by the literature.[17] In some areas such as housing management, local discretion has been very high — so much so that such vital issues as access and allocation to housing and the spatial distribution of different housing classes in public housing have largely been determined by local bureaucracies. Moreover, there is no evidence that democratic political processes — and in particular political parties — have influenced these bureaucracies. Expenditure studies do reveal the influence of party on overall public housing levels (with other things being equal, Labour councils building more units than Conservative councils) and on council housing rent subsidies, but no relationship has been established between party control and more qualitative aspects of housing management.[18] Generalising on the role of local parties in other areas of urban policy is even more difficult. Some evidence exists suggesting that Labour authorities are more receptive to transport protest activities than are Conservative authorities,[19] but in land-use planning, land values, inner cities and industrial location little relevant research has been undertaken. Of course, with regard to inner city and industrial location policies, the selective nature of central government programmes in any case falls mostly on Labour controlled authorities, so party differences at the local level have less application.

The British central/local system does involve a fair degree of decentralisation, so local authorities do have discretion in many areas, and as important, they do *bargain* with central governments both over spending levels and the procedural and substantive detail of policy.[20] In some instances (especially in housing and transport) local preferences and interests may limit the alternatives available to central governments. While accepting this, and the fact of some local power, it is also the case that the *basic* frame of reference within which local policies decisions are taken has been determined by national legislation. Urban containment, population dispersal, regional economic revival, positive discrimination, land-values policy and many aspects of housing policy derive mainly from *national*, not local, political and bureaucratic interactions. Rules, regulations and financial controls emanating from functionally distinct central bureaucracies profoundly affect, and often shape, local policy agendas. As a result, local bureaucracies play more of a of a reactive than an innovatory role in national urban policy making.

From our analysis it is clear that, in the case of Britain, theories which deny any independent reformist role for the state in urban society are oversimplifications. Claims by the more *dirigiste* Marxists that all state actions, bar those forced on authorities by protest movements, serve the interests of capital can be quickly dismissed. Although the evidence is not always complete, we can point to a succession of policies which owe much more to party ideology and competition and to the administrative complexities and confusion of government, than to some intended or actual link between policies and the interests of capital. Housing policies which reduce residential or occupational mobility, regional economic policies which put employment considerations before economic growth, land-use planning and land-values policies which restrict land supply and which in some instances have inhibited urban investment and growth on low cost city periphery sites, rather than aiding the capital accumulation which comes from rapid economic growth, have inhibited capital accumulation. A quick comparison with government policies (or sometimes the absence of policies) in these areas in other countries,[21] shows just how dramatically different the role of the state has been in different capitalist societies at roughly similar stages of development. Nor can we accept that the 'contradictions' in housing, land-use, land-values and regional policy have been a consequence of pressure from below. As we stressed, protest movements have had a marginal impact on policy, and the electoral link between policy and class interests has been highly tenuous. Admittedly, in housing, land-values and regional policy, Labour policies have been forged at least in past by a perception among party leaders that electoral factors were important. But often, as in the case of housing, this perception was misplaced or misinformed. None of this is to deny that private capital *has* played a major role in urban change. Clearly it has and any coherent urban policy has to face the problem of how and to what extent the market in capital and land can be harnessed, regulated or controlled.

Those who claim that urban policies (and indeed all domestic policies) have been profoundly influenced by macro-economic constraints deriving in the main from international factors are on much stronger ground.[22] Such constraints have affected urban policies in a number of ways. Expenditure on housing, roads, and urban development generally has fluctuated with the fortunes of the economy. Interest rate levels determined in large part by the position of sterling and the balance of payments have also varied greatly and thus have had a major effect on private and public development. Perhaps most importantly, central governments constantly under seige in the international economy may have been diverted away from radical (and possibly expensive) innovations in urban policy. This is almost certainly true of the *implementation* of policy in the period between 1974 and 1978, with Labour's housing, transport and land-values policies floundering for want of finance. But all governments in all contexts operate under economic constraints, and we were able to identify a whole range of policies which in *conception* owed little to macro-economic factors. The basic philosophies behind containment, dispersal, urban transport, housing, land-use planning and land values policies were not directly linked to macro-economic constraints. Even in implementation, a host of institutional and political interactions were identifiable which had an independent influence on policy.

When discussing urban policy we also referred to the role of 'ideas' — currently popular solutions to urban problems and inequalities deriving not from the programmes of political parties or from the vested interests of organised groups, but from 'outside' the political process — usually from the experience of other countries and from academic and expert opinion. It is, of course, notoriously difficult to trace the influence of ideas in the policy making process.[23] The positive discrimination programmes of the 1960s, for example, owed a great deal to contemporary views on poverty, but whether these views were in some way *independent* of existing power relations seems doubtful. Ideas, in other words, do not exist in a political and social vacuum. The popularity of an idea at any one time depends in part on its utility to those with decision-making power. Between 1966 and 1975, positive discrimination was popular because it seemed to offer a solution to urban problems at very low political and economic cost. The ideas which underpinned British urban policy in the period between 1940 and 1950 — regional revival, containment and dispersal — were similarly attractive to politicians and civil servants because they offered the chance of *planned* urban growth, a near consensus on which existed in this period.

In other words, to define ideas as an *extraneous* influence on policy is theoretically not very useful. A much more constructive way of incorporating ideas into explanations of policy is to examine who utilises ideas and for what purpose. This exercise is not so very different from asking 'who shapes the policy agenda?' or even 'who has power?'. Once again, this brings us back to the role of political parties for, as we have shown, parties played only a very limited role in shaping the policy agenda in the vital areas of land-use planning, urban transport and inner cities policy. Instead, policy was left very much to expert opinion and civil service advice. In such a situation, civil servants and experts became the key actors in deciding which ideas should influence policy and which should not.

In a recent article, Alan Cawson argued that Britain has already developed a dual system of decision making: one corporatist, one pluralist, and that the corporatist arena is gradually encroaching on the pluralist.[24] Our analysis of urban policies gives some support to this view. Certainly, the shared values of politicians, bureaucrats and organised interests in many of the areas studied looked very much like what has been defined as corporatism. Often this meant pursuing policies which were perceived to be 'economically rational', or seeking other, more specific goals such as 'containment' and 'balanced urban growth'. Pluralist decision making, defined either in terms of the interaction of representative groups,[25] or in terms of the successful working of the electoral and party political institutions of liberal democracy, was much rarer. Moreover, electoral and party political influences were much less significant in the more recently acquired (but by no means less important) areas of government responsibility, implying that corporatist decision making is likely to spread as government responsibilities increase. But neither was it obvious that when political parties *were* an important influence on policy, that this derived from them responding to the needs and demands of social groups or classes. On the contrary, their role seemed to owe more to

outdated ideologies which were only loosely related to their bases of
social support. Whether the parties can be reformed in a way which
allows them both to become the main influence on policy and to be
representative remains to be seen.

Is a National Urban Policy Possible?

Fashion in social science follows events in society with depressing
regularity. During the 1960s in an era of optimism and rapid economic
growth, planners, sociologists and economists talked with great
confidence of governments finding solutions to societies' urban ills.
In marked contrast, the fashion of the 1970s has been to emphasise the
limitations of government action. Whether it be 'overload', external
constraints, 'fiscal crisis', or popular opposition to government
intervention in society, we are bombarded on all sides by dire warnings
of the consequences of expecting too much from government. It is,
however, difficult to deny the relevance of many of these warnings for
our study. In the urban policy area governments have been and continue
to be seriously constrained by political opposition, by the complexity
of the policy process and by economics (but not, generally speaking,
by popular protest).

   To this list we should add a related and possibly more formidable
constraint: even within parties and governments policy makers are by
no means always agreed on what the goals of particular urban policies
should be. Since 1945 most policies can be accommodated within three
broad objectives: the reduction of inequalities (defined spatially and
between individuals), the enhancement of 'economic efficiency', and
the aesthetic improvement of the physical environment. Needless to
say, these three are not always compatible and many policies have
involved some sort of trade off between the three. Moreover, although
Labour governments have been rather more concerned with reducing
inequalities than have Conservative governments, this has not always
been their only or even their primary objective. The economic
environment may, of course, sometimes have shifted policies towards
the objective of economic efficiency, but this apart, Labour politicians
both within particular governments and between different governments
have often failed to agree on fundamental objectives. The same is true
of Conservative politicians who have vacillated considerably in such
areas as land-values and regional policy. And on some issues, notably
policy towards the inner city, Conservatives have pursued equality with
as much vigour as have Labour politicians.

   Given this daunting array of constraints and conflicting or confused

priorities it may sound idealistic to talk in terms of a new National
Urban Policy. But constraints on policy making change. It may be, for
example, that in the late 1970s Britain is about to embark on its first
sustained period relatively free of balance of payments crises since the
War. If so, long term planning in economic and social policy may be a
slightly more realistic goal than before. Moreover, many of the
inconsistencies and anomalies in urban policy which were catalogued
earlier in this book are in real need of publicity, and not all are so
intimately related to intractible political and economic problems that
they are beyond all hope of correction. There are two fundamental
failings in British urban policy which are in this category:

(a) The failure to relate and to integrate different policy areas. This is
almost the theme of the book. Time and again policies were shown to
conflict with one another. Housing estates have been built far from
employment opportunities. Regional economic and dispersal policies
have often worked directly against inner city policies. Land-values
policies have done little to help public housing and inner city policies.
The list could go on. Since the 1968 Town and Country Planning
Act and the introduction of structure planning the co-ordination of
housing, transport and land-use planning should have improved — at
least at the county level. But county (and region) wide planning remains
deficient because counties lack the powers to combat central and local
government bureaucracies intent on defending their jurisdictions and
responsibilities within functional policy areas. In addition, physical
planning remains divorced from economic planning. It would not be
misleading to claim that the very minimum requirement of a national
urban policy is the close co-ordination of physical and economic
planning. The creation of the *Metropoles d'équilibre* or balancing
metropolises in France and Holland's population dispersal policy were
made possible through the integration of physical, economic and
population policies.[26] As we saw, bureaucratic opposition to a central
planning agency has been critical in preventing the evolution of similar
policies in Britain. Now that we are entering a new 'anti-planning' period,
the opportunity for central planning may be lost. But the need is as
pressing as ever. By 1978 official population projections, although
indicating only small increases in total population, nonetheless still
predicted fairly massive regional population shifts from the North of
England to the Midlands, the South-West and East Anglia, as well as the
continuing depopulation of the central cities.[27]

Clearly planning is necessary, but would central planning help? French urban planning does, after all, have its faults and the Dutch are now concerned at the depopulation of their central cities in the Randstad.[28] Obviously there are potential costs involved in central planning. When mistakes are made they may be very big ones and many today would argue that what we do *not* need is more centralised government intervention, but *less* government or at least more citizen involvement and participation to make government more 'responsive' to myriad needs and demands. It may be, however, that the 'centralised decision-making versus public participation' dilemma is not as great as is often suggested. For one thing, public disillusionment with various urban policies has probably been directed as much at local initiatives as those deriving from central government directives. Complaints received by the Southwark Community Development Project Information and Advice Centre reveal the extent to which local redevelopment and housing management policies were a major source of citizens' complaints.[29] Redevelopment is, of course, related to national policy but had redevelopment been subject to closely co-ordinated physical/economic plans, it might have been much less insensitive to citizens' needs. Had, for example, regional economic policies been co-ordinated with transport, inner city and housing policies some of the more disastrous consequences of redevelopment — job loss, the creation of isolated anonymous council housing estates — might have been avoided. None of this is to claim that more central co-ordination of policies would not produce errors, nor is it to reject a role for local (or regional) governments. The recent emphasis on *partnership* between central and local authorities is encouraging, although unless it is to become simply a slogan, partnership will have to involve important changes in central and local administrative structures — not least the integration of central economic and physical planning and new local and regional planning bodies with the powers to adapt centrally agreed planning principles to local needs and demands.

(b) The failure to examine the welfare and distributional impacts of policies. 'Integration' and 'co-ordination' can also become slogans unless governments and politicians are aware of the *purpose* of government intervention. The failure to appreciate the interconnectedness of policies is closely related to the failure of governments and political parties to evaluate policies and in particular to measure their distributional or welfare consequences. It is almost as if politicians and officials have believed that because legislation authorising 'planning', 'public housing', 'dispersal', 'containment' and 'redevelopment' have been passed, that urban policies have by definition been successful. Yet it is obvious that without relating these objectives one to the other and without careful evaluation of their implementation experience there is no way of judging success or failure. Indeed, without evaluation the very purpose of the legislation is in doubt. For example, what *is* the purpose of council housing? To subsidise the poor? To provide good quality housing at low cost for working class families? To reduce class segregation? Unfortunately, neither Labour nor Conservative governments have provided clear answers to these questions — and this in spite of the massive sums spent on council housing and the major changes wrought on urban society as a result of public housing development.

Once governments do start to look at the consequences of programmes, then a host of critically important questions are raised. The Inner Area Studies, for example, by relating the effects of a variety of government policies both to each other and to general social and economic context revealed very clearly many of the inconsistencies in policy and the need to co-ordinate not only urban policies but all relevant policies. There is, after all, a wide range of government services — education, health, law enforcement, social services, civil rights enforcement, anti-pollution law and income maintenance — which have not been covered in this book but which have crucial consequences for urban society. A truly comprehensive urban policy would *have* to include these areas as well as urban policies proper.

What, in fact, an acceptance of the two broad requirements for a national urban policy — the integration of a wide range of domestic policies and carefully evaluated purposeful policy making — implies, is the acceptance of the need for a planned society. Whether this can be achieved given existing economic and political constraints, and whether, once implemented, planning can be both economically efficient and sensitive to citizens' needs and demands, are probably the most vexing questions of modern industrial society. Planning is not, of course, equivalent to socialism. On the contrary, many argue that the 'coming corporatism' will put economic growth first and other priorities — notably equality — second.[30] Certainly, serious conflicts of interests were shown to exist in many of our policy areas between social justice goals and those imposed by economic imperatives. Speculative profits from land can be considered beneficial to the

economy, as can redevelopment, massive urban road schemes, urban
sprawl and policies which accelerate the decline of the inner cities.
Neither does the adoption of modern management and decision
making techniques — PPBS, critical path analysis, area management —
which are often heralded as revolutionary by advocates of corporatism,
necessarily reduce inequalities or create more pleasing and functional
physical environments.[31]

It would be naive, however, to ignore the role of representative
institutions in any discussion of the prospects for planning. Samuel
Beer's 1969 comment that 'Corporatism cannot constitute a complete
policy and must be supplemented by some other source of will and
direction such has come in the past from party government,'[32] remains
valid. In our study we noted a variety of instances where party played
an important — and sometimes crucial — role. What prospects are there,
then, for a revitalised role for political parties in national urban policy?
Needless to say, we should not be encouraged by the experience of the
past. When parties have been active in urban policy they have often
proved inflexible and unresponsive, clinging to outmoded ideological
precepts which have little relevance to the stated purposes of policies.
A revitalised party role might lead to more responsive policy, but this
would not necessarily produce greater equality between areas or
individuals. Indeed, it could be argued that the main problem of party
government in Britain in recent years has been the absence of clear
bases of social support to which parties can respond with coherent
programmes. This may explain why parties have clung so tenaciously
to ideological positions dating from periods when class and group
structures were much simpler and susceptible to effective political
mobilisation. Of course, for parties to admit that they have no obvious
base of social support would be to undermine their very *raison d'être*.
The experience of modern industrial societies in recent years is that
when parties have found a new base of support it has been founded on
regionalism or middle class populism neither of which need lead to
greater equality. Tax revolt movements in Denmark and California,
indeed, have specifically demanded the redistribution of resources back
to property owning middle classes.

While accepting that there are risks involved in advocating the
revitalisation of parties, it probably remains our best hope. In the
context of a low growth economy and increasing public disillusionment
with government, the need for some sort of intellectual and moral
regeneration within the parties is urgent. Richard Rose has carefully
catalogued the ways in which party in government might be

strengthened.[33] Greatly improved party research departments, more and better political advisers and a political civil service are among the more important suggestions. It is essential to remember that parties *do* have some independent influence on policy; there is no 'iron law' which places some strict limit on what parties can do. Bases of social support are also volatile, and we have no reason to suppose that the complexity of our social structure will always result in what has been called 'government by directionless consensus.'[34]

The first and most basic requirement for a revitalised party role should be a new emphasis on political eduction — both for political élites and the public at large. In this way the most fundamental issues at stake in urban society will be debated and discussed, and at least the hope for a more sensitive and responsive state role will be established.

Notes

1. Manuell Castells, *The Urban Question* (Cambridge, Mass., MIT Press, 1977); C.G. Pickvance, 'On the Study of Urban Social Movements', in Pickvance (ed.), *Urban Sociology: Critical Essays* (London, Tavistock, 1976) discusses this question and the controversy within Marxist urban sociology at length.

2. See David Coates, *The Labour Party and the Struggle for Socialism* (London, Cambridge University Press, 1975), chs. 5 and 8; David Howell, *British Social Democracy* (London, Croom Helm, 1976), chs. 9 and 10.

3. See Donald E. Stokes, 'Spatial Models of Party Competition', in Angus Campbell *et al.*, *Elections and the Political Order* (New York, Wiley, 1966), pp.161-79.

4. See Murray Edelman, *The Symbolic Uses of Politics* (Urbana, Illinois, University of Illinois Press, 1964).

5. See J.T. Winkler, 'The Corporate Economy: Theory and Administration', in R. Scase (ed.), *Industrial Society: Class Cleavage and Control* (London, George Allen and Unwin, 1977) and sources cited; also, Alan Cawson, 'Pluralism, Corporatism and the Role of the State', *Government and Opposition*, vol.13, no.2 (spring, 1978).

6. There is little evidence that the public have much interest in the principle of public housing. For example, in 1967, 74 per cent of a national sample favoured the sale of council housing to occupiers, while only 17 per cent opposed the idea, George Gallup (ed.), *Gallup International Public Opinion Polls*, Great Britain, 1937-75 (New York, Random House, vol.2, 1976), p.918.

7. Peter Hall *et al.*, *The Containment of Urban England* (London and Beverly Hills, PEP, George Allen and Unwin, Sage, 1973), vol.2, p.454.

8. Donald Foley, *Controlling London's Growth: Planning the Great Wen* (Berkeley and Los Angeles, University of California Press, 1963). See also, Peter Hall *et al.*, *Urban England*, pp.35-8.

9. On this general subject, see S.E. Finer (ed.), *Adversary Politics and Electoral Reform* (London, Anthony Wigram, 1975).

10. Quoted in Foley, *London's Growth*, p.69.

86   *Politics, Policy and Urban Society*

11. Graham K. Wilson, *Special Interests and Policy Making* (London, Wiley, 1977), ch.9; Michael Moran, *The Politics of Industrial Relations* (London, Macmillan, 1977).

12. Wilson, ibid.; Richard Rose (ed.), *Studies in British Politics* (London, Macmillan, 3rd edn., 1976), contributions by Nettle and Peterson.

13. See Pickvance, *Urban Sociology*, pp.198-218.

14. See for example the contrasting approaches documented in John Ferris, *Participation in Urban Planning* (London, Bell Occasional Papers on Social Administration, no.48, 1972); Norman Dennis, *Public Participation and Planners' Blight* (London, Faber, 1972). I.M. Hall, *Community Action Versus Pollution: A Study of a Residents' Group in a Welsh Urban Area* (Cardiff, University of Wales Press, 1976); John Grant, *The Politics of Urban Transport Planning* (London, Earth Resources Research, 1977).

15. Hugh Heclo and Aaron Wildavsky, *The Private Government and Public Money* (Los Angeles, University of California, 1971), chs. 2-4.

16. Ibid., pp.378-9.

17. Kenneth Newton, 'Community Performance in Britain', *Current Sociology*, vol.26, 1976, pp.49-86 and sources cited; J.A.G. Griffith, *Central Departments and Local Authorities* (London, George Allen and Unwin, 1966).

18. Newton, ibid.

19. Grant, *Urban Transport Planning.*

20. Griffith, *Local Authorities.*

21. See James L. Sundquist, *Dispersing Population: What America can Learn from Europe* (Washington, DC, Brookings, 1975), chs. 3 and 5.

22. This is either explicitly or implicitly accepted by most Marxist and neo-Marxist critics of British society. See, for example, David Coates, *Struggle for Socialism*. But for a non-Marxist view, see also Neville Abraham, *Big Business and Government* (London, Macmillan, 1974).

23. See, for example, Anthony King, 'Ideas, Institutions and the Policies of Government', *British Journal of Political Science*, vol.3, parts 3 and 4 (July and October 1973).

24. Cawson, 'Pluralism'.

25. Following the American school of interest group theorists, in particular David Truman in *The Governmental Process* (New York, Knopf, 1951).

26. Sundquist, *Dispersing Population.*

27. As reported by Peter Hall in 'Planning for no Growth', *New Society*, 30 March 1978, p.723.

28. Sundquist, *Dispersing Population*, pp.210-13.

29. Alan Davis *et al.*, *The Management of Deprivation: Final Report of the Southwark Community Development Project* (Polytechnic of the South Bank, 1977).

30. See Winkler, 'Corporate Economy'.

31. For a good discussion of some of these techniques and their effects at the local level, see Robin Hambleton, *Policy Planning and Local Government* (London, Hutchinson, 1978), part 4.

32. Samuel H. Beer, *Modern British Politics* (London, Faber, 2nd edition, 1969), pp.427-8.

33. Richard Rose, *The Problem of Party Government* (Harmondsworth, Middx., Penguin, 1976), ch.16.

34. Ibid., p.414.

BIBLIOGRAPHY

Full references are given in the footnotes following each chapter. The purpose of this short bibliography is to provide readers with references to some of the more important sources available in the urban policy areas covered in the book.

Chapter 1

For general introductions to British urban problems and urban policies, see J.B. Cullingworth (ed.), *Problems of an Urban Society* (London, George Allen and Unwin, 1973) (vols.1-3); J.B. Cullingworth, *Town and Country Planning in Britain* (London, George Allen and Unwin, 5th edition, 1974); Peter Hall, *Urban and Regional Planning* (Harmondsworth, Middx., Penguin, 1976).

For comparative perspectives, see Arnold J. Heidenheimer, Hugh Heclo and Carolyn Tech Adams, *Comparative Public Policy: The Politics of Social Choice in Europe and America* (London, Macmillan, 1976); James L. Sundquist, *Dispersing Population: What America Can Learn from Europe* (Washington DC, Brookings Institution, 1975).

A good sociological perspective on urban problems is R.E. Pahl's *Whose City?* (Harmondsworth, Middx., Penguin, 1975).

Chapter 2

J.B. Cullingworth's *Town and Country Planning in Britain* (London, George Allen and Unwin, 5th edition, 1974) remains the best introduction to land-use planning, but see also William Asworth, *The Genesis of Modern British Town Planning* (London, Routledge and Kegan Paul, 1954); Gordon E. Cherry, *Urban Change and Planning* (Henley on Thames, Foulis, 1972). The most detailed overview of land-use planning with some discussion of policy, is Peter Hall *et al.*, *The Containment of Urban England* (London, George Allen and Unwin, 1973) (vols.1 and 2).

On New Town planning, see Ebenezer Howard, *Garden Cities of Tomorrow* (London, Faber and Faber, 1946); Frank Schaffer, *The New Town Story* (London, Paladin, 1972).

On the role of different political actors in land-use planning, see J.B. Cullingworth, *Environmental Planning 1939-1969, Vol.1: Reconstruction and Land-Use Planning, 1939-1947* (London,

HMSO, 1975); David Eversley, *The Planner in Society* (London, Faber and Faber, 1973); Arnold Goodman, *After the Planners* (Harmondsworth, Middx., Penguin, 1972); Gordon E. Cherry, *The Evolution of British Town Planning* (London, Leonard Hill, 1974).

For an introduction to the issue of public participation, see Norman Dennis, *Public Participation and Planners' Blight* (London, Faber and Faber, 1972); John Ferris, *Participation in Urban Planning* (London, Bell Occasional Papers in Social Administration, no.48, 1972).

For an insight into the role of local authorities in the policy process, see J.A.G. Griffith, *Central Departments and Local Authorities* (London, George Allen and Unwin, 1966).

Chapter 3

For an introduction to the economic problems of land values, see P.N. Balchin and J.L. Kieve, *Urban Land Economics* (London, Macmillan, 1977); A.J. Harrison, *Economics and Land-Use Planning* (London, Croom Helm, 1977); K.J. Button, *Urban Economics: Theory and Practice* (London, Macmillan, 1976).

For introductions to the social and political aspects of land values, see Peter Hall (ed.), *Land Values* (London, Sweet and Maxwell, 1965); *Report of the Expert Committee on Compensation and Betterment*, Cmd.6381 (1942); J. Ratcliffe, *Land Policy: An Exploration of Land in Society* (London, Hutchinson, 1976).

On the influence of actors in the policy process, see Oliver Marriott, *The Property Boom* (London, Gollancz, 1969); Peter Ambrose and Bob Colenutt, *The Property Machine* (Harmondsworth, Middx., Penguin, 1975), Malcolm MacEwan, *Crisis in Architecture* (London, RIBA Publications, 1974), J.B. Cullingworth, *Environmental Planning 1939-1969, Vol.1: Reconstruction and Land-Use Planning, 1939-1947* (London, HMSO, 1945).

Chapter 4

The best descriptive study of housing policy in Britain is Alan Murie, Pat Niner and Chris Watson's *Housing Policy and the Housing System* (London, George Allen and Unwin, 1976). David Donnison's *The Government of Housing* (Harmondsworth, Middx., Penguin, 1967) is somewhat out of date, but remains an excellent account of government's role in housing. A wealth of technical and statistical data are contained in *Housing Policy: A Consultative Document*, Cmnd.6851 (HMSO, 1977).

For accounts of council housing policy, see *Council Housing:*

Purposes, Procedures and Priorities (Cullingworth Report, HMSO, 1969). For a radical view of council housing, see CDP Information and Intelligence Unit, *Whatever Happened to Council Housing?* (Home Office, London, 1976). On council housing allocation, see Elizabeth Burney, *Housing on Trial* (Harmondsworth, Middx., Penguin, 1967); also, David Smith and Anne Whalley, *Racial Minorities and Public Housing* (London, PEP Broadsheet No.556, 1975).

On slum clearance policy, see John English, Ruth Madigan and Peter Norman, *Slum Clearance: The Social and Administrative Context in England and Wales* (London, Croom Helm, 1976).

A good case study of the legislative process in housing is Malcolm Joel Barnett's *The Politics of Legislation* (London, Weidenfeld and Nicolson, 1969).

Chapter 5

There is no single satisfactory text on urban transport policies, but see K.M. Gwilliam, *Transport and Public Policy* (London, George Allen and Unwin, 1964). William Plowden's *The Motor Car and Politics, 1896-1970* (London, Bodley Head, 1971) is comprehensive and perceptive.

For a study of transport planning in London, see Douglas Hart, *Strategic Planning in London: The Rise and Fall of the Primary Road Network* (Oxford, Pergamon, 1976).

For accounts of public participation in transport, see John Grant, *The Politics of Urban Transport Planning* (London, Earth Resources Research, 1977).

Transport Policy, Cmnd.6836 (HMSO, 1977), contains a wealth of statistical data on transport in Britain.

Chapter 6

The best general introduction to regional and locational policies is Gavin McCrone's *Regional Policy in Britain* (London, George Allen and Unwin, 1973). But see also, *Report of the Royal Commission on the Distribution of the Industrial Population* (Barlow Report), Cmd.6153 (HMSO, 1940); Gerald Manners *et al.*, *Regional Development in Britain* (London, Wiley, 1972); Graham Hallett *et al.*, *Regional Policy for Ever?* (London, Institute for Economic Affairs, 1973); Stuart Holland, *Capital Versus the Regions* (London, Macmillan, 1976).

On the political dimension in regional planning policy, see Jacques Leruez, *Economic Planning and Politics in Britain* (London, Martin Robertson, 1975); Alan Budd, *The Politics of Economic Planning*

(London, Fontana, 1978); Michael Shanks, *Planning and Politics: The British Experience, 1960-1976* (London, George Allen and Unwin, 1977); Michael Stewart, *The Jekyll and Hyde Years: Politics and Economic Policy Since 1964* (London, Dent, 1976).

The burgeoning role of new unemployment agencies is discussed in Brian Showler's *The Public Employment Service* (London, Longman, 1976).

A good bibliography on regional and sub-regional planning is Brenda White's *The Literature and Study of Urban and Regional Planning* (London, Routledge and Kegan Paul, 1974).

Chapter 7

A good summary of recent inner city policies is Clare Demuth's *Government Initiatives on Urban Deprivation*, Runnymede Trust Briefing Paper, 1977, but see also, Robin Hambleton, *Policy Planning and Local Government* (London, Hutchinson, 1978), chs. 3-5.

The various publications of the National Community Development Project are a useful (if sometimes tendentious) source of information on community action. See in particular, *Forward Plan, 1975-1976* (1975), and *Gilding the Ghetto* (1977). See also Ray Lees and George Smith, *Action Research in Community Development* (London, Routledge and Kegan Paul, 1975).

For a statement of government plans for the inner city, see *Policy for the Inner City*, Cmnd.6845 (HMSO, 1977) and for accounts of the problems facing inner areas, see the various *Inner Area Studies.*

INDEX

Abercrombie, Patrick 162
Acquisition of Land (Assessment of Compensation) Act (1919) 74-5
Action Areas 48
Addison, Lord 110-12
Agriculture, Ministry of 36
Allaun, Frank 134-5, 151
anomie 273
Assisted Areas 222, 224-5, 257
Automobile Association 164

Balchin, P.N. and Kieve, J.L. 74
Barker, Anthony 59
Barlow, Royal Commission on the Distribution of the Industrial Population, and Report 29, 194-7, 199, 203-4, 228, 282-3
Barnett, Malcolm 126, 128
Beer, Samuel 284
Benn, Anthony Wedgwood 172, 221
Better Homes, the Next Priorities (White Paper, 1973) 141
betterment 20, 35, 69-75
betterment levy 54, 85
Bevan, Aneurin 98, 117-20, 122, 131, 151
Beveridge Report 117
Boer, Anthony de 180
Bowley, Marian 111
Boyd-Carpenter, John 84-5, 88, 93, 100
breathalyser 174
British Leyland 216
British Rail 181-2
British Road Federation 164, 170, 174, 180, 186
British Transport Commission 161
Brooke, Henry 84
Buchanan, Professor 168-72
Buchanan Report (1963) 42, 168-72
building licences 200, 201
building societies 129, 144, 146, 153, 273
buses 160, 167, 173-4

CDP Information and Intelligence Unit 125, 135, 244

California 284
Callaghan, James 60, 180, 241
Carr, Robert 241, 245, 247
Castells, Manuel 191
Castle, Barbara 174-5
Cawson, Alan 279
Central Lancashire New Town 46
Central Land Board 77-8, 98
Centre for Environmental Studies 250
Centre Point 95
certificates of alternative development 38, 81-2
Child Poverty Action Group 137, 144, 254, 274
Churchill, Winston 163, 196
Civic Amenities Act (1967) 136
Civic Trust 39, 44
Civil Aviation 166
civil servants, role of 16, 35-6, 39-40, 44-6, 51-2, 61-2, 95-102, 181-2, 185-6, 196, 228, 242, 267-8, 272, 274-6, 279-80
Clay Cross (Derbyshire) 140
Clegg, Walter 134
collective consumption 18, 191
Commonwealth Immigrants Advisory Council 235-6
Community Development Project 238-48
Community Land Act (1975) 56, 59-60, 86-8, 94, 96-100, 102, 270
compensation (and betterment) 35, 69-75
compensatory education 235-7
Comprehensive Community Programme 249-55
compulsory purchase orders 31, 38, 75, 80
Confederation of British Industry 218-19, 221, 228
Conservation Areas 136
Conservative Governments 27, 28, 60-3, 76, 88-9, 102-3, 110-11, 114-16, 118, 148-53, 185-90, 225-32, 241-2, 286-8, 263-72; (1951-64) 36-45, 80-4, 122-30, 164-70, 201-7; (1970-74) 52-6,